ANDREW O'HAGAN was born in Glasgow, Scotland and was shortlisted for the Scottish Writer of the Year award for *The Missing*. *Our Father* was shortlisted for the Booker Prize and the Whitbread First Novel Award. His latest book is *Perso...* ...inated one of Granta's 'Be...

BELLA BATHURST'S f... ...nsons, was a non-fiction b... ...nson's family of lighthouse engineers. Her second book, a novel, *Special*, was published in 2003.

W.F. DEEDES is a columnist and former Editor of the *Daily Telegraph*. He is the Bill of *Private Eye's* 'Dear Bill' letters. He is the author of *At War with Waugh* and *Brief Lives*.

COLM TOIBIN is one of Ireland's most celebrated authors. Among his novels are *The Heather Blazing* and *The Blackwater Lightship*, which was shortlisted for the Booker Prize in 1999. *The Master* was published this year.

MONICA ALI'S debut novel *Brick Lane* was shortlisted for the Booker prize, the Guardian First Book Award and the Orwell Prize, and received a WH Smith 'People's Choice' Award. She was nominated one of Granta's 'Best of Young British Novelists' in 2003.

VICTORIA GLENDINNING has written biographies on Anthony Trollope, Vita Sackville-West and Rebecca West and has also published a number of novels, *The Grown Ups*, *Electricity* and *Flight*.

SIMON GARFIELD is a prize-winning journalist and author of, amongst others, *The Nation's Favourite: The True Adventures of Radio 1* and *Mauve* which was described in the *Daily Telegraph* as 'a book about science which also happens to be a miniature work of art'. His next book, *Our Hidden Lives*, will be published later this year.

IRVINE WELSH'S books have made him a cult figure within the writing world since the 1990s. Several of his books have become best sellers and all have a mixture of comedy, drama and hard-hitting issues. He has written *Porno, Trainspotting, The Acid House* and *Filth*.

SAM MILLER Sam Miller is a journalist and writer based in Delhi. He was previously head of the South Asia region at the BBC World Service, and has worked as a journalist, producer and manager in television, radio and online. He is also a widely published writer on the politics and culture of the Indian subcontinent.

MICHAEL ATHERTON became captain of the England cricket team at 25 and is one of the most successful batsmen in the game. He played professional cricket for Lancashire and England for 15 years. His autobiography *Opening Up* was published in 2002.

JENNY COLGAN is a best-selling novelist. Born in Ayrshire, her novels include *Amanda's Wedding* and *Looking For Andrew McCarthy*.

TONY HAWKS is the author of *Round Ireland with a Fridge*, which was followed by *Playing the Moldovans at Tennis*, both books inspired by obscure bets. His most recently published book is *One Hit Wonderland* in which he attempts to have a hit record – in Albania.

THE WEEKENDERS ADVENTURES IN CALCUTTA

THE WEEKENDERS ADVENTURES IN CALCUTTA

BELLA BATHURST

W.F. DEEDES

COLM TOIBIN

MONICA ALI

VICTORIA GLENDINNING

SIMON GARFIELD

IRVINE WELSH

SAM MILLER

MICHAEL ATHERTON

JENNY COLGAN

TONY HAWKS

EBURY PRESS

First published in Great Britain in 2004

10 9 8 7 6 5 4 3 2 1

Copyright © *The Night Fishing* Bella Bathurst; *A Hundred Different Lives* Bill Deedes; *Mercy* Colm Toibin; *Knife* Monica Ali; *Emails to Ed* Victoria Glendinning; *The Hotel Calcutta* Simon Garfield; *Reality Orientation* Irvine Welsh; *Going Underground* Sam Miller; *Waking up from Your Father's Dreams* Michael Atherton; *An Indian Marriage Lives* Jenny Colgan; *Laughter is a River Too* Tony Hawks

First published by Ebury Press
Random House, 20 Vauxhall Bridge Road, London SW1V 2SA

Random House Australia (Pty) Limited
20 Alfred Street, Milsons Point, Sydney, New South Wales 2061, Australia

Random House New Zealand Limited
18 Poland Road, Glenfield, Auckland 10, New Zealand

Random House South Africa (Pty) Limited
Endulini, 5A Jubilee Road, Parktown 2193, South Africa

The Random House Group Limited Reg. No. 954009

www.randomhouse.co.uk

A CIP catalogue record for this book is available from the British Library.

Cover Design by Two Associates
Text design and typesetting by Textype

ISBN 0091895782

Papers used by Ebury Press are natural, recyclable products made from wood grown in sustainable forests.

Printed and bound in Great Britain by Bookmarque Ltd, Croydon, Surrey

Contents

In January 2001 Calcutta officially changed its name to Kolkata. However, not everyone has been quick to use the new pronunciation and spelling. *The Weekenders: Adventures in Calcutta* reflects this, with both spellings being used.

Acknowledgements

The decision to publish this book was made on the night that the first Weekenders won the WH Smith Travel Book Award. The charity to whom the royalties had gone, had an event that same evening and we moved seamlessly from one to the other, celebrating at both. When the hangovers receded we were left with the serious decisions of how and where. In both, we were lucky.

Firstly, Andrew O'Hagan, whose short story had been so compelling in the first book, agreed to edit Weekenders 2. Andrew's brilliant and deliberately light hand on the tiller transformed this project. His understanding of tone and pace, his ability to direct the authors without stifling their freedom and his sheer enthusiasm made this book the success it is; all the authors loved working with him and it is to Andrew that Weekenders 2 owes the greatest debt.

Secondly, the choice of Calcutta as our destination proved perfect. It offered the two things we needed most: a rich source of inspiration and a network of friends whose knowledge, help and good company made it possible to see and do more in five days than most visitors achieve in five months.

All the writers from the first book were asked to contribute and new authors were sought. Bill Deedes, who played the lead role in selecting writers first time around, was introduced to Monica Ali by Andrew at the Hay on Wye literary festival. He asked her to join us and she responded immediately, saying that on her one visit to Calcutta she had found it to be 'more Indian than the rest of India put together. Colm Toibin, Bella Bathurst and Sam Miller, all highly respected writers and journalists, were brought on board by Andrew, and Jake Lingwood at Ebury introduced us to Jenny Colgan and Simon Garfield.

There was only one story line missing: no book on Calcutta would be complete without referring to cricket. Again we could not have been luckier: Michael Atherton, who once described Calcutta's main park, the Maidan, as the spiritual home of cricket, writes for the *Sunday Telegraph* and agreed to write his first piece of fiction for us. I travelled with Athers, Monica and Bella on the last of the writers' trips. Athers was mobbed everywhere we went, even at two in the morning at the burning ghats (funeral pyres). The only person in India who failed to recognise the former England cricket captain was the taxi driver with whom he spent two days. He even visited the man's home where they were playing cricket in the courtyard.

In this trip, as with all the others, our cicerone was Tim Grandage, whom I had got to know when the *Telegraph* chose his children's home for its annual Christmas Charity Appeal. It was not gratitude that drove him to spend all day – and most of the nights – with the writers, but a love of the city and its people. He once told me that he had founded Future Hope 'not out of pity for the street children but out of admiration for them'. It is in the same spirit that this book has been written and Calcutta could not have a better ambassador, or the writers a better companion, than this unassuming, intelligent, caring man. He knows everyone from the leper who 'works' the street corner, the prostitutes and the children sleeping rough at the stations, to the police chiefs, politicians and captains of industry. He introduced the writers to his friends and took us everywhere, showing us every contrasting face of this amazing city; the flower market, the burning ghats, the Raj Bhavan, the ceremony of Id on the Red Road, the Maidan, Eden Gardens, the new market, the jazz club, a clerk's offices, the palaces and the slums, the temples and the stations. He and his lovely wife Erica could not have done more for us all. We are also indebted to Tarun Dutt, the former chief secretary of West Bengal, and Supratik Bhattacharjee for having the patience to share their deep knowledge and under-standing of Bengali history and culture with us.

We also need to thank Bob Wright, who used his vast network of contacts to act as chief tour operator, enabling us to stay at the Tollygunge Club and Bengal Club, even when they were fully booked. He also introduced us to 'Mr Baz', the safest and nicest driver in Calcutta.

The third couple who so generously opened up their home to all the Weekenders was Sunita and Naresh Kumar. In the chaos that is Calcutta, they provided an oasis of elegance and serenity for which we were all grateful.

As before, all the authors have given their time and their stories free. So too have all those people working behind the scenes, including our wonderful agent, Andrew Nurnberg. Ebury offered terms unheard of in the normal business world so that royalties which go to Unicef will be three times the usual figure. Our thanks go to Claire Kingston, Stina Smemo and Dawn Burnett at Ebury for all their hard work, and most of all to Jake Lingwood, our editor there. It cannot be easy working with a newspaper, a charity, 11 authors and an editor, but if it was difficult, Jake never let it show and his support throughout has been much valued.

Much of the credit for getting the book off the ground goes to Laura Boardman, who transformed a late-night party decision into reality. Laura travelled with Andrew O'Hagan, Irvine Welsh and I on the first recce and she set the template for this collaboration. We also had a wonderful time.

Thanks also to Charles Moore, the then editor of The *Daily Telegraph*, who supported this project wholeheartedly. The *Telegraph's* formidable reputation as a supporter of charitable ventures developed under Charles's editorship largely because he was always open to any suggestion; if it was a force for good he would back it. I am grateful also to our current editor, Martin Newland, who has continued the paper's support, and to Sarah Gent, who has handled most of the administration here.

Finally, a personal acknowledgement to Eric Willis, had he not passed his love of Calcutta on to his daughter this book probably would have been set elsewhere for such things determine fate. When pooling our ideas for a destination I could think of no more exciting or inspiring place – nor one whose reputation was so in need of balance. In Britain, Calcutta is defined by its poverty and destitution in India its epithet is 'the City of Joy'

Susan Ryan, Managing Editor, Daily Telegraph.

Introduction

Howrah Station is on the quiet side at 7.38 a.m. A sheet of dust lies on the surface of Platform 13, and there, just under a sign for Horlicks ('the Great Family Nourisher'), a pair of yellow birds peck and bounce in yesterday's stomped chewing gum. The people will come in a minute: the thousands of clerks on trains from the suburbs, and the familiar dust will cover their shoes and the birds will scatter. But at 7.38 the station is quiet. Three small boys are sitting in the space between the tracks, their dirty limbs gathered round a fire of loose coals and plastic bottles. Together they are eating something, and together they watch for the day to present something new.

An hour later, in Rowland Road, on the other side of the river, a second group of Kolkata boys are tucking in their white shirts. They too used to live in Howrah Station, before being taken away one night and washed and given a bed and a place in the Future Hope charity school. Raju Bose, aged ten, has his hair in a neat side-parting; he can remember Howrah Station, but nowadays he likes cricket and trigonometry and he doesn't have any reason to cross the bridge. 'Okay,' said a woman in a green sari. 'Protocol says you must be standing up for the National Anthem at the beginning and at the end.'

'He came from a poor background and he built the nuclear rockets,' says Raju.

'Good,' says the headmaster. 'When you meet the President don't be too afraid. Tell him your hopes for India.'

The first time I went to Calcutta I recorded these two scenes in my notebook. I have never forgotten them – the dirty boys in the railway station representing everything we thought we knew about Calcutta, and the second group in their white shirts, boys making ready to visit Raj Bhavan to meet the President of India, showing something new, something amazing and redemptive. The journey from one to the other – from the past to the future, from the hopeless to the glorious – might be understood to provide a definition of modern Calcutta, a miraculous city of human dramas and troubles occurring in the present tense.

The idea of this book is to enter fully into that present of Calcutta – or Kolkata, as it is now called – to allow writers to take you to the imagined heart of the world's most misbegotten city, and, in doing so, to amplify your sense of its wonders. The book is a travelogue and a thriller, a tone-poem and a colour-chart; it is a portmanteau of Calcuttan delights and horrors, and a book in which one writer's material is allowed to bleed into another's, creating encounters, echoes, organic connections, proving in its own way how a book of good writing can become like a city itself – a thing of patterns, sounds, coincidence, memorials. *The Weekenders* (since the first book set in Sudan) are now making a habit of overstepping the boundaries of ordinary travel writing, taking authors and their readers over the threshold of their own outsider status to make them suddenly intimate with the life of places known more by reputation than by understanding.

Calcutta has always been a place of stories. From the

Bengali to the Colonial, from the art-song to the cinema: the city is a matrix of remembered narratives jostling for air and space. It is part of the life of any living culture that those narratives be inflected and changed from one generation to another, and that, for me, is one of the things that gives *The Weekenders: Adventures in Calcutta* its flavour and its colour: here is Kolkata as imaginative writers see it now, a place where the past still murmurs and the future beckons like never before. Kolkata is a perpetual dream, and now, in this book, occasioned by eleven short visits by eleven of our best authors, we may enjoy a further fermentation of the writer's art – we see Kolkata's reality affecting the minds of these authors, while, at the same time, we see the writers' imaginations touching and altering the reality of Kolkata. That seems the fairest and most exciting exchange in the pursuit of truth and the excavation of life: we may ask nothing more of a place on earth, and nothing more of our writers.

Andrew O'Hagan
London, 2004

The Nightfishing

BELLA BATHURST

THIS river is not a river. Not a river in the European sense, anyway. It may look like rivers ought to look – a wide brown belt of water flowing slowly through a landscape – but long before it got to this place, it became something else entirely. This is a liquid road, a strand of Shiva's hair, a blessing and a gravemouth. This is the beginning and the end. Without it, nothing exists; no birth, no death, no regeneration, no God. As it moves across the country, it divides and multiplies, becoming simultaneously a source of food and drink, a home, a place to bathe or worship, a refuge and a petro-chemically polluted environmental disgrace. It doesn't have the best views in the world, or the sweetest taste, or the longest history, but it remains the holiest of holies. For most of its length it is thick with silt and the colour of dishwater coffee, but without it you do not live and you can never properly die. Though people are actively discouraged from drinking or preparing food from it, one drop is said to wash the human soul clean for a lifetime. In the country, new-born children are immersed in it and when each family member finally dies, their ashes will be sprinkled on its waters. And while it and all the other rivers still flow, India will be all right. This is the Hooghly, one of Mother Ganga's many daughters, as she passes through Calcutta.

And frankly, it's only a twenty-first-century European who could be idiotic enough to find any of the Hooghly's multiple personalities surprising. Of course rivers give life to the places they pass through, of course they are more than just moving water. It's obvious. So obvious, in fact, that you only have to look at a town plan – any town plan, in any part of the world – to see it. Almost every major international city is built on or close to a river; they have always relied on those rivers for their historical and commercial success. Rivers were once an absolute precondition for existence, the one non-negotiable fixture for all aspiring urban spaces. Without them, there would be no London, no Paris, no New York. So it isn't India's faith in her rivers which is peculiar, but our apparent disillusionment. To us, the Clyde, the Seine or the Tiber have become just pieces of scenery, mildly diverting attractions. The rich might buy a ten-foot sliver of riverside view in Richmond or Greenwich, but they're thinking of the water as a trophy, not as an asset. They don't want to use the Thames, they just want to look at it. But the rivers of India are still very much alive. The last 200 years have changed them too, and the version of the Hooghly that exists now is only a ghost of what it must once have been when this city was the capital of the Raj, and when half the tea in India came via Calcutta. Even so, there are still things going on along the banks and in the stream of the Hooghly that Europe forgot long ago.

Anyway, it's no use talking about ends without starting at the beginning. Once upon a time, Ganga was the eldest daughter of the Lord of Snow, the mountain-god Himalaya. When all the gods in heaven came to Himalaya and asked if he would resolve a long and painful dispute between two of them by sending one of his daughters down to earth, Himalaya chose Ganga, but when Ganga heard she was to leave heaven, she was furious, and vowed to drown the earth in the floods of her rage. The god Shiva took up Ganga and held her in the coils of his hair until she had quietened, and then released her strand-by-strand as the seven sacred streams of India. In the Sanskrit texts, Mother Ganga has 108 separate names, from Bahu-ksira ('The cow which gives much milk') to Svarga-sopana-sarani ('Flowing like a staircase to Heaven'), to be chanted devotionally by all Hindus. She is still worshipped all along her length, from Haridwar up in the mountains of the Himalayas where the faithful float lighted lamps in the river to Varanasi and the confluence of the Ganges, the Yamuna and the Saraswati at Prayag. This is the site of the vast Kumbh Mela festival which takes place every twelve years, and where – according to the faithful – the river transfigures from water into nectar. Any river which, like the Hooghly, flows from or into the Ganges is considered divine, though there are also rivers with no geographical connection to the Ganges which have almost the same blessed powers as she does. Every stage of life, from the brahmin's thread ceremony to marriage to each of the different annual *pujas* (the festivals celebrating one or other of the Hindu gods) will involve the river in some way. A good Hindu should not only observe all the ceremonies, all the texts and all the pujas, he should at some stage in his lifetime try to visit all of India's most sacred rivers, and participate in as many of the different melas as possible.

Part of Ganga's holiness is connected to its purity. From source to sea, the river is 1,500 miles long, and for most of its length is extremely fast-flowing. The speed of its descent through the continent helps to keep it clean, but as it moves through the plains and marshes and reed beds before it splits into its various different tributaries, it filters itself. Bottled water from the Ganges is supposed to keep longer than ordinary water, and all along its length there are people filling jerry-cans of soupy liquid to keep at home for first blessings or last rites. At Jangipur, a few hundred miles north of Calcutta, Ganga unravels a strand of itself southwards down the Bhagirathi, a tributary which until the construction of the Farakka Barrage during the 1980s once ran dry for much of the year. By the time it reaches Calcutta, the Hooghly has thickened with ripped-out silt, and is slowing as it nears the sea.

As it passes through the city, the river is wide, as wide as the Severn estuary, muddy, and pocked all over with small patches of water hyacinth. At first glance, the life along its banks looks much like the life of the Thames or the Clyde – the station, the bridges, the big ugly civic buildings, the cargo boats and tugs moving up and down on some unidentifiable mission of their own (like people and their mysteries as they move through the city, like people and their ailments as they flow down the corridors of Dr Catchatoor's hospital). But all along its length, from the idol-immersion strands at the top to the dockyards of downstream Kolkata, the Hooghly has bathing ghats; a few steps down from the street to the water, a tilted slipway, a line somewhere or other on which to dry saris, and perhaps a platform of some description on which people can wash their clothes or themselves. And every single ghat, at every single stage of the journey, on either side of the bank, is full of people pounding cloth or gossiping or just standing in the water staring down towards the sea. It's winter, and therefore not particularly hot – warm to anyone come directly from a dank November London, but chilly to a native Kolkatan – but still there are always people around, talking, pouring the urns filled with the ashes of their relations into the sacred water, splashing through the shallows.

Upstream, the river has a domesticated air. On the right-hand bank, there are old colonial buildings now sprouting plaits of green weeds up their chimneys, the Nimtala burning ghat, the railway line, a couple of wooden cargo boats so overloaded with hay that they look like fish with bad wigs, a construction-sand wharf, the decrepit remains of a canal system that once ran all the way to Bangladesh, and a large and beautifully maintained temple. From here, it's possible to see the old warehouses and colonial buildings being reabsorbed into the ground almost as fast as you pass. The colonnades and classical pediments are embellished with thick green vegetation, their façades obscured by a latticework of lianas and roots. With many of the buildings it is difficult to work out whether the plants are parasites or hosts; if they are pulling down the buildings or keeping them standing. Everywhere there is the menacing sense that the swamp is only ever inches away from taking over again, that Kolkata exists by the skin of its teeth, and that one day even its stones will vanish below the tides. But, just as everything decays, so it also finds another role. There's an organic quality to this city, a habit of using and reusing which goes beyond the usual Indian brilliance for recycling. Nothing – nothing at all – is wasted. At Burrabazzar wholesale market, there is a small quarter where the street people bring the scraps of cardboard, glass or metal that they have found discarded. Each thing, however small, is sorted and restored in some way: the metal melted down, the glass recycled, the paper pulped. Everything, even religious doctrine, is reused. One god is never one god, but is recycled as three. One life is never one life, but a potentially infinite set of reincarnations. Those imperial architraves and wrought-iron verandas are only on their second or third life in an eternity of recurrence.

Before arriving in Kolkata, all I knew about the place – aside from black holes and missionary positions – was a memorable section I'd once read in James Cameron's book *An Indian Summer*, in which he describes the place as 'the most irredeemably horrible, vile and despairing city in the world'. In his opinion, 'anyone who has lived in Calcutta can never again find serious fault with anywhere else'. He points out that Calcutta's namesake and 'patron saint' is not the domesticated Durga or the learned Saraswati, but scarlet-tongued Kali, the Black Mother. At the Kalighat temple, a goat is sacrificed most days of the week and a buffalo twice a year. The place drips with vermilion dye and a huge black lingam stands in a corner like a threat. Kali herself, unsatisfied and atrocious, stares out between the bars of her shrine at the passing pilgrims. In human form, Kali-Ma is usually depicted with four arms, one holding a sword, another the head of a slain giant, and the last two encouraging her worshippers. Her earrings are fashioned from cadavers, her necklace is of human skulls and her girdle is a belt of dead men's hands. Her face and breasts are smeared with the blood of her victims, and she stands on the prone form of her husband Siva.

Kali's legend takes several different forms, but in essence, she is the mother-goddess Durga reincarnated in warrior form to fight darkness on earth. When she saw that the world was overwhelmed by darkness, Durga transfigured herself into Kali and took on the forces of evil. When the battle was over and the ground littered with the corpses of her victims, Kali was so overjoyed at her victory that she began dancing. She danced and danced; she danced so hard that the ground shook and Siva begged her to stop. Lost in her frenzy, Kali did not notice him. Unable to attract her attention, Siva lay down among the bodies in protest. Kali danced on until she looked down to see that she was trampling on her own husband. Realising what she had done, she stopped dancing and thrust out her tongue in shame and self-disgust.

To anyone accustomed to a British God of sandals and moderation, Kali's bloody visage seems extreme; a black-and-scarlet goddess for a black-and-scarlet city. Kali is undoubtedly ferocious, but she is also both wifely and maternal. She is also Kolkata's protectress, keeping the city against the worst the world can throw at it, making bad blood into good. The city she guards is extreme, but then so is London, so is Monrovia, so is everywhere except perhaps Livingston or Belgium. And certainly you can expect to travel directly from a dinner during which you are served a dessert covered in gold-leaf to the local state hospital, in which 400 people share a single drip, a single bed and a single bandage. All the wealth and all the poverty coexists in a way that Englishmen accustomed to dissembling find altogether too naked for comfort. But Kolkata doesn't have the time or the inclination to mind. When it wants to – when, for instance, one of the important annual festivals comes round – it brushes down the streets, puts the dust aside, takes out its cleanest clothes and parties like every night was the last one. And when there are too many people and too much to absorb, it creates spaces in the filth, zones of silence amid the grumble of the car horns and the eviscerating smog. It has to. For half of Kolkata, there is no choice but to sleep or wash or take a wank right there by the side of a shopfront or under a tree. But at night, when the rickshaws are slid neatly into each other's arms by the side of the street, the shutters of the pavement shacks are closed, and the street sleepers are concealed under a small square of traffic cones and scaffold-netting, it looks more orderly. There is still plenty of activity – down at the vegetable market, people are sorting aubergines into beautiful, icy baskets, and a crocodile of men sway like landsick sailors across the road with a ton or so of potatoes resting on their heads. The dogs who creep and loiter during the day come out to chase off any stray cars, and the police take their long sticks to the backs of the sleepers in the station. The roads become roads again instead of vehicular free-for-alls, the stations become stationary, and the river flows on, only interrupted by the faint splash of a death or a sale.

Besides, Kolkata is used to people examining its dirt. That's what Kolkata does, that's what it's famous for. You go to Paris for spring, you go to Rome for the Pope, you go to Kolkata for dirt. You go there, you expect filth, squalor, despair. That's what you come to see. Except, of course, that nobody does go there, and nobody does see, because Calcutta has had everyone from Kipling onwards come to diagnose it, to tell the city that it's got every known and unknown tropical disease from cholera to falling sickness, that it's got no more than minutes to live, and – as one final parting insult – that it's unquestionably the worst case they've ever come across. It's had people from Rumer Godden to Geoffrey Moorhouse write whole books picking over its symptoms. And, of course, it's had Mother Teresa, who might have been considered saintlike (and is currently well on the way to beatification) but whose effect was to confirm the city's reputation as a place of iniquity, a hellhole in which all the world's poverty, dirt and violence were somehow gathered together in one vast urban nightmare. Even now, Kolkata's citizens speak of the city in the tones of a parent with a beloved but intransigent child, complaining that if only Kolkata could get over its filthy habits, its wastrel lifestyle and its penchant for gambling with all it should hold precious, it just might salvage something of its greatness. And every one of the voices has had its effect. Until the 1960s, there were still about 6,000 whites left over from Partition. They left when the communists came in. Now, there's only a few hundred ex-pats, and almost no tourists. Apart from our group and a few stray characters in the Oxford bookshop, I don't think I saw a white face all week. Which, in its own way, is both wonderful and disheartening, since if any city deserves the aimless millions from international tourism, it's Kolkata.

The most recent census put Greater Kolkata's population at 13 million, but the number is probably a hopeless underestimation, given its nomadic nature. Every day, something like a million people pass through the two stations, Sealdah and Howrah, coming in from Bihar and the surrounding countryside to work and, if there's a square patch of pavement left unoccupied, to sleep as well. Those who actually service the city are usually Moslems and rural commuters because West Bengal is the white-collar state and Kolkata is its babu capital. As 'sahib' was for the whites, so 'babu' was for the Indians, the honorific title once given to members of India's gentry. The name still holds its old respectful connotations, though its use is broader and more affectionate now. Though other parts of India may consider it a double-edged compliment, to have joined the Kolkatan babus is to have entered a papery state of grace.

That fondness for deskwork was, for a while,

Calcutta's undoing. When the Communists first took power in the early seventies, they inherited a city in decline. Calcutta had lost its status as the Indian capital in 1911 when Delhi took over the role; by the sixties, the city was losing its industry as well. The foreigners left and took their businesses with them, union power ran out of control and bureaucracy smothered everything under six-foot drifts of paper. For a while, the combination of babu culture and Marxist doctrine had the effect of petrifying everything exactly as it stood. The unions had absolute power, the babus had absolute authority, and West Bengal had an absolute right to consider its history far too good to improve on. Which, in practice, meant that nothing much started before 11 a.m., and then only managed an hour or so of desultory paper-rearrangement before going out on strike. Thirty years on, pragmatism has replaced dogma. Kolkata's idea of communism has become one capable of incorporating religion, property ownership, state collaboration with big business, and an enthusiasm for privatisation bordering on the Thatcherite. Today's leaders appear to be doing all they can both to encourage business and to keep union power under control. Things work. Admittedly, they work only with the addition of a lot of rubber stamps, but the general mindset is now a can-do one, rather than a can't-do-and-particularly-not-if-it-interferes-with-lunch one. In 1984, the city gained India's first metro system, a single line running straight from north to south. It has become part of Kolkata's pride now, one of the cleanest, cheapest and most effective underground systems in the world. Along with the tentative return of big business and the increasing numbers of women in the workplace, the metro has become a physical symbol of the city's regeneration.

Like many of the old industrial cities of Britain, there are growing signs that Kolkata has picked itself up and is ready again for a higher reincarnation.

Not that the casual visitor would ever have seen much evidence of inertia. Napoleon might have considered the British a nation of shopkeepers, but he'd evidently never come to Kolkata. On every pavement and every street corner, there is someone selling something; a garland of marigolds, a pan of samosas, chai in small hand-turned terracotta cups, silver strings of washing-powder packets, sweetmeats, bracelets, children's toys, paan, rice, coconuts, daal. Within the space of a block, you can find everything from saris to luggage to shoeshine boys. Somewhere in the few hundred yards between the hotel and the metro station, you can get your moustache clipped, a full set of luggage, a brace of malfunctioning lighters, a three-course meal, a set of Bollywood posters, and enough tea to float Darjeeling. All of it is somehow rendered beautiful merely through the act of replication. The hawkers sell their wares, and the children sell the hawkers' scavengings. Someone, somewhere is always offering something. The effect of so much steady enterprise is to make all other nations seem lame by comparison.

Back out on the water, the light is stronger than on the streets, but even here it never sharpens completely. Avijit Bagchi is both the boat's owner and our guide, though he confesses at the end of the journey that he would prefer to get rid of all three of his elegant wooden launches, since they swallow money and attract less and less business with every passing year. We sit in the centre of the stream, and watch the city begin to blur at the edges. Like most other Indian cities, Kolkata has a breathtaking pollution problem. Most vehicles in India drive on low-grade petrol or diesel – not four star, not even two star, but some kind of vicious sub-continental minus-star. The mixture of private cars, Kolkata's native ambassadors ('bowler hats on wheels', according to the writer Geoffrey Moorhouse), buses farting poisonous fumes, lorries painted with the face of Shiva or Krishna or Ganesh and the legend Horn Please OK all combine to produce a form of pollution which reeks like sin. If you listen, you can hear it killing everyone around you. Regular drivers have a cough – small, tight, not the usual theatrical hawking – which you know is the kind of cough that, sooner or later, became a choke and then a death-rattle. The pollution has two effects. First, it changes the light. Colours are muted, views are softened, and all lamps – no matter how powerful – seem to be dimmer by a good 40 watts or so. At night, car headlights form perfect cones of brightness through the gloom, and during the daytime it feels like watching life go by behind a veil of mosquito netting. And secondly, it means that everyone has to wash more frequently. Which, presumably, will make Kolkata's water run out all the faster. The city already had one of the highest population densities in the world; now it also has an impending drought problem as well. At the moment, Kolkata can afford to be relatively profligate both with water and with electricity. In the street, there are standpipes and fountains spurting 24 hours a day, and at night, the lights come on like a permanent Diwali. Even the hotels do not include the usual polite notice to conserve water or to keep your towels for another day. People wash themselves as often as they can, even in winter. In the past, the monsoon would replenish the supply. Now, with the increase in population and the prospect of changes to the planning laws, the water table is going down and is not being restored. In ten years or so, the water may well be gone. Kolkata and all its 15 or 20 million souls will run dry.

The launch moves downstream, underneath the thick steel webbing of the Howrah bridge and down towards the new toll bridge at Prinsep Ghat. Along both banks, there are warehouses, stations, landing-places; evidence of Calcutta's past vitality and its present significance. Downstream, there is Howrah station, the warehouses which used to service it, the two bridges, and – on the right bank – mile after mile of derelict history. There are dockyards, two merchant and one naval, a sawmill, the Moslem quarter, an oil refinery, and the remains of the largest tea-wharf in India. Unlike the main stream of the Ganges, the Hooghly is comparatively slow, and has to be dredged frequently in order to keep it open. Several of the shipyards along its length are still working, but since the river in Kolkata is no more than 15 or 20 feet deep, it is impossible to build ships of more than 20,000 tons. On the other side is the Botanical Gardens stretching for miles downstream, the terracotta chimney stacks of the brick kilns, and a cattle-shed. If you look closely, you can see all Calcutta's past written here along the banks, in the warehouses now sliding back into the jungle, the bathing ghats, the shipyards, the steel mills, the old colonial houses flowing with bright saris and the riverbank notice – covered in quick-growing creeper – on which there is written the single word, 'Wreck'.

The remains of the warehouses also serve as a reminder of another river in another country. A century ago, it was said that a man could have walked from one bank of the Thames to the other over the backs of all the merchant vessels moored there. In 1800, London's river was estimated to support half a million individuals, from shipowners to mudlarks. Children picked through the filth on its banks in search of brass rivets or old iron, while above them in the city's sandstone palaces the bankers estimated that the Thames generated £10 million in revenues for London every single year. Patrick Colquhoun, who set out the original scheme for a separate Thames police force, claimed that in 1800 there were 40,000 journeymen and labourers employed full-time loading and unloading the incoming vessels, and that at least 1,250 fishermen were taking their living from the Thames. Much of that revenue, and almost all of those ships, arrived in the Thames direct from the four quarters of Britain's empire. In the first two decades of the nineteenth century, the East India Company was exporting goods valued at over £5 million per annum, most of which came through Calcutta. What flowed out of the Hooghly then flowed into the Thames. Jute, cotton, steel, silk, tea, jewels and stones moved in a steady, unending procession across the ocean; as one city emptied, so the other filled up. Now, Kolkata's empty slipways and rusted gantries also have their direct counterparts in London. Though 90 per cent of Britain's imports still arrive by sea, the Thames long since stopped being their main port of arrival. Londoners wanting to get from one bank to another would have to walk on water now.

But it is also down here near the oil refineries that the parallels with the Thames begin to run out. Here, the similarities are not with London, but with cities further north. In many ways, Kolkata's fortunes mirror those of Glasgow or Liverpool – once-great industrial and manufacturing cities with huge and literate migrant populations, working rivers and superiority complexes.

As in Glasgow, you're quite liable to find yourself having a discussion about Tagore or theology or the meaning of the new hotels with a taxi driver or a bank clerk. And as in Glasgow, there are also the old dead industries, the unionisation, the politics, and the sod-you sense of identity. Since the Empire pitched all its cities into direct competition with each other, the parallels are hardly surprising, but they do also serve as a reminder that, when and if the Raj worked, it did so because there is a particular affinity between the British character and the Indian one. Ask people now about colonialism, and they say, 'better the Britishers than anyone else', the thinking being that at least the British were impartially brutal. They were also non-sectarian, and much less interested in obscure points of Hindu or Islamic doctrine than in making money, which – given the Indian capacity for enterprise – is at least one common language between the two races.

Perhaps the British didn't bother with theology because, being products of a monotheistic culture, India's sheer generosity of choice made it impossible for them to take it on. Part of the difficulty with Hindu mythology is that, like Mother Ganga's names, there are at least 108 possible variations of every story. The trinity of gods, Shiva, Vishnu and Indra, each have their own accounts, and each has the capacity to appear in a variety of different incarnations. Attempting to go from nought to sixty on the essential Sanskrit texts in a week is therefore a bit tricky. I did, however, discover a faster path to enlightenment. Perhaps uniquely, it isn't to be found on the river at all, but on Calcutta's roads. Those wanting to understand India should take a drive at any time of the day or night, but should preferably do so during the morning or evening rush-hours. On it, you will learn that there are always at least three possible ways of approaching any route (backwards, forwards or sideways), that you should never on any account look behind you, that a strict but invisible hierarchy operates in all things, that an untimely death is only a passport to a better life, that it is necessary to hold fast to a belief in karma, that the true believer must pray with frequency and fervour, and that enlightenment is to be reached by first passing through several subsidiary stages – bewilderment, terror, intimate awareness of one's mortality – on the way to a state of almost trance-like peace and acceptance.

Even this technique is not enough to prepare anyone for Kumartuli, the place where the river gods and goddesses are made. On the launch a couple of days previously, Avijit had explained the process by which the clay idols were made. Each of Calcutta's regular annual pujas celebrated a different god, and each of those gods had their earthly manifestations. At Kumartuli, sculptures representing Durga, Kali or Saraswati would be modelled out of clay, bamboo and hay. When the time for their particular puja came round again, the models would be decorated, worshipped and then immersed in the river. From Avijit's description, I had an impression of these idols as something quite crude and temporary, small things almost like corn-dolls assembled out of a bit of river-mud and a few spare sticks. I should have known better. Guided by Amar and Jeevan, two Future Hope alumni who knew and saw more of this place than I could ever hope to understand, we take a trip across the city. Stepping off the main street and down a small alleyway, we enter a quarter filled with busy stalls on either side of the road. In the first few stalls, scaffolders crouch, trussing lengths of bamboo together to make the bones of a figure, or to provide the supports for their final positioning. A few paces past them the straw-men are overlaying the bamboo with thick muscles of hay, fleshing out the figures' limbs, adding a recognisable gender, giving them four legs or ten arms. Beside them, their newly clad figures stand sinewy and headless by the edges of the narrow street. Their limbs are bound with string, and their bamboo skeletons poke out bonily from wrists and ankles. Beyond them, there are the sculptors who apply the first layer of river mud – a thick, sticky clay with the consistency of grey plasticine – over the hay. The clay goes on in several stages, layer over layer, and all along the street there are drying figures standing or reclining on plastic picnic chairs as their limbs crack slowly in the shadows. And then there are people who make only hands, or only feet, or only the avatars on which the gods will stand. Finally there are the finishers and painters who apply two or three final coats of mud, and then paint and decorate the sculptures.

And these things are neither crude nor small. Some of the sculptures were double my height, and delicate as spun glass. Round a corner, and you are confronted by a dozen amputated hands, pointing or gesturing or lying with open palm outstretched. Go another few feet, and a life-size lion crouches in mid-spring, Aslan turned to clay. Look up, and you are staring into the glazed eyes of Mother Teresa, twice as aged and twice as cracked as she was in real life. On the other side is a footless sadhu, his clay hands bound together in perpetual prayer, while round his feet scurry tiny clay rats. Up above, a figure with four arms, a vastly pregnant stomach and the tusked head of Ganesh stands as if in conversation with a rearing, wild-eyed horse. One workshop has begun taking on private commissions, and three sculptors sit below the figures of an Indian cricket captain, a full-size model of St Christopher carrying his human burden over his shoulder, a coconut-breasted bust of a woman, and a laughing Chinese man dressed in a magician's waistcoat and mandarin's velvet cap. Beyond them, the idols wait like their makers' petrified relatives for the next stage of their many incarnations, and for their separate festivals to bring them to life. From September to January, there are several pujas, each belonging to a different god or goddess. September and October (the date depends on the timing of the full moon) is Durga puja. Durga is either represented as a ten-armed demon-slayer riding a lion, or as a sweet-natured and obedient wife. Shortly after the end of Durga puja, there is Kali puja, and lastly, in January, there is Saraswati puja. Saraswati is the goddess of learning, and is usually shown holding an instrument like a sitar and riding on a swan. When each separate puja comes round, the idols are carried down to the river, worshipped, rotated seven times and then immersed in the water. Some dissolve almost completely, but others take no more than a brisk skinny-dip and emerge from the river with a bit of damaged paintwork and a peeled backside. The unmelted ones are hauled out onto the bank, dried out and taken back to the Kumartuli workshops for restoration. The work goes on all year round, and it is both logistically and theologically awesome.

Another side of Kolkata's relationship with the river can be seen a few streets away, down on Strand Road. The Strand is Kolkata's Lover's Lane, a place where courting couples can come in search of a few hours of peace and perhaps the chance to do something a bit

more western than just holding hands. Halfway along
its length is the Millennium Park, an area of green and
sculpted pathways, climbing-frames and river views,
where couples and families come to promenade in the
French manner. Until it was built a few years ago, this
patch of land was waste ground between the river and
the street, bisected by the railway tracks (not that any
land, however small, is ever truly wasted in Kolkata.
Everything from the steps of the landing ghats to the
market kerbsides shaking with the weight of delivery
lorries supports someone, somewhere, concealed under
makeshift palm-leaf roofs and plastic walls or using a
single sheet of newsprint for a mattress). Now, at the
end of Ramadan, the Millennium Park has turned into a
parade-ground for Kolkata's finest family fashions.
Women in their newest saris and salwar kameez sit
watching the drifts of passing weed while their children
spin dizzyingly round and round on the bars of the
climbing frames. Groups of men in shiny new-style suits
huddle and laugh together, while in a corner behind a
tree, a man and a woman lean into each other,
oblivious to everything around them. A group of
teenage girls dressed in jeans conspire from one of the
stone benches. In the past five years, the fashion for
Western clothes has spread quickly. Although there are
still certain taboos – no exposed arms, no exposed legs,
hair never flowing free – very few women have their
heads covered, and even in winter there is still
considerable scope for suggestion. It is, as it should be,
completely impossible to tell who is Moslem and who
Hindu. The end of Ramadan is a cause for celebration,
and Kolkatans generally couldn't care less if the
celebration belongs to someone else. One of the city's
distinctive virtues is its lack of angst over religion.

Under the Communists, West Bengal is ostensibly secular, which means in practice that all creeds are considered equally valid and that the explosive tensions present in other parts of India rarely reach Kolkata. Now, as Islam breaks its fast, the Park has become a place for Hindu, Moslem, Catholic and Sikh to mingle in one great amorphous swirl of colour. For once, they're not looking to the river, but at each other.

Meanwhile, out in the stream of the river, the sun begins to dip down into the thickening smog. Even at dusk, there are still signs of activity; the splash of a dolphin or a porpoise, the widening rings of a fish rising, the splash of something only sensed. All along the Hooghly's length, there are prawn fishermen at work who will either sell their catch at the nearest ghat or take it down to the Burrabazzar. Bengal consumes more fish than any other part of India, and as Avijit explains, 'prawns is a very preferred fish for Bengalis'. Most of the fishermen would work and sleep on their boats for ten days or a fortnight, fishing up and down the river and then returning to their homes in Bihar. The boats are no more than about eight or ten feet long, elegant little slivers of wood shaped like floating banana leaves. They seem to have almost no draught at all, but each has a tiny slatted deck and underneath it a water-filled hold where the fish are thrown as they come from the line. Halfway down the boat's length is a palm-thatched semi-circular shelter where the fisher-man and his son will sleep. Up in the bow is a cooking pot, a few lengths of line and a pan full of bait, while down on the stern the fisherman's son pokes his way along the banks. The best fish is either ilish or becti, varieties exclusive to the Hooghly and much beloved by Kolkatans. It's a fat, flat sort of fish, with a grey back, a white underbelly, large silver-pink scales and the snout of a foreshortened boxer dog. The flesh is white and light, like sea-bass or sole, and tastes exquisite.

Down at the New Market, the wholesalers sell the day's catch to shops and restaurateurs. Pacing through the gloom, the buyers point and barter while on each stall one man sits crouched over a pad and calculator, and another man bisects each specimen with the speed of long practice. Shivaji Ojha, purveyor of at least 1,000 kg of fresh fish every day to Kolkata's restaurants, instructs one of his helpers to show me each variety's place in the social and economic hierarchy. The helper lays them out in a long neat line on the floor, a fine two-foot becti at the top, then a silver and a rock-salmon (both thinner and spikier than their Scottish counterparts), a fat haddock, two kinds of red snapper, two carp, and then a series of cheaper, bonier fish, each with the high pikey snouts of the becti. Right at the bottom of the line is a leatherskin, mackerel-spotted, spiny, and corrugated with a line of spikes up the flat of its back. The buyers can take the fish whole or – for a premium – filleted, and Ojha does steady year-round business. During the wedding season (November through February) and the monsoon (June through October), prices rise from 140 rupees per kilo whole to 350 per kilo. Becti is, he says, 'a very speciality fish', a sweet-water treat to be produced at weekends and by the rich. In the monsoon season it is joined by ilish, a seafish which, like salmon, lays its eggs in rivers and will be netted while spawning. Over on a corner of the fish-market floor next to a basket of discarded leatherskins, two men crouch on a polythene sheet, taking the discarded offcuts and chopping off any remaining flesh on a blade shaped like an upright scimitar. Over on the other stalls, dealers are weighing out five different types of prawns, from maggoty-white shrimps through huge, whiskery tiger prawns. They, and the various seafish, will have been caught 30 miles away out in the Bay of Bengal, but the majority of the fresh-water specimens will have been caught out in the Hooghly amidst the factories and the ghats.

Thinking about it afterwards, I don't know why it should seem so strange for that night's fish supper to come straight from a city-centre river, but it does. It was, after all, only two or three generations back that Britain expected just the same from the Clyde or the Mersey, and the recent return of trout to the Thames has been widely advertised. Besides, one of Southern India's most famously photogenic images is of the Chinese fishing nets at Kerala, and it is only when you get there that you realise the nets are eternally dipping and lifting into a major shipping channel. Attempts have been made to get the factories and generating stations to treat their outflows into the Hooghly, though – as with many things – the success of the regulations varies from place to place, and from source to source. Contaminated, neglected and exploited it may be, but even then the Hooghly remains as part of Kolkata's present life, not a part of its history.

Almost the last river-visit we make is to the Nimtala burning ghat. Here, the corpses of Calcutta's dead are carried shoulder-high on garlanded biers down the street and in through a small stone archway to a place smelling of incense and over-cooked meat. Directly in front of the archway is the landing-stage itself, its sloping stone walkway sprinkled with water-weed and reminders of the things which have passed this way; a hank of human hair, a beaded bracelet, a smear of henna, the wilted remains of a garland. On both sides of the ghat are raised platforms covered with hoods, their floors marked with four shallow six-foot indentations. Two of the pyres are full of ashes, and two are covered with what looks at first like no more than a well-constructed bonfire of logs, burning white under the afternoon sun. A pair of human feet poke out at the end, swelling and yellow beneath the flames. The toes and soles have begun to ripen from the heat, and each toe has become perfectly round, like a puffball mushroom before it pops. The fires are watched over by a small group of crouching attendants, poking at the burning branches or just sitting on their haunches gazing into the flames. Richer corpses will be burned quickly on logs of sandalwood, poorer ones on cheaper, slower wood. The very poorest will not be burned at all, but cast into the river whole, unblessed and untouched. The victims of snake bites are considered to have had their souls stolen by the snake god, and thus to have reached a state similar to purgatory, unable to move forward into the next life or backwards into this one. They will be put on rafts, covered with cloth, and floated off down the river as offering or appeasement. The Doms – those who tend the dead – are considered both the lowest of the untouchables and worthy of great respect, shepherding their charges from this life to the next. On the other side of the archway, the family sit and watch. Relatives bend together to murmur taut words at each other, the Doms mutter between themselves, and the ubiquitous children splash and play down at the edge of the ghat, watched but not attended. Around them and behind, you can hear Kolkata talking to itself; the car horns, the shriek of rusty brakes, the intermittent pinging of a bicycle bell or a boat's klaxon. The burning ghat is quieter than most places in the city, but even here, there's still movement and conversation. Women are allowed to come to cremations, but only briefly, since observing the dissolution of one's closest relations remains a predominantly male task. I've seen human corpses before, but there's still something startling about watching the equivalent of your cousin or your mother flame-grilled before your eyes. Sitting in Presbyterian silence in the chapel of Mortonhall cemetery waiting for the hydraulic whirr of the coffin-slide and the disappearance of Auntie Morag through the eau-de-nil curtain is not the same as this. At least there is no space left for imagination here.

Oddly, it is not here that things feel funereal. That comes a few days later amongst the abstracted silence of Londoners. It may well be that returning from India always feels this way. It's probably completely normal to walk directly into a typhoon of images and impressions and strange, hyper-sensational experiences hurled towards you without order or form – cycles of life, death rituals, the floating past, night-fishing – and then just as abruptly to find yourself back amidst the shrivelled calm of Britain. It probably doesn't help to have gobbled far too much information all at one go, and thus to find myself dealing with a painful case of indigestion back at home. But perhaps such monumental sensory overload is no more than a suitable acknowledgement of both Kolkata and her river. If the Hooghly has a thousand incarnations, then the only way to do her justice is to see her through a hundred different lives.

A Hundred Different Lives

W.F. DEEDES

IT had been a terrible summer, and a flash flood wiped out the early seedlings. Ashish Mondal liked to believe he had farming blood in his veins, but like his hair, the old blood was thinning now, and he had come to feel different from his beloved father, who had enjoyed a better life with the land. Abdul's two brothers had some of the newer wisdom: when father died, they took their share and moved to the city as soon as they could.

Ashish didn't want to move. He would rather have taken other jobs to supplement the farm work, but there was no regular work, not for his kind, the low caste. Work in any government service was ruled out. There were too many applicants for menial jobs, and, as Shefali gently reminded her husband, he was not a persuasive character. But things got worse when Shefali became sick. When the local doctor came to look at her, he shook his head. (He did this to most of his patients.) It was not because he didn't know the answer, but because he knew what was wrong but lacked the resources to put it right. Dr Bose was not the greatest of doctors, but he was a good man and preferred not to mislead his patients.

The doctor shook his head after looking at Shefali, explaining gently that she was suffering from the sort of respiratory problems that could lead to tuberculosis. No, she hadn't got TB, only a ticket in that direction. He could have added something about malnutrition, but the good doctor stopped short, aware that it didn't make much difference as food and drugs were equally scarce.

There was a robbery, though as robberies go it was no big deal. They had gone to a distant market in hope of getting a better price for what they had. The journey had taken most of the day. The three children had spent the time in care of a friendly neighbour. So the thief had an easy time of it and had taken several hundred rupees which Ashish had saved and some trinkets belonging to Shefali. Ashish had persuaded himself that the rupees were safely hidden in a place no thief was likely to look but it proved to be the first place the thief searched. He knew what he was doing. A local social worker who knew all about him had once asked him why he was a thief. 'Because thieving is what I do,' he answered simply.

The theft went very deep with Lillian for reasons she found hard to explain to Ashish. She felt all her final privacies had been invaded; she felt exposed by this stranger and his skill. Ashish, resigned to hardships and disappointments, sought to reason with her. It might have been so much worse, he pointed out. One of the children might have been taken, the house might have been burned down or damaged. But Shefali had resolved in her own mind that it was time to move away. It was true that she thought more often and deeply than Ashish about their children. Sunil was in school. The three teachers there were good-hearted but unqualified, and the sum of Sunil's knowledge was that of a child two or three years younger. This grieved his mother: she wanted for her son what she had never had for herself. Ashish, supposing, in his way, that farming blood ran in his veins, considered it less important. Rina, the daughter aged five, and Subhas, four, were not yet part of the great problems of spelling and arithmetic.

Looking ahead, Shefali saw the village as empty of promise for her children. She knew that none of them was getting what they needed to eat. The children were not starved, but there was never enough. Sooner or later, she told herself, for the sake of the children, they must abandon this smallholding and venture into the world. She knew she must take her time: Ashish would not be captivated by the idea. On the contrary, he would resist it. He would see it as a failure of his stewardship. He would plead that the children were too young.

Her intuition was sound enough, but the stars move mysteriously, and it was Ashish, in fact, who first raised the subject with her. He had been talking to his friend and neighbour Ashok Saha, who also ran a smallholding. Saha and his wife had only one child, a son of eleven. He was of an age when boys of all races become socially inquisitive, and he had been asking his father questions. Ashok Saha had explained rather clumsily why they held lowly status within the village. It was tradition, it was to be expected, it was inevitable. The boy had not taken this well. Bruised by some encounter in the village, he had turned to his father for reassurance but had been told instead that history required him to see himself as inferior and learn to put up with it. When his mother Gita heard of this, she feared that her only son might well be tempted to run away from home.

She knew this happened often: young children, running, running, disappearing. Moreover she remembered cousins in a village not far away who had moved to Calcutta. It was a long way away, more than 500 kilometres, but it was said that the people of what was now Kolkata were closer together socially than they were ever likely to be in her village of Pukurtala. 'There is a tolerance here,' her cousins had written to say after a long interval. 'People treat each other as equal.'

'Ashok and Gita are leaving us,' Ashish said to Lillian one night.

'It is not the worst thing,' she replied. 'There is nothing for us now in the village. Nothing in the fields. The school is nothing. We are nothing.'

The plans for a move began to take shape. There were long discussions about the drawbacks; the journey would be arduous for a woman in poor health. It would have to start at the bus stop which was seven kilometres from where they lived. They would need this bus to take them to the railhead from which trains go to Kolkata. And on reaching Kolkata, where would they live? Ashok claimed to have a friend on the southern outskirts of Kolkata who had won temporary accommodation by offering to help the landlord to finish the construction of the building.

Neither Shefali nor Gita thought this sounded very promising. Men were always so much more optimistic about such propositions. But the sale of their small properties in the village had been put in hand, and the hopes of both families had gone too far. A local agent had booked their tickets on the bus and the cheapest accommodation on the train. Of course, the bus had been overbooked. Some sixteen people in the village (including children) had bought tickets, but only seven seats proved to be available; yet somehow Ashish, rising from his habitual mood of resignation to all hardships, had secured a seat for his wife and two of the children, and they set off from the tiny bus stop.

The sun was setting and then darkness fell soon after the journey began. Five miles on, the driver announced a puncture in one of the front tires. The luggage could remain where it was, he said, but all the passengers must dismount. Ashish sighed, and fixed his mind on making sure that when they set off again his wife would be restored to her seat. Shefali, who often thought a little ahead of Ashish, wondered now if the bus would ever reach the railhead in time for the night train.

The invisible hand which sometimes stretches out to human beings in their hours of need began to make itself felt. The bus sped into the night; the train was late leaving. With unexpected ease, Ashish and Shefali, their three children together with Ashok, Gita and Samir were able to find seats in the long train, stow their luggage, and settle down. Journeys are unknowable: minutes and hours and great swathes of darkness pass by the window while the two families dwell in the innocence of sleep. The children woke first with the daylight while the train was still some 20 miles from Kolkata. Ashok had assured them that his friend from the suburbs would meet them. Ashish felt doubtful about this, Shefali even more so, but they looked about them expectantly as the train drew in to Howrah station. Their expectant eyes seemed to draw a strange young man towards them. 'Forgive me,' he exclaimed. 'My name is Thornton Hill. I'm a correspondent for the *Times-Herald* of New York. Can we get acquainted?'

Ashish returned a blank look. The rest of the party ignored the young man and began hauling baggage out of the train. Lillian had not left her seat and Thornton Hill turned towards her. He seemed to have a young woman with him, and she was a better speaker. The woman turned to Lillian with a bright smile.

'You must forgive us,' she said in broken Hindi. 'You look exhausted. Maybe I can help a little. I used to work here and I'm on holiday, looking round Calcutta. Thornton is a journalist interesting himself in people moving into Calcutta. He's looking at case histories.' The woman paused. Shefali had understood some of it and grasped none of it. But instinct suggested that this was a friendly pair of human beings. Ashok's friend was nowhere to be seen. So she smiled back wearily, saying nothing.

Thornton Hill, older and smarter than he looked, was reaching conclusions of his own. The weight of baggage told the story. These were prospective settlers. He had spotted Mary Hind in his hotel a couple of nights earlier dining with a group of Indian friends, had reckoned she might be helpful and had told her of his assignment. 'The place to start,' she had advised him, 'is one of the railheads where they come in from the East. That's where you'd find the rural migrants venturing into the big city. I can guide you.' Standing on the crowded platform, Ashok was making excuses to Ashish for his friend who had failed to appear. He would be helping his landlord get a roof up. He was not entirely his own master. For the time being he had to do what he was told. Ashish listened patiently: his low expectation of life had led him to foresee this, himself and Shefali and their three children stranded on a platform at Howrah Station, islanded indeed, all of them surrounded by piles of baggage with no means of moving it anywhere and no fixed address to which it could be moved. Looking about him, however, Ashish saw a pool of labour clamouring to assist the two families.

Thornton Hill turned to him. 'Where ya for?' Mary Hind interpreted this. Ashok drew from the pocket of his jacket a folded slip, on which was written:

113/17A, Tiljala Road, Kolkata
(Bariwala Manoj Das).

She showed the slip to Thornton. 'From recollection of earlier days,' said Mary Hind, 'I fancy that encampment is newest, and quite one of the nastiest.'

'Meaning?'

'There's this ring of shanty, or bustees as they call it here, round much of the city.' She was half-whispering to the reporter. 'The small landowners make a killing by offering space to new arrivals. It's like a camp without any order at all. The migrants arrive, rig something up, get settled, live in squalor, psychologically further from the city than when they started from home. Then the kids get sick – run away.'

Mary Hind shrugged her shoulders as Ashish and Shefali, Ashok and Gita and their four children began to move off with boys who, unasked, were shouldering the bags.

'We know where they're heading?' said Thornton. 'They'll take a while to get there. We'll go later. I need breakfast.'

'You'll be lucky to find them again in that jungle,' said Mary lightly.

They returned to Thornton's driver waiting outside the station, and drove to the nearest hotel for toast and coffee.

Later, lifting up a sugar spoon, Mary Hind's mind turned to the four children they had just seen, particularly the two elder boys Sunil and Samir. 'You saw the faces of those two older boys?' she said to Thornton.

'Vaguely.'

'We none of us pay enough attention to what children want to tell us,' she declared. 'It never enters our heads they might see further than we do, might have useful advice to offer.'

'Part of the social worker's doctrine?' said Thornton with a disarming smile.

'I've worked with children most of my life,' she said. 'Long enough to know that we don't take them seriously enough. We don't have to conform to all their wishes, but it's sometimes useful to know what their wishes are.'

'Wishing. We're all wishing.'

'You had to read their faces.'

'To see?'

'Doubt. Doubt, primarily. Have we come to the right place? Was this a sensible move by mother and father?'

'Children never enjoy change,' argued Thornton, munching toast. 'They live by routine.'

'I'll bet you a day's fee,' said Mary Hind, ignoring his observation. 'Those boys saw further into the future than their parents did. Kids grow up fast in this country. That's why there are around a hundred thousand of them loose on the streets of Calcutta.'

'That's a fair number.'

'Well, I don't think anyone knows the exact number. It's what the Indian societies who try to cope . . . Thornton, are you interested in that group we met?'

'Sure. I'd like to follow them into that . . . what did you say . . . slum?'

'Bustee. Yes. Let's give them a day or two to settle. A day or two. If they ever settle.'

Three hot days had passed. Two of Mary Hind's Indian friends did social work in the Tilijala area. 'Locating them may not be all that difficult,' said one. 'There's a kind of pecking order for new arrivals in this particular dump and they will be on the eastward side.' They left Thornton's hired land cruiser and walked down a track until they reached a clearing in what had once been a wood. Almost all the trees had been hacked down to make firewood for cooking. At first it looked as if they were approaching an abandoned camp. Decaying vegetables and empty cans lay beside rigged up tarpaulins. The lucky ones enjoyed a canopy of corrugated iron.

In a sure-footed style which surprised Thornton, the Indian women picked their way down rough tracks, stopped, took fresh bearings and walked on a few yards. Ashish, who had been vainly trying to comfort his wife since dawn, looked up with astonishment to see the vaguely familiar face of Thornton Hill staring down at him. He turned instinctively towards the two social workers, began to speak rapidly, glancing from time to time at the face of his wife. The story was soon told. Both boys, Sunil and Samir, had disappeared. Ashok Saha joined the group, perpetually shaking his head. Mary Hind's quick mind at first wondered why the two mothers were not together comforting each other. It emerged that in the shock of finding the boys gone they had fallen into a grievous misunderstanding as to which boy had been the likely ringleader.

Thornton Hill took a step or two back. He assumed, in his way, that this was a scene best left to women. Mary Hind and the two social workers sat down on the ground, made a sympathetic gesture which appealed for calm and began to gather particulars. Ashish and Ashok recited all they knew. The boys had been there, when, after the roughest of evening meals, the two families had lain down and sought sleep. Shefali, with her heart-rending face, sat listening, nodding and wiping her eyes. After twenty minutes, Mary Hind rose and signalled to Thornton and the Indian social workers to draw a little apart. 'The boys will shortly become untraceable. There are tens of thousands . . .' She paused, as if to consider. 'They're looking for something better,' she said, 'without a clue how to find it.'

The social workers spoke up. They were saying a lot of people were on the lookout for house boys, who in effect became slaves. Even law enforcers used these children. Child labour was being reduced, but it still happened. One of the social workers had a profession-al way of counting things off on her fingers. 'There were 40,000 sex workers in Kolkata, a fifth of them under the age of 14,' she said. Thornton Hill smiled when necessary and took careful notes in a pad from Smythson of Bond Street.

Mary Hind returned to Ashish and Ashok. 'We'd like to help if we can. We think it's unlikely your sons have simply run away – more likely they're on some kind of search.' Ashok looked puzzled. Ashish wore his habitu-al look of submissiveness. A surge of irritation suddenly broke over Mary: these Indians and their incurable infe-riority complex! 'Now,' she said. 'We think they'll be back – no, not immediately, but maybe sooner than you think. Meanwhile, don't on any account move from here. If you move, they can never find you.'

Mary returned to Thornton, who was looking around him, note-taking, looking uncomfortable. 'They haven't a pump, they haven't a drain,' he exclaimed. 'And some bastard is getting rent for this?'

'I'm kicking myself,' said Mary Hind. She drew a small digital camera out of her bag. 'I bought this for my Calcutta holiday and I had a mind to photograph those two boys on the platform. That might have been useful now.'

Ashish's uncle lived in Kolkata. He had not been seen in a long while, but they knew he was there, and they knew roughly where he lived. Could it be that this was where Sunil had gone? Ashish expected the answer to come from someone else. What did they think about it? Mary said. 'The bustee in Calcutta is everywhere, not just on the fringes.'

'You assume my uncle lives in a slum?'

'No, I don't.'

Ashish returned to his wife.

On the following afternoon Shefali listened again to what the social workers had to say, nodding her head and then repeating to Mary Hind some of what she had been saying to her husband. He was a good son. Within their economic limitations she and Ashish had striven to be good parents. The love they had for their son and his love for them formed a bond that would not be easily broken. He had had virtually no education but he had unusual understanding for his age.

Over a late supper of curried fish and Indian-bottled French claret, Mary discussed this encounter with Thornton Hill, who had spent his day exploring the role of the small landlord in Kolkata's extensive bustees. 'I'll grant,' said Thornton briskly, 'those boys probably went off with good intentions. But it's going to take much more than a mother's faith to bring them back.' Thornton sipped his wine and gazed into the glass. 'You seriously think those boys have got a chance?'

'I wasn't discussing what *I* thought,' said Mary firmly. 'I was telling you what one of their mothers thought.'

'You believe that stuff?'

'She has her faith. Who am I to discredit it?'

'You believe any kind of divine force pervades this goddam city? You should have been with me today where they wash under a pump and queue twenty minutes for the toilet.'

'Once upon a time, I worked in this city!' said Mary drily.

'My simple heart refuses to believe that maternal love is going to draw a boy back to his mother like some kinda magnet. The age of miracles is dead.'

'Thanks for supper,' said Mary.

On the morning after their arrival in Kolkata, both Sunil and Samir, awakening at dawn, had observed half a dozen other boys in the camp going to bathe in the river a short distance away. As they had not seen water since leaving their village, the idea had strong attractions. They had risen stealthily, left their sleeping parents and joined the bathers. Bathing done, most of the boys had drifted aimlessly away from the squalid camp and were kicking a ball on a neighbouring property when angry shouting was heard, men with sticks appeared and a chase began. As it entered a narrow road the chase was joined by a policeman who was passing on a motorbike. Sunil and Samir ran with the rest, who, after a while, scattered expertly to confuse the policeman.

'We must return quickly,' said Sunil to Samir breathlessly when it seemed safe to stop. 'I'm sure I know the way back.' But it was soon apparent that he did not: they were lost in an ugly part of Kolkata's shantyland. Every squatters' camp of bamboo poles and rough awning looked the same. A few women were astir, working round small wood fires and cooking pots, but it was pointless to ask them for directions for neither boy could remember what the place where their families had settled was called.

They walked anxiously towards the rising sun, looking for a solid road. Neither was yet unduly distressed. Boys of eight and nine in India develop independence faster than their brothers in the West. The solid core of self-assurance within both of them held firm, yet both realised their unexplained absence would alarm their parents. It was important to find a way back soon. A mile or two on they came to a road. At one end of it there appeared to be something like a bus stop. As they hastened towards it, Samir realised that neither of them carried a single rupee in their pockets. Perversely, the bus stop displayed signs that at least one bus ran to a railway station.

'There might be money to be made at the station,' said Sunil, 'but we need to reach the station.'

'Ride the outside of the bus,' suggested Samir. By the time they had been ordered off the bus, they were within walking distance of the station. They joined a strange company of hawkers, beggars, travellers and boys of their own age who treated the station's platforms as home. They drifted round, attracting no attention until a young Indian woman eyed them doubtfully. She felt drawn to do this because she was a trainee in a little Indian society which had recently been set up to care for the needs of platform children at this particular station. It was the society which Mary Hind would be visiting two days later.

'You have just come here?' she said. Samir had reached a point when anxiety about their predicament was beginning to invade his self-confidence. He was also hungry. It entered his mind that they might both save themselves a lot of trouble by telling this friendly-looking woman how they came to be where they were. In which case this tale would soon be ended. But Sunil thought differently. 'We work here,' he explained.

'Begging?'

'No,' said Sunil with dignity, 'we are vendors.' Samir saw it as his duty to nod at this. The young trainee hesitated. She was there to offer help to platform-children in need, offer them night shelter in small dormitories which her Society was setting up and to suggest ways in which they could reach schools. She paused, smiled, and passed on. Sunil and Samir looked at each other. 'She wanted to put us away,' said Salwan stoutly. 'Narrow escape!'

'Sunil,' said Samir, 'I am very hungry.'

'That is because we have no money to buy food.'

'That is true, Sunil. But how do we get money?'

'We beg.'

They looked for a place that was not already taken. The sun seemed to wink at them both through the dirty glass of Howrah station's roof.

The Indian trainee returned to her tiny office close to the station. She glanced at papers on the table. She was hardly to know that a message about two missing boys, one of them in rust-coloured shorts with a yellow band, would soon be coming over the fax, but was not yet with the papers on the table.

Thornton Hill had gone back with an interpreter to the rough camp which housed Ashish and Shefali Mondal, Ashok Saha and Gita Saha. The main thrust of his enquiries was the growth of India's megacities and its human consequences. He talked with some of the new arrivals, listened to stories of their travels and their future dreams. He was struck by how few of them felt disappointed to find themselves in worse conditions than the ones they had left. They felt this was a staging post. The city beckoned. The schools there held promise for their children. After a while, he encountered the Mondals where Shefali mysteriously seemed to have supplanted her husband as head of their little family. Ashish seemed stunned by the disappearance of his eldest son and was not making much sense, but Shefali was calm. When Thornton murmured through his interpreter of his genuine sympathy for her, she had responded with a sad little smile that was almost reassuring.

Thornton Hill set out for the bustee early the next morning. If the day was going to be a scorcher, he reasoned, best to face the stink of the bustee early on. His hire car had travelled half a mile when the driver halted, turned with a broad smile to Thornton and announced, 'I have puncture.' His voice sounded almost triumphant.

'Sod it!' said Thornton and dismounted. They examined the wheel together, which was flat. The driver shrugged.

'Wait! I call other car.'

'How long?' Another shrug.

'Blast and damn,' shouted Thornton.

'No!' An empty cab was passing. 'Change of plan.' He glanced at his watch. It was quarter to six. He gave the driver directions back to his hotel.

He found Mary Hind finishing a cup of coffee in the breakfast room. 'Surprise, surprise,' she murmured. 'I thought you planned to get going before dawn.' Thornton smiled grimly, sat down and waved at a waiter.

'I'm a victim of the pneumatic tyre,' he said.

'You won't enjoy a morning at Howrah station much,' Mary warned him, 'but we're glad of your company. Unescorted females are glad of male companions in that station.' As they pulled up outside the station, Mary glanced at her watch. 'I suggest,' she said, 'we separate. I'm starting with a very small body that has its being outside this station and offers medical help here. I want to talk about the ailments these children suffer from – and it's not your cup of tea. Take a look round, case the joint, and we'll meet at the entrance to platform 14 in an hour. Meanwhile a journalist of your talent should be able to find ample copy in this hellhole.' Thornton dismounted, saluted and made his way into the station's main entrance.

'Come back, New York Grand Central,' he murmured as he entered the station, 'all is forgiven.' Kolkata's rush hour was coming up to peak. Everyone who had business to transact in Howrah station had arrived. The licensed vendors, unlicensed hawkers, beggars, thieves, travellers, and countless children for whom the station was home, swayed to and fro. It put Thornton in mind of a disorderly opera scene. Best to locate platform 14 first of all, take his bearings from there. Then he would case the joint. Mary had been right, there was some colourful copy on offer. He moved towards the entrance to a platform where a train was coming in, discharging a thousand city workers, drew out his notebook and set down a description of some of them.

'Hello, mister, how are you?' Two small boys clutching tins confronted him.

'Sod off!' shouted Thornton, scribbling in his book. There was an unexpected silence. One of the boys was staring at him intently. Thornton momentarily raised his eyes, glanced at the boy, began to move away. As he did so, a nearby train hooted. It triggered in his brain recollection of a similar sound at Howrah station some days earlier. He glanced at the boy again. Christ! That family with the baggage . . . Steady! Real life didn't go like this. He'd fallen into some kind of trance. It must be the heat. He was dreaming.

'Kaka, Kaka, Kaka, ami Sunil (Uncle, uncle, uncle, I'm Sunil)'

Thornton shook himself, grabbed the boy's arm. 'You're—' Well, who the hell was he?

'Hello, mister, I am Salwan.'

Thornton caught both boys by the shoulder. He was suddenly seized with an irrational dread they were about to run away. 'You'd like a drink, sumtin' to eat?' He gestured at a vendor standing not far away.

The transaction did not pass unnoticed. An elderly Indian who had just come off a train made a gesture of disgust to his wife. 'The sex trade in this city takes all shapes and forms,' he confided in a low voice.

A surge of doubt came over Thornton as he watched the boys tuck in. They had left their parents. Maybe they didn't want to go back. So when they had had their fill, would they slip away, become lost again, this time for good? Desperately, he waved his notebook at them and pulled a wad of rupees out of his hip pocket. Would the penny drop, cross the communication barrier? Both boys stared at him, mystified.

'I want to draw sketches of you both,' babbled Thornton. 'I'll pay you to sit for me.' In earlier life he had attended art school. He turned a page in his notebook and drew out a pencil. Both boys, conscious of having at last met someone in Kolkata who recognised them and might be able to lead them home, had formed a firm inner resolve not to part from Thornton. To that end, they would go along with this odd man's eccentricity.

Thus at five minutes to seven Mary Hind found them close to the entrance to platform 14. Thornton, with sweat streaming off his forehead, was crouched against a pillar sketching Siddu. Both boys were watching Thornton with puzzled faces. 'Hello, miss. How are you?'

'We'll take them straight out to the families,' said Mary Hind. After an emotional five minutes, Thornton straightened his back and wiped his face. He felt he had been running the Marathon. He turned to a fresh page in his notebook. Reunion with the mothers would be amazing copy.

Two hours later, Thornton Hill and Mary Hind were in the land cruiser moving back into Kolkata. 'We stop at the nearest grand hotel and celebrate with a drink,' said Thornton scribbling away on his pad.

'It would be appreciated,' said Mary Hind, 'if you felt able to work a modest reference into your copy to the work done by Indian social workers in this saga. They do what they can for Calcutta's lost children – though not always so sensationally.'

'Sure,' said Thornton. 'Mother India's care for her children gets a couple of hundred words in the first thousand words of my two-thousand word piece.'

'Good. What's the other eighteen hundred words about?'

'"Triumph of an Indian mother's faith in her son" . . . "Children know best" . . . "Twenty-first-century miracle of Calcutta" . . .' muttered Thornton, scribbling fast.

'So you've seen the light?' said Mary Hind.

'Not me', said Thornton Hill. 'I'm a journalist, remember? Seeing the light is other people's business.'

Mary smiled at him, then Thornton slowed down and ducked out the window, saying, 'Look, there's a hotel.'

Mercy

COLM TOIBIN

THE old woman's monument is a quiet, well-kept place, a hospital with an air of deep spirituality and practical hard work. Those who labour here have a light in their eyes as well as a distinct businesslike spirit. At the entrance, there are directions to the Pain Clinic and a timetable for the immunisation services.

The doctor is clearly busy. This is, she says, the only hospital in Asia run by women for women. It was set up in 1981 by Dr Marie Catchatoor, who died in 1996 and was of Armenian origin. No, she herself, the doctor says, does not take a salary. She is a retired professor of medicine who trained in Calcutta and studied in England. All the doctors are volunteers. They charge the patients, she says, but the fees are very very small, almost a token, and most people can afford them.

'You give me the money,' she adds, 'and I will provide it free.' There are fifty beds; the hospital delivers babies and does surgery, whatever the patients need, it is a complete hospital, the doctor says. The only women they will not treat are those with more than three children. 'If you have more than three children, we will not give you any medical help.' In this male-dominated society, she adds, the husbands, whether Hindu or Muslim, are not keen on their wives having information about contraception. The hospital offers such information.

Dr Catchatoor's hospital is a few doors down from the Mother House of The Missionaries of Charity, set up by Mother Teresa. 'Oh yes,' the doctor says, 'they often send us people. Not as much now as before.'

What is the difference between the legacy of Dr Catchatoor, who gave up her life to this work, and that of Mother Teresa, who did the same?

'Oh,' the doctor says vehemently, 'the difference is total. We are a hospital. They run homes for the destitute and the dying. We give people medicine and medical care.'

When I ask her if she has any literature about the late Dr Catchatoor, she shakes her head. No, she says, there is no book about her or pamphlet or memorial committee. The hospital merely organises a lecture in her memory each year, but it is highly specialised. It is never about the doctor as a person or the work she did. Last year's was called 'The Changing Scenario in the Management of Breast Cancer and its Psycho-Social Impact'.

'Why do you spend your retirement in this city working for nothing?' I ask her.

She becomes stern as she studies me to make sure I am listening. 'We had our life,' she says simply. 'Do you do it out of love?' I ask her. 'Out of dedication to the nation,' she says. 'What do you say when you go upstairs? You have to announce to God what was your contribution to humanity.' She thinks for a moment, before continuing. 'In any case, I don't want to come back in the next life as a spider or a rat.'

A few doors away lie the mortal remains of Mother Teresa, cased in a large tomb in the middle of a chapel which is a shrine to her memory. All around the walls the story is told of her life and her works. It tells us that she was born in 1910 in the former Yugoslavia, that she joined the Loreto Order of nuns, living in Ireland for some time before arriving in Calcutta on 6 January 1929.

'I observed the life in the streets with strange feelings,' she later said. 'Most of the poor people were half-naked, their skin and hair glistening in the hot sun. Clearly, there was great poverty among them.'

On 9 September 1946, while on a train, a call came to her, something mysterious and powerful, that she should work with the poor and destitute of Calcutta. On 12 April 1948, she got permission from the Pope to leave the Loreto Order and set up The Missionaries of Charity. Between August and December of that year, she did some basic medical training, and then she rented two rooms in the city, one for a school and the other for the sick and dying. The first novice joined her order the following year and the order grew as her fame grew; she became synonymous all over the world with selflessness and charity and care. She became an Indian citizen in 1960. When she died in 1997, she was given a state funeral. Her body, the story written on the walls tells us, was taken on the same gun carriage as that used for Gandhi and Nerhu. Her favourite prayer was the Memorare. ('Remember O most gracious Virgin Mary that never was it known that anyone who implored thy aid or sought thy intercession was left unaided.') Early in the history of her order, she promised God that she and her nuns would say 85,000 Memorares, the story on the wall tells us.

The photographs of Mother Teresa in old age, her eyes shining with an ascetic missionary zeal, or her head bowed humbly in prayer, made her famous. She is loved all over the world; many books have been written extolling her virtues. 'Her impact on the public imagination,' John Cairns writes in his foreword to a book of her sayings, *A Simple Path*, 'has been compared to the ripples a stone makes when it is thrown into a calm pool of water. For many non-Christians, Mother Teresa

represents a form of Christianity they can wholeheartedly respect.'

Sunita Kumar worked with Mother Teresa for more
than thirty years, and was spokeswoman for the Order,
and helped, through her connections in the West, to
make Mother Teresa's and her work famous. In her
book of pictures of Mother Teresa, she writes: 'Mother's
life was unique. She lived very simply and humbly like
the poor . . . Her room was small, approximately twelve
foot by eight, with only one window . . . Her diet was
frugal and similar to what the poor in Calcutta would
eat.'

In becoming famous, Mother Teresa made Calcutta
famous too, for its poverty, its destitution, its squalor.
For many who lived in the city, however, or for out-
siders who liked Calcutta for its richness, variety and
complexity, the notoriety she gave the place, and the
fame she won while doing so, and indeed the seeming
madness within her medical methods, have made them
less than impressed by her legacy.

The history of the city itself may go some way towards
explaining the controversy about Mother Teresa's reputation, about whether she is the saviour of the city or an
aspect of its decadence. Calcutta was built by the
British; it was a colonial outpost in the eighteenth and
nineteenth centuries, but more than that, a centre of
trade whose growth was unplanned and unstructured,
'chance-erected, chance-directed', in Kipling's phrase.

From 1813 English goods, with the exception of
alcohol, could be imported paying only a two and a
half per cent tax, while a much heavier duty was
imposed on locally produced goods. Also, each time
locally produced goods underwent a change of form,

from raw material towards final consumption, a duty was payable. No such duty was payable on foreign imports. At the end of the First World War, more than 95 per cent of the joint stock companies had only British directors. All fifty jute mill companies were under British managing agencies. 'It seems not only a wrong,' Rudyard Kipling wrote in *City of Dreadful Night* (1890), 'but a criminal thing to allow natives to have any voice in the control of a city adorned, docked, wharfed, fronted, and reclaimed by Englishmen, existing only because [of] English lives and dependent for its life on England.'

Yet Calcutta remained the richest city in India. The Bengali population who became wealthy did so not by keeping apart from British-controlled enterprise, but by working as clerks and middlemen, manipulators and arrangers. They took cuts on the deals the British made; they became moneylenders rather than traders; they invested in land and property rather than ships or perishable goods. The Indian share of the total tonnage of ships over 80 tons registered in the port of Calcutta was 5 per cent in 1805, 4 per cent in 1817 and 8 per cent in 1825. In *My Reminiscences*, Rabindranath Tagore remembered his brother saying that it was 'a great shame that our countrymen had set their tongues and pens in motion, but not a single line of steamers'.

It was clear that money could be made by those who could keep ledgers and accounts, read orders, write letters. For the native population, literacy was thus one of the few roads to solvency. Education in the nineteenth century became a primary asset for Bengalis. Slowly a rich culture grew around the written word. Slowly, too, a class of disaffected men with an education but no proper employment developed. 'While the

Bengali middle class literati had made itself, and the city in which it lived, the unchallenged centre of cultural leadership for the state of West Bengal,' wrote Partha Chatterjee, 'it had virtually no participation in the industrial and commercial bourgeoisie which dominated the economy of Calcutta.'

As the city changed and grew, and a native middle class emerged, gradually too an artisan class, and a class of messengers and deliverers, people with roots in the countryside, moved into the city. A rich popular culture, using a rural oral tradition, but ready to smarten and change in the crowded city, emerged in the poorest parts of Calcutta with extempore poetry competitions, singing contests, satirical shows and farces, street theatre and dance and primitive painting. This sense of an intact and dynamic Bengali culture which was all around them was to have a powerful impact on the richer and educated Bengalis who had become more British than the British themselves. In the second half of the nineteenth century, through their reading of European writers and their experience of popular culture and through the distancing of the colonial experience, they grew increasingly self-conscious and nostalgic about the romantic associations of their roots and their traditions. The more urban and urbane they became, the more they became interested in the rural and the simple. The movement they established, which was to have immense cultural and political implications, was called the Bengali Renaissance.

What happened in Calcutta in the second half of the nineteenth century has astonishing echoes of events in Ireland and Catalonia during the same years. The three cities of Calcutta, Dublin and Barcelona were port cities in nations which were not states, deprived of political power by colonial forces, and increasingly alert to ideas of nationhood. After 1850, in all three places, a culture which depended upon ideas of a native tradition began to replace political apathy and powerlessness, until that same culture actually became politics. All three cities produced a persuasive idea. They represented the native culture as older and purer than that of the so-called conquerors, and now they were ready, using whatever technology they could lay their hands on, to combine that ancient culture with modern systems. Thus the Catalan architects would use Romanesque motifs and also steel frames; thus the Irish Literary Renaissance would use modern theatrical skills or modern idioms with constant references to Ireland's heroic past. So too Bengali intellectuals used the printing press, Marxist philosophy, and any European and American influences – including, after 1930, film – they deemed worthy of their attention, to bring back to life what was, in their dreams, an oral and rural culture.

Both in Ireland and in Bengal in the second half of the 1890s scholars and amateurs applied themselves to study of medieval texts and the collection of folklore to establish the rich and ancient roots of their pre-colonial heritage. W.B. Yeats referred to Lady Gregory's version of the Cuchulainn legends as the most important book to come out of Ireland in his lifetime. Five years earlier, in 1896, when Dineshchandra Sen published his *Bengali Language and Literature*, based on a collection of early and medieval manuscripts which he had gathered, Tagore wrote: 'We did not know there was such a vast entity as early Bengali literature.' Such discoveries and the pride surrounding them in both Ireland and Bengal were to have enormous political implications.

The leaders of these movements in Ireland, Bengal

and Catalonia were deeply implicated in the very colonial experience which they sought to undermine. The Catalans had made fortunes out of Cuba; the leaders of the Irish Literary Renaissance, themselves deeply alert to what was happening in Bengal, were mainly Protestants, members of the ruling class, many of them landed; the leaders of the Bengali Renaissance also came from families who had become rich by associating with the British and serving British interests. In both Ireland and Bengal, these leaders were exceptional; rather than representing their class, they stood out from it; they used its power, and to some extent betrayed it. They also sought to establish a native spirituality against the materialism of the oppressor. Thus W.B. Yeats and his friends in Ireland approached mysticism with the same zeal as Gaudi, the leading figure in the modernist movement in Catalan architecture during the same years. In Calcutta, spirituality set the natives, rich and poor, apart from the mere traders who came from outside.

It is easy to imagine, therefore, James Joyce's story 'The Dead' taking place in the Barcelona or Calcutta of the early years of the twentieth century, places where musical life could be conducted with a peculiar intensity, and songs and singers handed a strange power. In all three societies, two languages were in conflict, so it is easy to imagine our Calcutta intellectual being attacked for not writing in his native language, Bengali, and being married to a woman from the countryside whom he, so urbanised and deracinated, will come to misunderstand and almost fatally desire. In all three societies, from the 1870s onwards, there was a fetishisation by poets and playwrights and painters, and then by intellectuals and politicians, of the countryside itself, the remote landscape where the nation's source was at its most pure, the uncontaminated, uncomplex life of the village.

Ireland and Bengal had other things in common. Both places were troublesome, even in the early years of the nineteenth century, although Calcutta was, according to Lord Macauley who lived there between 1834 and 1838 and took a dim view of the native culture, less trouble than Dublin. 'We have agitators in our own small way,' he wrote. 'Tritons of the minnows, bearing the same sort of resemblance to O'Connell that a lizard bears to an alligator. Therefore Calcutta for me, in preference to Dublin.' Both places were partitioned by the British, Bengal by Lord Curzon in 1905, Ireland in 1920. Both places suffered devastating famines, Bengal in 1943, Ireland in 1846. In both Ireland and Bengal, the city was not to be trusted either in art or in politics and those who trusted it, such as Sean O'Casey in Ireland and the filmmaker Mrinal Sen in Bengal, carried the atmosphere or the aftertaste of the village to the metropolis, made in the phrase of the Calcutta sociologist Ashis Nandy 'an ambiguous journey to the city'. The slum, Nandy wrote, 'is left forever trying to re-invoke a remembered village under different guises.'

Once the British moved their capital city to Delhi in 1911, then Calcutta would be left to its own ambiguous devices, to decay as much as it pleased, to become even more overcrowded and unsanitary and chaotic. The historian Sumit Sarkar has written of the Bengal Renaissance:

Calcutta . . . often had a negative image, a city somehow basically alien, where the gentleman would have his *basa* [residence or lodging] as against his proper *bari*

[home] in the village or small town of his birth or retirement . . . Bengali high literature in the 19th century did
not develop any distinctive ways of imaginatively visu-
alising the new experience of life in the great
metropolis, as Dickens did with London or Baudelaire
with Paris. And as for the semi-popular literature of
farces and tracts, or the Kalighat paintings, there
Calcutta often became the city of Kali, the epitome of
the degenerate present.

Bengali intellectuals and artists lived in the city by day,
but when night fell they imagined, or in certain cases
tussled with, a rural idyll, a dream community, all pure
and unsullied, and they felt nostalgic for it, even though
many of them had never experienced it.

In the city built on trade to which the masses came in
search of opportunity, there is no pity. Even still, the
medical services in the city are rudimentary, often non-
existent. Mother Teresa's reputation rests not on the
efficiency or size of the service she provided, but on her
rhetoric of service and mercy, elevating the poorest of
the poor to the most exalted level in a place where
there was, from the beginning, no system of help for
those who fell by the wayside.

In the period I stayed in the city I spent time in a
house owned by Europeans. A young man who had
been working in the house, but whom no one had seen
for a year, came back during my stay. He sat hunched
alone in the garden on a low stool sheltering from the
sun. It was clear that he was dying. His face was all
bone; his eyes were blank. No one went near him
although several greeted him; he was too weak to
return any greetings. No one asked him where he had

been or why he had gone away and not made contact
for so long; everyone knew he was back because he
had nowhere else to go now. His luck had run out.
What happened to him over the next two days was a
lesson in why a figure like Mother Teresa stood out in
Calcutta and why the services she offered and the atti-
tudes she articulated were so badly needed.

It was clear from the way the young man coughed
and his general weakness that he could be suffering
from several diseases, among them open TB, which
meant that he could be infectious for anyone coming
even close to him, breathing the same air. It was likely
that he had been moving around the city with the
disease. He had come back here merely because he was
at death's door. He looked sad and weak and dejected
as he sat alone away from us while his fate was
decided.

He could not stay here, because others could become
infected. There was a special public TB hospital where
he could be taken; we moved across the city with him,
keeping him in the back of the jeep facing outwards.
He could barely walk. It became clear as soon as we
arrived at the hospital that being white, from the British
Isles, still means a great deal. You can swagger into
places, make your presence felt and demand to see
whoever is in charge. But when it was announced that
we had a local boy in the back of the jeep who needed
a hospital bed now and was suffering from TB at least,
the officials made clear that he could not stay. He
would need x-rays; he would need an appointment; he
would have to come back the next day; no, nothing
could be done now, even though it was obvious he was
very sick, and dangerous if he came close to people
who had no immunity from TB. The officials were

implacable and oddly hostile. We would have to take him away.

There were other ideas; other locations to which our patient could be taken; and these offered a strange key to the city, its levels and layers and history and legacy. Everywhere we went then in this jeep, two white men with this skeletal boy in the back, men of every age stood and stared at us, openly, unembarrassed, never for one moment averting their eyes. Once on the street, you were public property, every aspect of you to be taken in. I began to stare back and sometimes I smiled, and the starer would smile back, a smile of warm resignation, as if to say – here we all are in this puzzling universe, what can we do but stare, what else is there, except smile, maybe laugh?

Two Europeans in a jeep seemed to offer the street life of Kolkata enormous interest as we ferried the young man next to an American voluntary hospital, the Mission of Mercy Hospital on Park Street. We brought him with us into the small main office, knowing that someone should have immediately put a face mask on him, or kept him in isolation, but they were busy and full, and too preoccupied in trying to find a way to help us to notice the danger.

As they took down the details, I walked out into the hall and noticed smashed windows, and then everything I saw seemed to have been broken, an ambulance had had its windows smashed, there were signs everywhere of recent violence. I asked one of the staff, who explained that two days earlier the hospital had been attacked by members of the local Muslim community, whom the hospital served. The Muslims were angry at first because of rumours that members of their community had died unnecessarily in the American hospital, but angry then because of the American presence in the city at all, and had smashed up the place in their anger. It had never happened before. The staff wondered if this was the beginning of new hatred in a city which had not known such things for a long time.

They could not keep the young man, they said, they had no space and no expertise in TB, but they could do x-rays and give them to us for a very small payment. The x-rays confirmed that the young man had open TB, and this meant that it was essential that he be put in isolation and treated by specialists as soon as possible. The hospital still said that there was nothing they could do. As we drove across the city again, I was fascinated by the staring eyes along every street corner and at traffic lights, taking their time to study us as we stopped in the traffic jams which clogged the city. The driver was increasingly worried about the patient, and the patient sat inert, expressionless and immobile in the back of the jeep. It was possible, the driver said, that no one in the city would take him in and that would be a catastrophe, one that happened every day in the city, but no less worrying for that.

While the first hospital we visited had been built since Independence, and was a cluster of one-storey sheds and outhouses, and the second hospital had been built by the Americans in the 1960s and was bright and functional, the next hospital, the largest in the city, had been built by the Victorians and, a maze of additions and extensions, was sturdy in parts, the rest falling down, rotting slowly in the sun. It was hard to find the centre of power, the admissions office, the place where decisions could be made, but eventually we found a room full of men who were not doctors, one seated at a desk and the others clustered around.

No, there was no room, they said, and no isolation ward. The chief shook his head; there was nowhere for the patient. Could he see a doctor? We asked. No, the chief said. It was too late. Maybe come back tomorrow. Five men stood and watched as we begged and bargained. It was clear that the chief could not give in; he could direct us lazily, almost contemptuously, to the admissions office, where there were doctors, but it would be no good, he said. We asked him to write his name down, while thanking him for his help. He found a piece of paper and wrote his name.

With this piece of paper as our key, we attempted to open the labyrinth of buildings and bureaucracy that was the largest public hospital in Kolkata. We found an admissions unit and made our way into the inner office, x-rays in tow. The patient was still outside in the jeep. As a doctor told us to wait, I looked around me. On the top of a metal cupboard in the office was a set of huge old ledgers. They looked as though no one had touched them since Edwardian times; damp and fetid, they were festering, mouldering. I had a terrible urge to get a black bin bag and remove them, and I looked at every member of staff who arrived, wondering why they did not have the same idea.

We showed the chief's signature to the doctors and said that he had said they could help us. They looked at the x-rays, but hesitantly, carefully, almost doubtfully. They did not ask to see the patient. I wondered what would happen if I touched the ledgers on the press, if the grime and dust of a whole century would engulf us all. In all the years, surely one doctor might have asked what was in them, and could they be thrown out, or stored away? They looked like a very contagious disease in themselves. Soon, the medical team said that the patient would need hospitalisation, but they had no beds for that night. He would have to be brought back the next day and they could take him then. We pointed out how infectious he was, and dangerous if left at large in the city. They nodded in agreement and said firmly that they could not take him until the next day.

It was getting late and the traffic was building up. There was still only one place where we could go, the driver said, but it was miles away. It was better, he added, not to use the telephone. It was easier to turn people away by phone; it seemed to me easy to turn people away in person as well, but the driver said it was worth a try. He knew someone who knew someone who worked in the next hospital so we drove to find this guy and convince him to come with us. This was the last stop.

Along the way, I asked the driver and his friend why we did not try one of Mother Teresa's hospitals. They said that was where we were going now to a place called Naba Jeeban, but there was no guarantee they would take us in. It was a hospital which dealt with some TB patients, but with limited resources, and not a place used to taking people in for one night. The home for the destitute and dying in the city centre, also run by the Sisters of Charity, would not be suitable, I was told. Our passenger needed hospital treatment rather than the basic shelter provided there.

The hospital was a small, dingy, dimly lit place, and we were greeted with suspicion because what we were looking for was irregular. It was clear that my two friends were ready to be insistent and not go away without an argument. Just one night, they emphasised, as the Brother, a member of the men's branch of The Missionaries of Charity, looked doubtful but said nothing. When it was promised that the young man would, without fail, be collected in the morning, the Brother offered a sort of nod, a tacit assent, meaning that he did not disapprove enough to send us away. But still he did not say yes. So a game had to be played of standing around, making small talk, shifting from one foot to another, while the patient still remained in the back of the jeep. Tea was had and many matters were discussed before finally the subject could be broached again: Could the patient be brought in and was there a bed ready for him? In the end, assent was given and the poor patient after his long day's travelling could be taken in and put in the TB ward.

As we were finishing, a Brother from the Order came in, and he was introduced as a senior and influential figure within Mother Teresa's organisation. He was uneasy at first when I asked if I could speak to him alone. The Order, he explained, have not had an easy time with journalists recently and have tended to avoid making statements to the press at all; it was easier to get on with their work. But, nonetheless, he invited me to come to a room upstairs and agreed that he would speak off the record.

I asked him first about the allegation that his organisation has no medical expertise and that standards of care within the Mother Teresa institutions are less than ideal, which is strange considering the wealth of the organisation. I was expecting him to walk out of the room, but he grew thoughtful and quiet as he considered the question. It was partly true, he said, because the organisation had been set up when conditions in the city were at their very worst, and the act of merely taking people in, giving them shelter when they were dying, was an act of rare mercy in the Calcutta of the late 1940s and the 1950s. It still was today, he said. Which is why people still threw themselves on the mercy of The Missionaries of Charity at Nirmal Hriday, the centre for the destitute and dying.

The organisation was not perfect, he said, but it had done more good than harm; more lives have been saved than lost. The poorest of the poor, he said, were treated as holy by The Missionaries of Charity without making any effort to convert them; the focus was on the person and this might seem nothing in a European city, but here, with so many living in the most appalling and degraded conditions, being offered shelter and treated with kindness was immensely important. But it was, he admitted, a drop in the ocean. The aim was not to cure the problem, but to come as witness, as a way of serving Jesus. The work is not a failure if we cannot reach everyone in Kolkata, he added. Our aim is to be a friend of those caught up in poverty; we are not claiming to have the best approach.

Was it true, I asked him, that needles were reused in the medical centres? It was true in the past, he said. In the old days, he added, if a needle was sharp enough to get through a piece of cotton, then it was reused. But not over the previous ten years, he said. Once HIV and hepatitis became rampant, you couldn't go on doing that. Now there was more attention to the medical side of things, while trying not to lose the spiritual care; the organisation was changing, he said, and it was also important to remember that most of the written attacks on The Missionaries of Charity came from people who had seen only Niram Hriday, the centre for destitute people in the centre of Calcutta. There were other centres too, he said, which journalists and so-called witnesses never visit.

I asked him to give me an example. Such as Prem Nivas, the centre for leprosy treatment, he said. It's a good distance out of the city, and hard to get there, but you should go there, he insisted. Would someone from the Order take me there, I asked, or talk to me when I got there? Probably not, he said. We have had too much negative coverage. But don't write about us without going there, he warned. His laugh was friendly but dismissive when I asked him again for directions there. I can't help you any more, he said. But if you want to tell the truth, visit Prem Nivas, the centre for the treatment of leprosy along the railway line at Titagarh. That'll open your eyes for you, he concluded.

In the morning we took the patient back to the largest hospital in the city and left him in a huge ward where he would begin a course of treatments and tests. I noticed that all around the hospital were bookshops and book stalls and I spent the rest of the day there because I had a list of books I wanted to buy. Some of the books were out of print and almost unobtainable; this meant that time could be spent talking to the booksellers and waiting in the bookshops as messengers were sent to other booksellers. Most of the booksellers were old and trade was now mostly in schoolbooks and textbooks. The booksellers remembered a time when Bengali literature was still glorious and the printing presses of the city were busy with new volumes of poetry and prose by the great figures in their culture; as early as the 1780s type foundries were set up for Bengali characters and a thriving publishing industry was in place until as late as the 1930s.

These men's fathers had shaken the hand of Rabindranath Tagore, who was born in 1861 and died in 1941; they had handled his books as they came fresh from the press, they had heard his poetry and his songs and read his stories and seen his plays in the years they were written. Tagore was, Ashis Nandy reports (echoing Auden on Freud), 'not merely a person or an institution, but a climate of opinion'. Tagore's books are still on sale everywhere; he remains to this day a powerful presence in the life of the city. His family background and his writing tell us much about Calcutta and its hinterland in the years of Bengal's cultural flowering.

The Tagore family made their fortune from working for British businesses and from money-lending. They were enormously wealthy; in the early nineteenth century they formed part of the 'pattern of conspicuous consumption and waste of resources . . . characteristic of the new rich of Calcutta', according to the historian Sabyasachi Bhattacharya, creating 'an impression in public memory of great wealth – while eroding the very basis of wealth'. They diverted 'from business towards land purchase . . . a means of acquiring social status to set the seal on the new wealth earned in business'. The Tagores stood apart, however, because of their interest in Bengali society and culture. Dwarakanath, Rabindranath's grandfather, was active in promoting education and social reform; his sons were interested in philosophy and religion and literature. His grandchildren in turn became artists and writers and philosophers and reformers. One of them invented a system of Bengali shorthand and became a leading feminist; another founded an important literary magazine; the women in the family were as educated as the men and several of them became writers as well. Tagore himself set up the rural university, Shantiniketan.

Tagore was educated by private tutors and by his talented siblings. His account of his childhood offers an extraordinary version of luxury coupled with a family environment dedicated almost entirely to cultural pursuits, the writing of poetry, the learning of languages, travelling, theatre. The Tagores were steeped in Bengali culture but also highly Europeanised. 'Tagore,' Ashis Nandy has written, 'spoke both the languages of continuity and discontinuity.' His family seemed to see no distinction between the need for social reform and the need for servants, the need for new songs and poems and plays in their native language and the need for travel in Europe. The painter William Rothenstein, when he visited the family house in 1911, thought that 'their collection of Indian paintings was the best I had seen, made, as it was, by artists'.

Tagore's output runs to 29 large volumes; the 2,000 songs he composed have the status of folk songs in his country. He won the Nobel Prize for Literature in 1913. He writes with much greater tenderness about village life and the beauty of the countryside than he does about Calcutta itself, even though he was in 1899 the first novelist in his language to set a novel in the city. In his letters, he wrote about his joy, akin to Tolstoy's, at running the family estates in rural Bengal and being out of the city. In July 1915, he wrote: 'After long years I have come among my tenants, and feel, and they also, that my presence was needed. It was a great event of my life when I first dwelt among my own people here, for thus I came into contact with the reality of life.' The following year he wrote: 'Coming away from Calcutta, I have come to myself. Every time it is a new discovery for me. In the town, life is so crowded that one loses the true perspective.' In an interview in 1935 he said: 'Being a landlord I had to go to villages, and thus I came in touch with village people and their simple mode of life . . . The river system of Bengal, the best part of this province, fascinated me . . . At first I was quite unfamiliar with the village life as I was born and brought up in Calcutta and so there was an element of mystery for me.'

It would have been impossible in these years of political ferment for Tagore's work not to have political implications. At times he became directly involved, writing patriotic songs to oppose Curzon's partition of Bengal in 1905; in 1919 he returned the knighthood the British had given him four years earlier in protest against the Amritsar Massacre. At other times, by remaining strictly in the cultural realm, by passionately supporting literature in his native language, his political influence became all the greater. On his visits to London he became close to the Irish poet W.B. Yeats, another city boy who had found his inspiration in the rural landscape, who understood also the power of poetry and theatre in a nationalist movement. 'As in our country,' Tagore wrote, 'so too in Ireland, there has for some time been an endeavour to give the inner powers a distinctive character . . . In its efforts to express its distinctive spirit, Ireland turned to its own language and legends and mythical tales.' In 1917 the Abbey Theatre in Dublin put on Tagore's play *Post Office*. Tagore had come to know Thomas Moore's *Melodies in India*. 'I often listened to their enraptured recitation by Akshay Babu. The poems combined with the pictorial designs conjured up a dream of Old Ireland. I had not then heard the original tunes, but had sung these Irish melodies to myself to the accompaniment of the harp in the pictures.' In 1921, in London again, he followed events in Ireland very closely: 'Things that are happening in Ireland are ugly,' he wrote. 'The political lies that are accompanying them are stupendous.'

Tagore continued, even from his country estates, to edit literary magazines for distribution in Calcutta and publish small journals in the city. The history of the city from his beginnings as a writer in the 1870s until his death in 1941 includes intense cultural activity. Pradip Sinha has written about the city in the 1930s as a golden age

> with a thriving commercial theatre, a pioneering film industry, Bengal's own tradition of music, the leisurely conversational sessions, football, politics, good scientists and Indologists, the spiritual legacy of the nineteenth century, terrorism, musclemen, the Bengali circus, novels of sentiment, the comparative freedom of women, and over the entire scene, the presence of Rabindranath Tagore, the ultimate civilised man. But the idyll was less than total, and simple regret or nostalgia would be an inadequate response to an inevitable end. The real time of truth was soon to come, when war, famine, riots and Partition struck the city and the nation.

The days of glory are long gone now; the booksellers belong to a tradition which is over. But the days when culture mattered in Calcutta did not end with the famine of 1943 or Partition in 1947. Satyajit Ray was born in the city in 1921. He too came from an old family known, as Ashis Nandy writes, 'for its enormous contribution to Bengali literary and cultural life'. Ray's education was more British than Bengali, however, and, according to Nandy, 'he started life poorly acquainted with Bengali literature and Indian music and unacquainted with Indian village life, later so closely identified in world cinema with his films. His familiarity with Western literary classics and music, on the other hand, was deep and abiding.'

Ray thus belonged to a central strand in the life of the city: cultured, middle-class and ready to work with the British, if work were available. Ray was employed by a British-owned advertising agency as a graphic artist. His move from the city to the country, from a deracinated culture to the place close to where tradition was being invented, is similar to that of John Millington Synge in Ireland, who also moved for his dramatic subject from a cosmopolitan world, which he viewed as jaded, towards the vibrancy, as he saw it, of a remote culture. Ray's first film, a strange masterpiece called *Pather Panchali*, was made in 1955. In 1976 in his book *Our Films, Their Films*, he wrote: 'Looking at "Pather Panchali" today, I am upset by errors of detail which keep blurring the social identity of some of its characters. I know this was caused by my lack of familiarity with the rural scene.' In a diary kept while filming in the Bengali countryside in 1956, he wrote: 'One just wants to go on absorbing it, being chastened and invigorated by it.' Yet he loved urban improvement: he once told a young journalist that to understand Indian modernity one had to contemplate the Calcutta subway.

Ray's career as a Bengali filmmaker working in Calcutta in the 1950s and 1960s makes clear how complex this society remained even in the years of economic decline. He writes about the significance of a film festival in the city in 1952, about Jean Renoir's coming in 1949 to make a film in Bengal, about film clubs, film magazines, the availability of foreign films. Yet by making his films in Bengali, Ray was limiting his Indian audience, the language being understood by only 15 per cent of the population. In Bengal itself, as he worked on his films, since only 20 per cent of the potential audience was literate, then the market for a serious film was very small indeed.

Nonetheless, Ray's career was almost as varied as Tagore's. He wrote about film with acute intelligence, alert to his own strange cultural circumstances as to movements in European and American cinema. He worked until his death in 1992 in a number of styles, moving from the rural to the urban for his later films, from the starkly beautiful rural images to versions of Ibsen set in the city. He was awarded an Honorary Academy Award by the American Academy for his life's work. His background is typical of the world which gave us the Bengal Renaissance; his father and his grandfather were distinguished writers and illustrators for children, and his grandfather was also an important innovator in printing techniques in Calcutta; both men were friends and supporters of Tagore.

The career of Tagore and Ray as central figures in the rich and complex life of Calcutta and its hinterland spans more than a hundred years. Their work was passionate and sophisticated as it sought simplicity and a return to roots both real and imagined; they both had been superbly educated, with an equal sense of ownership of their own culture and that of Britain. They both discovered freedom and inspiration in the rural heartland where their best work is set. Both were fascinated by Bengali music. For the old men who sell books now in the old city and for their customers, this is the legacy of Calcutta, its true value, what the world should know. For them, the idea that the city has become synonymous, to the outside world, with the life and work of an elderly Catholic nun, Mother Teresa of Calcutta, who did nothing except look after small numbers of the poor, is both absurd and insulting. They cannot understand why this has come to pass.

The Gandhiji Prem Nivas centre for the treatment of leprosy, run by the Brothers of the Missionaries of Charity, set up by Mother Teresa, at Titagarh is about an hour from the city. You travel by metro until the end of a line and then wait for the train. The train is crowded beyond belief, with people sleeping flat-out on the ground while others struggle to push through the packed bodies to get out at the next station. There are no seats: these are cattle wagons. Everyone remains polite, even though, at each stop, the shoving and crushing means that many of us are lifted off our feet.

At Titagarh there are miles of low warehouse buildings down one side of the tracks. In another context, this could be a refugee camp, hastily built, or a prison camp. This is, in fact, the centre for the treatment of leprosy. The director, a brother, shows me to the pharmacy. The disease is treatable, he says, especially if you get it early enough. The problem is that there is a real stigma attached to it, so that people deny to themselves that they are infected, they disguise the symptoms, they let them go until it is too late. Most hospitals won't admit them, and the ones that do are afraid even to touch them. Often, their families want nothing more to do with them. They are destitute, cast-out, alone, penniless.

That is when they come here. The object, the director says, is not only to cure them but to love them. To give them medicine and dress their wounds and then try and prepare them for the world again by giving them work in the small workshop which is part of the complex. And making clear to them that they are not outcasts, not untouchable. The director talks about different doses of medicine and different combinations used for different degrees of the illness. We go through a list of the treatments and the length of time they take. Patients live here in the clinic until they are well enough to go – it sleeps almost seven hundred – and then return once a month for medicine until they don't need it any more. Those who get early treatment, the director says, can get an early cure, and late treatment means a late cure. Although the clinic can usually prevent a relapse, he says, sensation in the damaged tissue will not return and deformity caused by the leprosy often cannot be reversed. The director makes clear that although he is a Catholic, and the Missionaries of Charity is a Catholic organisation, they never question people about their religion. Conversions, he says, are very, very rare.

This emphasis on the physical condition of the patients and the need to use medical science as much as spiritual care surprised me, as it seemed far away from the rhetoric surrounding the treatment of the dying and the destitute in which Mother Teresa and some of her supporters had specialised. It was practical; it sought to cure as much as comfort. I asked if I could see the inside of the hospital, the wards and the treatment facilities. The brother led me across the railway tracks from his office to the clinic. All around us, families, living in shacks and hovels just on the edge of the track, were cooking on open fires, children were playing.

We entered the dark building. In one of the wards, men sat on their beds or lay there quietly watching us. Some of them had bandages on their hands and feet. In the corner bed, one man sat motionless, studying us. He could have been in his late forties, early fifties.

He looked like a connoisseur of something, fine wines perhaps, or paintings, or prose style. He gazed at us, evenly, closely. If someone had told me that he was a distinguished novelist, whose work combined a deep understanding of the comedy of human affairs with a dispassionate interest in our propensity for self-delusion, I would have understood. In this dark place, he exuded moral intelligence and a mixture of bottom-less sympathy and a knowledge bordering on cynicism. Nothing would shock him, I imagined, least of all his own bandaged foot. We took each other in across the dimly lit room. I nodded towards him and he smiled at me patiently, never for a moment losing his poise, the sense that the real world, whose foolishness had not escaped him, was here in front of him, having been assembled for his contemplation.

I asked to see the clinic itself, the place where patients were treated. The brother warned me that I might find what I saw difficult and I knew what he meant as soon as I came into the room. Two brothers were working with patients while others waited. They found me a chair and let me sit watching them work. They were cutting the dead flesh from the fingers and feet of the patients, using small, sharp knives. The patient looked on, clearly used to this procedure. The flesh was dead, it had no feeling, there was no pain, but there was blood. The knives had to be carefully dipped in disinfectant after each cut, and the blood wiped with clean cotton wool, also dipped in the disinfectant. Finally, when the dead flesh had been cut away, and the skin was all raw and bleeding, the wound was ban-daged, using new bandages. Then the next patient would come, proffering their foot or hand, as appropri-ate. No one cried out or complained. The work was done with an extraordinary care for hygiene, and with great precision. Later, I toured the depressing work-shops where patients could earn tiny amounts of money as they got better and prepared once more to go into the world. As I took the train back to Kolkata, I came to the view that if anyone wishes to canonise the entire Missionaries of Charity for offering this service to people suffering from leprosy, then it is all right with me.

It is early in the morning of Good Friday in Kolkata. The nuns of The Missionaries of Charity have asked to see me. They have read one of my books and I know that they want to tell me that they do not wish me to write about Mother Teresa. The nun who makes such deci-sions is a bit surprised when I tell her that I merely wish to pray with one of the Sisters downstairs in the chapel where Mother Teresa's body lies. If there is a sister down there, and she is free, then I can ask her, the nun says. I take my shoes off and go into the chapel. All the nuns speak English and they have been ordered to smile if anyone approaches. As I come towards a young nun who is praying in the corner, she smiles gently. I wonder, I ask her, if she could say the Memorare for me, which was Mother Teresa's favourite prayer. She nods and we both kneel down. She begins: 'Remember O Most Gracious Virgin Mary, that never was it known that anyone who implored Thy aid or sought Thy inter-cession was left unaided. Inspired with this confidence, we fly to Thee, O Virgin of Virgins. O Mother of the Word Incarnate, do not despise our prayers, but gra-ciously hear and answer them. Amen.' When she finishes she smiles again. I have not heard anyone say-ing these words for almost forty years.

Not far away, those who implored aid and sought intercession are lying in the grim space of Niram Hriday, the home for the destitute and the dying. As soon as you open the door from the street, you walk straight into the ward. There are other wards too, but it is astonishing how small this place is, as it is the central location in Mother Teresa's dream of mercy, and how modest it is against the teeming, massive city outside. It is clear that what has mattered more to the world has been Mother Teresa's image of ascetic self-sacrifice, her words about the poor, her intentions, her aura of holiness, than any set of actions, any great buildings. If you visit Shishu Bhavan, the home for children she set up, it is also amazing how small it is and how few are looked after there. The gap between Mother Teresa's reputation and the buildings which house her projects is like the gap between a landscape and a map of the landscape made to a very diminished scale.

What she did in 1948 was brave and visionary. The Loreto Order in Ireland, where she had first come as a novice, is known for its grandeur. It educates the upper middle classes, teaching manners and deportment to young girls. For a nun from that order to decide to work only with the poor, to offer them comfort in a climate of tragic mayhem and deprivation, and to get permission from the Church to do so, was an heroic act.

The year Mother Teresa set up the Missionaries of Charity is often taken to be one of the worst years in Calcutta's history. The famine had caused the deaths of millions, and Independence and Partition had meant the withdrawal of British capital and the narrowing of the hinterland. But things became dramatically worse after 1948. In fact, something occurred in the city which is almost unheard of. As wages decreased and unemployment rose, vast numbers of immigrants still arrived each year in Calcutta. They came from the countryside where there was a continuing slump in the value of agricultural produce. Eastern India was in such a poor economic state that Calcutta could offer low wages and yet have an inexhaustible supply of workers. The slum population as a percentage of the total population rose from 22 per cent in 1961 to 41 per cent in 1981. 'These people began their lives, without exception, in the villages,' Raghap Bandyopadhya has written. 'They came here lured by the city's gold, and this was the end of their rainbow. They have adopted a curious, mixed, half urban life style. They illustrate a special history and a special social mobility.' Bandyopadhyah also writes about the large number of pavement dwellers in the city. 'The pavement dweller is a truly "unaccommodated man". He has no special skill by which to earn a living: sheer physical labour is his only asset. Nearly all his kind can tell a tale of destitution, or natural or personal calamity, sickness and death.'

This is the world Mother Teresa worked in for two decades before the world took notice of her – Malcolm Muggeridge's famous interview with her was not until 1969. As things became worse each year, it is easy to understand how she had not developed sophisticated or imaginative plans for a modern hospital in Calcutta. She made one great leap into the dark; it is impossible to expect that she should have made another and developed independent views on birth control or politics or health care. Yet in all the years of her power and fame no one can remember her ever pleading the case for treatment for an individual patient, or demanding that rich doctors in the city should take in someone and cure them. She continued as she began, offering shelter and meagre comfort at a time when no one else was doing so.

The city itself continues to change and grow. It is the evening of Good Friday and the beggars and the pavement-dwellers have settled down in allotted patches in the city centre. One of the most expensive restaurants in the city is full. There are no tourists; these are all locals, many in large family groups. How do they manage to afford such meals? I asked an astute native of the city who has studied its mores. Watch the computer, he advised me, watch the phone. Very often, he says, if there is a large family, the meal is being paid for by credit card from the absent son in the United States, who is working in Silicon Valley, or for one of the computer firms in New Jersey. He will book the restaurant, he may even see the menu, I was told, and he will pay the bill.

In the years after Independence, the old middle class who had emerged as clerks and middle managers in the nineteenth century, using literacy as a route to solvency, did not go away. It was as in Ireland where education was the key to success, where no one inherited capital, where becoming a teacher or a clerk was, in many families, the highest ambition. Thus when the revolution in technology came, the American computer firms would make Ireland the second largest exporter of software in the world because Ireland's best and brightest had been educated and were ready to work for others; they longed for an indoor job with a monthly wage, they were intelligent and reliable. So, too, with the Bengali middle class, whose sons were in great demand by the new technology firms who could not locate in Bengal due to the poor infrastructure; instead, they imported the Bengalis to the United States in large numbers.

These bright young men cannot be present at family meals; they hang out in cyberspace instead where they can read the menu, see what everyone is having, and pay the bill.

Too much food comes and I can eat only half of what is on the dishes all around me. The waiter smiles. What should I do with the food? I ask him. It is up to me, he replies. It can be wrapped and I can decide who to give it to among those waiting on the street outside, or the restaurant will do it for me. Nothing will be thrown out, he says. I pay the bill and tell him that I will leave the matter in his hands. He nods in approval. Outside, the poor of the city wait for the food to be distributed. Others lie sleeping, or sitting in groups, watching the world go by, at everyone's mercy.

Knife

MONICA ALI

DEEPAK went inside the station to watch television. It was turned off. That meant it was broken and would stay turned off for a few months. When it was mended it would stay on for a few months, until it broke again. Deepak put his hands in his pockets and went to find Ganesh at the tea stall.

'Hey,' called Ganesh, who had no customers, 'can't you see I'm busy?'

Deepak didn't even slow down.

Two of the little ones had hold of a foreigner. The woman wore a long dress, a big bag on her back, and a tattered smile. The little ones tugged her dress. They pointed to their mouths and sang 'rupee, rupee'.

The woman wanted to get away. She also wanted to look kind. And she didn't want to give money.

Deepak shook his head. He'd grown out of such things.

A man shouted at the little ones to leave the foreign woman alone. They held on to her dress with two blackened hands apiece. A khaki uniform appeared, and sent the little ones skittering.

Sankar stood in his kiosk. He offered 'everything that the traveller needs' and – judging by how long they'd remained on the shelf – quite a few things that the traveller can do without. Sankar was giving Deepak some trouble.

'Don't bother me about prices. What is it to you? The price of this penknife is not something you need to know.'

Deepak put the sole of his right foot against the glass cabinet. He tried to make the glass squeak by wriggling his big toe.

Sankar bent over to see what he was doing.

'Get away. I'll have you thrown off this station!'

Deepak could run faster than the police. He wasn't worried. But he took his foot off the cabinet.

'Okay,' he said, 'make me a good price.'

Sankar laughed. 'Good price. Good price.' His voice, Deepak noticed, had gone high, like a girl's.

'Yes,' said Deepak, staying cool.

'It's not one or two paisa,' said Sankar. 'This is a many-function penknife. The best. It's so costly, you can't even afford to look at it.' Sankar shielded his eyes with his hand, as if the penknife would rob him blind too.

'One hundred rupees.'

'Two hundred,' said Sankar, before he could stop himself.

'One hundred and twenty.'

'Why am I even talking to you? One hundred and fifty.'

Deepak smiled. 'Keep it to one side.'

On his way over to platform eight he stopped by the poster outside the non-veg dining room. No one ever remembered to take it down. The writing on the poster had faded. Deepak could never read it. Now nobody could.

Deepak knew what it said though. He asked someone once and they told him. It was about a jewellery shop. It showed a photograph of a woman wearing a lot of gold at her throat and ears. In spite of all the gold, she looked nice. A long time ago, the first time he saw her, she reminded him of his mother. The poster lady was saying this: 'I never compromise.'

Over the years Deepak said it over and over to himself. He didn't know what 'compromise' meant, but he bet that it wasn't very nice and that was why the lady never did it. He bet his mother never did compromise either.

Deepak put a hand on the lady's cheek. 'I'm going to buy that red penknife,' he told her. Then he ran, because if the Rajdhani Express was already at the platform then someone would take over his bogey and clear it out before he even got there.

The Rajdhani Express was one hour late. Deepak was smoking bidis with Mintu and Salman on ten. They ran over the tracks to eight. Three schoolboys jumped off a local train. Deepak looked at their white shirts and shining hair. They were about the same age as Deepak, which was – he guessed – around nine or ten or eleven.

Mintu pulled his brush out of the back of his shirt and crawled along, sweeping under the seats. Some people threw him a rupee. Other people stood on his hands. Salman picked the bottles and left the paper to Deepak. They worked their three bogeys like this. It wasn't a bad pitch now because they had inherited one first-class AC compartment (three tier) from Vikram who had gone for a roof ride on the Chambal Express and leant out too far over the side. Deepak tucked his t-shirt into the back of his shorts and slid some newspaper down. He could get up to two kilos down there before the elastic on the waistband gave way. About twelve rupees worth.

Salman picked up a half-empty bottle of Coke and emptied it down the back of his throat. 'Let's go to the movies.' Salman always wanted to go to the movies.

Deepak started to say 'okay' but remembered just in time that he was saving for the penknife.

Mintu shook his brush too hard and all the twigs fell out. He picked them up and tied the bundle together again. 'Let's go and see the pantry guard.'

Every day they went to see the pantry guard to ask for the leftovers. It was good food. Spicy. Most days the pantry guard shouted at them to go away. But some days he let them have rice and dal and even – sometimes – mutton.

Afterwards Mintu said, 'His wife let him do the you-know-what today.'

'What are you talking about?' said Salman. 'When do you think the train left Delhi?' Salman grabbed Mintu's head and tucked it under his left armpit. He drummed on it with his free hand. Salman had a fine, soft throat, a small head and a baby's mouth and nose. New boys were always fooled by this. Salman liked to fight, and he usually won.

Mintu twisted his neck and made a face. His hair stood up thickly, as if he'd been using that to sweep under the seats. 'Aah,' he said. 'Maybe not his *wife* then.'

Salman swung around and dumped Mintu on the floor. It took Mintu a few moments to get up because of his bent legs. 'Listen, Sunny,' said Salman. He didn't add anything. He just wanted to say 'Sunny' because Sunny was what they used to call Mintu before Mintu decided that he wanted a real name.

Mintu did not know his own name because his parents were gungas. Deaf and dumb. They took Mintu around from village to village, begging, until Mintu had enough and ran away from home. 'But you can't run and you didn't have a home,' Salman told him.

'Even in spite of these difficulties, I still did it,' Mintu answered. He always wanted the last word.

They walked to Das Nagar and sold what they had. Salman and Mintu went to see a movie but Deepak walked all the way back without spending a paisa. He rolled his rupees tightly and slid them into a hole in the hem of his t-shirt, and he liked the way it felt against his stomach.

After a couple of days the hem unravelled. Deepak worked the seam at the neck and pushed the banknotes into that. Salman saw him. 'You want to get your throat slit?'

Deepak shrugged, as if it really wouldn't matter to him.

Salman kicked him on the back of the knees so his legs went under him. 'I'm lying down next to you. We're both asleep. Only I'm just pretending and you are really asleep. Then I take my blade and cut the seam. But my hand slips – like this.' He made a *whooshing* noise and flung his arms about to show how the blood would spurt from Deepak's neck.

Deepak rolled over and sat on Salman's chest. Then they both rolled out of the way of a trolley-load of green beans. Salman saw the tendons stand out on the porter's skinny legs. His official red shirt stuck to his back. His lower teeth bit into his white moustache.

They had almost rolled into Tripti, who was feeding her baby. The night the baby arrived everyone thought 'murder'. But it was a life coming, not going.

Salman said he was going to ride the buses. Deepak had some thinking to do. Inside the main hall he sat down by the poster. He didn't need to look at her face. It was okay if she was just there, behind him.

Once, she had reminded him of his mother. That didn't work now. There wasn't enough left, enough memory, to make it work. He knew it was stupid, but it was more that *she* was his mother. It was stupid. It was better than nothing.

Salman never said anything about his parents. Deepak asked him if he knew where his home was and Salman rubbed his baby nose with the palm of his hand and said, 'It's better here. That's what I know.'

Deepak watched a coolie with a banana mountain on his head and saw that he had to keep moving or else sink beneath the weight. He watched the shoeshine boys, the businessmen with their mobile phones, the clickclacking housewives and Guria who was the best pickpocket, though she was only a girl, slipping in between them.

It wasn't good to keep money. If you have nothing, you lose nothing.

Deepak thought of something. He jumped up and ran to check the knife was still there.

'My best customer,' called Sankar. He was really fat. There was barely space for him to turn around in the kiosk. 'Come to do business with me today?'

The knife was very beautiful. It had four blades, all pulled out at different angles, and a silver ring at the opposite end that could slip over a belt, if the owner happened to have such a thing. The handle was curved, dark red.

'Save it for me.' Deepak pelted away. 'You promised. You promised.'

Ganesh had no customers. He poured tea for Deepak. 'Always pestering,' he said. 'You're putting everyone else off.'

Deepak drank. He liked watching Ganesh's face when he talked. Ganesh had no teeth and that made it interesting. His cheeks could go in any direction.

'Big raid is coming,' said Ganesh. 'Don't sleep tonight. They'll catch you and put you in a home with all the other no-goods.'

Deepak had been in a children's home for a few months. He escaped with Salman when the guard was drunk one night. Mintu appeared about a week after that and they didn't mind him being around.

Deepak drained his tea and stuck the little clay pot in his pocket. 'Look how fast I am,' he said, and ran.

He went down the tracks. A woman had a fire going between the gauges. She dropped leaves into her pot. She was not right in the head. He went further, but not as far as the first bridge where the druggies kept together. He looked around. A goat was watching but that was all. He dug with his hands, wrapped the banknotes in a bit of orange polythene he'd found floating down the platform, scooped the earth over and some stones and then used the clay pot to make a red mark. He wiped his hands on his shorts.

The raid didn't come. The first couple of nights they took turns to keep watch. Then they forgot about it. Salman started talking about Mumbai again. 'Ooh,' said Mintu and batted his eyelids. 'Film star!' Salman jumped on him. Mintu looked funny on his back, his crab-legs waving in the air. 'Make love to me!' he shouted, until Salman sat on his face.

The money was getting bigger. Deepak kept hoping to find some on a train, but that had only happened once, when he was about so-high and a bigger boy had it off him two minutes later. But the money grew anyway. Deepak spent extra time in the morning at the ghat, diving for coins. People threw them in for the gods, but Deepak knew the gods didn't mind him having them. *They* never collected them. Ganesh counted the coins up and changed them into banknotes. One morning Deepak got 35 rupees and Ganesh's cheeks really flapped. Another day he carried a bag for a foreigner who gave him 20 rupees. He was lucky not to get a beating from the porters for that. The knife, he thought, was getting a really good owner. Not many owners would go to all that trouble.

'The one who goes the furthest,' said Mintu, 'is king all day tomorrow.'

They were sliding down the ticket hall. After midnight a man came with a hose to wash down the floors. It was ideal for skating on. When Deepak first arrived he didn't know about the hose and it was winter. The hose man never stopped for anything. Deepak nearly froze. He was so small then that even though he knew the water would come, he couldn't always stop himself from falling asleep. It wasn't too bad in summer. He trained himself to stay awake until two or three in the morning. But when he woke, most of the time he had wet his own shorts. That wasn't too bad in the summer either.

'Get stuffed,' said Salman to Mintu. Mintu had an unfair advantage. As well as his legs bending out, he had funny splayed feet like big paddles. No one could beat him at sliding.

'Chicken,' said Mintu, sailing past them.

'Listen, Sunny,' said Salman.

Deepak went to check on his savings. He was almost at

the place, could see the stones with the red clay mark, when he heard someone call him. Pankaj caught up and put a hand on Deepak's shoulder. 'Where you going?'

'Nowhere,' said Deepak, passing the place.

Pankaj walked alongside. He was tall as a policeman now but only half as wide. His trousers were held up with a piece of rope and his shirt was stiff with dirt.

'Me too,' said Pankaj.

Deepak used to be with Pankaj, who was a few years older, and didn't mind Deepak hanging around him. Then Pankaj started with the Dendrite and Deepak tried it but it burnt his throat too much. Pankaj had other friends and they could manage the glue, so Deepak got left behind.

'I'm going back now,' said Deepak.

'Okay,' said Pankaj and turned around as well.

When Deepak was washing, down at the ghat one day, someone had stolen his clothes. He had to go about naked until Pankaj got him another pair of shorts and a shirt. Pankaj always dared to do anything. Deepak never dared to steal.

'See you later,' said Deepak, and stopped on the platform by the black and white tiled water fountain.

'Yeah,' said Pankaj, and he kept on walking.

Deepak thought about Pankaj late that night, when he was trying to get to sleep. Salman snored on one side of him and Mintu thrashed about on the other. Mintu often woke with bruises. Deepak wondered if Pankaj knew something about the money. He didn't see how. He thought about the time he'd first seen Pankaj on Dendrite and what a strange feeling it had given him. Then he thought about the poster lady, who never compromised. He closed his eyes and saw her bending over to give a kiss to a boy. He saw that the boy was him, and smiled and crossed his arms over his chest. Deepak tried to get his father into his head. All he could get was a man crouching in the corner of a room. It was hardly even a man, more a shadow, a shape. How did he even know it was his father? It was better to think about the knife. The knife had colour and substance and weight. He knew how it would feel in his hand. Salman's breath whistled in his ear. Deepak turned on his side and went to sleep.

After he'd done the trains and been to the rubbish tip at Das Nagar, Deepak went to sit with Ganesh for a while.

Ganesh said, 'Just because nobody is queuing right now, that doesn't mean I'm not busy.' He rubbed a grimy rag over the kettle. He took off the lid and threw in a little more sugar.

Then he sucked hard and the bottom half of his face almost disappeared. Deepak turned to see what he was looking at. A policeman had turned over a dallah and was swiping absentmindedly at the bottom of the basket with his stick. The fruit vendor, to whom the dallah belonged, ran around after his oranges and waved a crumpled piece of paper in the direction of the policeman.

'For the likes of us,' said Ganesh, 'a simple licence is not enough. That man is a fool. Better to pay than pray.'

'What's the matter?' said Deepak.

'That policeman wants a little something,' Ganesh explained. 'Doesn't he have a family to feed?'

An orange rolled next to Deepak's foot. He picked it up and held it behind his back. It was a bit squashed. No good for selling.

Over by the seating a family was beginning lunch. They each sat on a piece of luggage. Mother, father and two sons unwrapped paper parcels and made a start on the stuffed rotis. The girl, who did not have her own parcel, took a bite from the parents' and then moved to her brothers. They held their rotis out of reach. The girl began to wail. Slaps all round. Then the mother broke some bread for the daughter.

Deepak watched. He slipped the orange into his shorts, to share later with Salman or Mintu. Whoever was around.

Not long – a few months maybe – after he came to the station he watched another family taking out their lunch. Deepak was very hungry. He came quite close to the boy, who was eating crisps. When he throws the packet, thought Deepak, I'll pick it up and taste it. The boy threw the packet and Deepak swooped. The crumbs tasted good. The boy smiled, showing his teeth. Deepak stood a little closer. The boy had a big samosa. He held it out. Deepak reached for it, and the boy pulled it away. The boy smiled again. Now he was going to let Deepak share. He offered the samosa. Deepak felt the saliva behind his lips. He put his hand out. The boy snatched the food away. 'Here,' said the boy, offering again. 'Try it.' Deepak slowly raised his hand. When he nearly had his fingers on the pastry, the boy jumped back.

Deepak turned and made his legs move. The boy called after him, not wanting the game to end, but Deepak didn't look. Every day since he came to the station Deepak had cried. Sometimes he thought the tears would wash the eyes straight out of his head. But after this day, this boy and his game, nothing ever made him cry again.

There was nearly enough money. For a few days

Deepak couldn't save anything, only had enough for half-plates from the kichuri vendor. Today he had ten rupees and he had put it with the rest. He always looked around carefully first. Nobody cared about a boy poking around in the dirt by the tracks. He took the piece of clay pot out of his pocket and rubbed it over the stones, making the red stand out a bit, but not too much. When he stood up he almost knocked into Pankaj. Deepak stepped back, covering the stones with his feet. That was the wrong thing to do. He stepped forward. Then he stepped back again. Pankaj said, 'What you doing?'

'Nothing,' said Deepak.

'Me too,' said Pankaj.

He wanted the knife very much. The want was shocking. It was like he had grown something, a hump on his back, a third leg. He had never wanted anything before. That was how it felt. He thought about it. A long time ago. He had wanted something. He wanted to be found.

Deepak's parents had taken him to the big temple. It was a special day. The temple was a long walk from the village. It took most of the day to get there. Deepak rode on his father's shoulders. He remembered being up there, his father's hands around his ankles. He wished he had been older. If he had been older he could have walked more, held his father's hand and looked up, seen his face and remembered it always.

There was a big crowd at the temple. 'Stay close,' his mother said. Deepak tried to stay close but the crowd seemed to carry him off. He wandered around without a care. There was a beautiful building in front and he went inside. He saw a big metal thing, like a huge red snake. When he got closer he saw that it was like a row of huts, all joined together. He climbed inside and touched all the smooth, shiny seats. Lots of people started to come in and he thought that probably there must be a wedding.

When the train started to move Deepak got a fright. He pushed his way between legs and looked out of the window to see what was happening. The world was rushing past. Then it wasn't scary any more. It was the best fun he'd had all day. For a couple of hours he went up and down the train and looked out of the windows. Then he remembered about his mother and father. And he felt a bit tired. Deepak started to cry. 'Don't cry,' said a man sitting with his feet up on a cage of chickens.

'Come and sit with me.' He freed a little corner on his seat. Deepak sat down and cried some more. 'I want my mummy,' he said. The man did a trick where it looked like he could take his thumb on and off. Deepak stopped crying. The man did some more tricks. He could wiggle his ears.

The train stopped and the man took his chickens and got off. Deepak watched him go and then he started crying again. He walked up and down the train shouting for his mother, even though he knew she wasn't there. It grew dark outside and only a blackness rushed by the windows. Deepak was tired from crying and he was very hungry. A woman called to him. She was on the floor, almost lying down. She held out the end of her sari and said 'Come, come.' Deepak crawled up beside her and she folded him into the sari. Deepak closed his eyes and just pretended he was home.

When he woke up the woman was gone, it was light outside and people were stepping over him to get off the train. Deepak climbed down the steps into a river of people. The noise hurt his ears. He pushed back up the steps and waited by the side of the door. He waited for the torrent to turn into a trickle and then he got off again.

Deepak couldn't think what to do. He stood by the train and thought very hard. Nothing came into his mind. His tummy was hurting a bit and that probably didn't help. He sat down on the floor and then he thought that if his mother and father came looking for him he would be harder to see, so he stood up again. He stood for a long time, until his legs hurt as well as his tummy and then he cried and cried. He was still crying when he noticed the boy next to him. The boy wore a shirt that came down past his knees and he held a bunch of bananas. 'I'm hungry,' said Deepak, and howled. The boy gave him the bunch of bananas and Deepak ate four straight off.

He stayed with that boy for three days and did whatever he did. Then the boy disappeared and Deepak looked out for him for months but he never came back. Deepak followed a group of four other boys and they let him tag along. That was how he learnt his new life. And in the beginning he did want something. He wanted to be found. And after a while, quite a long while, he knew that wanting was not part of the new life; there was nothing in it, nothing to be gained, and much to be lost.

'Get up. Get up.' Mintu was shaking him by the shoulders. 'Raid,' Mintu hissed. 'Get up.'

Deepak jumped to his feet. Salman had already gone. Deepak looked around. He knew Mintu was going to slow him down. He could see three policemen. But it was okay, they were already dragging two boys each.

Deepak held the sleeve of Mintu's shirt to show him he was not going to be left behind. They went to the vegetable market and found some muri sacks to sleep on. They talked about staying there every night. There were more rats but sleeping on the sacks was like being cuddled all night. It wasn't home though, and they knew the talk was only talk.

Every time he turned around Pankaj was there. He had enough money now. But he couldn't get to it, not with Pankaj hanging around. Salman and Mintu decided to go to the movies. Deepak said he didn't feel like it. He tried to shake Pankaj off by saying he was going down the tracks because he needed the toilet. Pankaj came with him so Deepak squatted down somewhere though he really didn't need to go. Then they wandered into the station and it was hours before Pankaj trailed away and Deepak could go and check on the knife.

Sankar said, 'Price is going to start going up.'

Deepak gave him a look.

'What?' said Sankar, spreading his fat hands. 'Inflation. You never heard of inflation?'

Deepak never had but he didn't like the sound of it.

Sankar laughed. 'Go on,' he said. 'So serious! A deal is a deal. I'll wait all my life for you.'

He ran into Salman and Mintu on the platform. Salman said, 'We're going to Mumbai.'

'How?' said Deepak.

Mintu screamed. 'How? How?' He pointed all around. 'How do you think?'

'I know,' said Deepak, who had just been taken by surprise. 'I mean – when?'

Salman made fists and drummed on his thighs. 'You know they are always looking for "extras". You don't have to have experience. You just have to look right.'

Mintu pretended to preen his hair. 'Salman thinks he has the right look.'

Salman ignored him. 'I heard this one boy, they took him off the street and now he's travelled all round the world.' He put his hands in his pockets and kicked at something that wasn't there. 'I don't mean that's going to happen. Not to us. But the film people, they always need extras. Thousands of them.'

'Why be so sure?' said Mintu. 'Let's go and be film stars.'

Salman took another kick, this time at Mintu's backside.

Mintu rubbed his arse. 'Train goes early. We'd better not sleep tonight.'

Deepak thought of the knife, going all the way to Mumbai with him. He had to get it now. 'See you back here,' he called and jumped off the edge of the platform.

He kept on digging, even when he knew it was hopeless. There had only been a little layer of dirt. The stones had been turned over, but he was sure this was the place. He didn't need the red mark any more. He knew the shapes of the grooves on the track, knew the weeds alongside. Pankaj, he thought, and dug his thumbs into the soil as if he were gouging out his eyes. He dug just because he had to do something with the surge of energy, but when he stood up his legs were shaking. He'd taken only five or six paces before he noticed the goat. The piece of orange plastic sticking out of its mouth matched almost exactly the shade of its eyes. With a roar, Deepak scooped a handful of stones and hurled them at the devil. The goat chewed once, side to side, ducked its head to dispense the plastic, and sprang away, treacherous and carefree. Deepak fell on the orange wrapper. Half the money was still there. Half of each note.

He knew he wouldn't sleep that night so he let the others put their heads down. He tried not to think about the knife but it would not leave him alone. If he could only have it in his hands for a few moments, he would cut himself open and rip out the thing that was hurting him, that was squeezing him to death from the inside. He thought about a giant knife. He wielded it with four blades open and hacked to pieces a goat that jumped into his path. Mintu jerked on the ground next to him. Deepak put a hand on his forehead and Mintu quieted down. Deepak left his hand there anyway. He closed his eyes, just for a few moments. He knew he wouldn't sleep.

He dreamed first of goats. They nibbled at his shorts, at his shirt, and when they had eaten through those, they began to nibble at his flesh. Then he was running, running naked in a field and there were other children running with him and they were not running away from anything; they ran because they could and because it pleased them. He ran all the way to his house and stood in the doorway while his eyes adjusted to the dimness of the light. In the corner squatted a man and the man was working at something. Deepak stepped inside.

'Come and see,' said his father. Deepak went closer. His father raised his head from his work and Deepak saw his face. 'Do you like it?' his father said. He held up a wooden elephant, still a little rough around the ears and trunk.

'Yes,' answered Deepak and held out his hand for it. 'It's not ready,' his father told him. 'Go and play.' He bent his head again and picked up his knife. He blew wood dust from the blade and ran his thumb along the curved, red handle.

'You'll miss it,' called Salman, hanging off the train.

'No,' said Deepak. 'I can run fast.' He tore down the platform, into the station.

He put his hand on the poster, all along the woman's cheek. He had thought he had to tell her something before he left, where he was going and why. Now that he was here there was nothing really to say. It was only a poster. He went towards the train and didn't look back until he got to the edge of the hall. He waved then, long and hard, because he knew if he never saw her again, this much at least he had done.

Emails to Ed

VICTORIA GLENDINNING

Ed – I'm sending you the draft of my report as an attachment to this message. Some useful things in it for us but honestly, like we were saying, these international conferences don't really deliver. Best not tell Her Upstairs though or we'll never get sent on another. Do what tweaking you want on the report and come back to me. Wish I'd been going back to Dhaka like you instead of flying straight home tomorrow. I really appreciated our late-night talks. Funny how you only get to know someone properly when you're away from the usual context. I ended up feeling a bit of an anorak though. Some of the things you said, like 'risk-averse', and a romantic, etc. etc. Oh well. M.

Thanks very much, great idea. If it's really all right with you and the office, that's exactly what I'll do. It does seem stupid to be in Calcutta, I mean Kolkata, for the first time in my life, and to leave having seen virtually nothing but the inside of the Oberoi and the Tollygunge Club. I've got masses of leave owing, and there's nothing in my diary for the next two or three weeks that can't be rescheduled. I'll get in touch with Marcus to sort it soonest. Presumably you won't be back in London anyway until next Monday. Have you had time to look at my draft? I'm just off to meet old Kumar for a drink at Petercat on Park Street. Great being a free man! M.

God, Ed, I am in the shit with Charlotte. We were meant

to be going up to see her parents in Durham next week-end, a big deal. I'd no idea she would mind so much. I feel really bad about it. I'll be emailing her every day, and I've told a slight lie. I said I had to stay on to check local statistics for the report, so when you see her, will you back me up? I've even looked out some numbers from our briefing papers to impress her. Bet you never read them properly. I hadn't till now. Did you know there were 13 million people in this city? And 80 million in West Bengal? And that about a quarter of the babies under three are malnourished? Well, Charlotte does now. M.

Re report: No, Ed, I don't think that 'exuberant' would be better than 'lively' on page 13, para 3. I'd have writ-ten 'exuberant' if I did. But you're probably right about cutting the very last para. Got a bit carried away. I'm feeling pretty lively, or exuberant, right now. This morning I moved out of the Oberoi – it's almost empty except for a few grey-faced men in suits doing business with locals who look like they could run rings round them. And the grey men's fat white wives reading mag-azines round the pool. I'll miss the spaciousness and getting my clothes laundered, and oh God the air con-ditioning. Where I am now, I'm back in the 1950s. It's just off Sudder Street, not so far from the Oberoi, but another world. Luckily there's an Internet shack just along the street, which is where I'm writing this.

There's a skinny little girl who hangs around just out-side the overgrown kind of garden in front of my guesthouse. At least I suppose she's a little girl. She's completely bald. She's got on a raggy yellow dress that's much too big for her. When I go out, she walks along beside me chattering, and holds my hand. I tell her to 'go home', like one would to a dog, and she does, or at least she goes to the guesthouse, she's always there again when I get back. She looks about five, but I suppose she could be nine or ten. M.

Yes, Marcus says he can reschedule the meetings, so I'm in the clear. How do I know the sizes of children? My sister has five kids! There are all these miniature humans like stick-insects on the streets here, talking a blue streak, me of course not understanding a word, and begging very professionally. They aren't any taller than a three-year-old back home, and half the weight. Kumar says he will show me the red-light district this evening. That should be really interesting. I am SO HOT. The shower here is just a dribble. Let me know what Her Upstairs says about the report. M.

That's all right then. I'll do a bit more work on the transportation section if she really thinks that's necessary. I'm quite glad in a way because I can tell Charlotte that too, and it's not a lie. Today I decided to buy a lungi to wear 'at home'. Kumar says it's much the coolest, and everyone on the street wears them. The poor people, that is. Like the lunghis they all wear in Dhaka. I went into one or two shops that sold men's clothes and they just looked at me pityingly and shook their heads. So I went to the New Market. It doesn't look very new. An enormous crowded warren of stalls and shacks and what you might call 'units', all on different levels. Still didn't see any lungis. A smartish man with a briefcase asked me in good English what I was looking for. He was very friendly. He said his brother sold the best lungis in Kolkata, and just round the corner. We walked for miles, twisting and turning through the market. I'd never find his brother's shop again. Anyway I bought two lungis. They turn out to be just strips of checked cotton, with raw edges and not stitched down the side into a sort of tube like Kumar's, which is the only way to be sure you're decent. So I'm not much better off till I find someone to stitch them for me. M.

No Ed, I know I didn't tell you anything about it. But I will since you say you're interested, 'sociologically'. Duh! But here goes. We took a cab for part of the way. It would have been quicker to walk, the traffic jams are terminal. Then on our feet we turned into a narrow unmade street, and a smaller street off that. No, not a street at all, a passage. Squalid. The buildings each side decrepit. Women squatting against the walls all the way down on both sides. Some pretty, some ugly, some thin, some fat, all ages. Some of them had silky saris and lots of glittery jewellery, some didn't. There were little kids running around. I didn't see any men. When we walked down the narrow space between the women they smiled up at us, or most of them did. I felt very self-conscious – and very interested. Near the end of the alley Kumar stopped outside a doorway and said he had a good friend in that house, she was sick, would I like to meet her? I chickened out and said, perhaps another time. Is this the sort of thing you want to know? M.

OK so I'll keep you posted. We agreed we could tell each other anything. The alley, since you ask, is called

Seth Bagan, and it's off Nandy Mullick Lane. There are other alleys just like it round there. You're right, it's certainly not for 'rich white men', but then there's very little high-end trade here apparently. Kolkata is not a sex-tourist destination. I'd guess there are some fancy callgirls in apartments somewhere for really wealthy locals. But how should I know. M.

Today I saw the worst things I have ever seen. I've been around, I've roughed it, I know about slums, but being in there is different. It changes you. Kumar took me back to the alley to see his sick friend. We took off our shoes at the entrance. The inside of the house is a dark, filthy, cramped ruin all on different levels, with the women and their families sort of camping in the rubble. The sick girl was sitting on the stone floor in the 'kitchen', which doesn't have any furniture or anything to cook on, nor a roof. What can it be like when the rains come? She can't walk because she has a sore on her leg – a round patch of flesh, or ex-flesh, about four inches across, rotted right down to the bone. A crater. She was putting some powder into it that someone from a clinic had given her. Kumar interpreted for us. They don't say 'AIDS', they call it 'the illness'. This girl doesn't know, or doesn't want to know, that she has the illness, though she has been sick a long time. She told me the sore was an insect bite. She's very young. She was smoking a cigarette and had three more laid out in a row on the ground in front of her. I left her my packet. M.

Stayed in most of today on my rock-hard bed, sweating buckets, smoking, scratching my bites, and reading

P.G. Wodehouse. I liked your story about Marcus's run-in with Her Upstairs; from here she seems as surreal as Aunt Agatha in my P.G. Wodehouse. Yesterday after that visit I went on my own back to the Oberoi, which was cool and calm and grandiose as ever, and sent my emails to you and Charlotte in comfort from the Business Centre there, and then had a curry, and two Kingfishers, and about a litre of watermelon juice. I guess that's why my stomach is upset today. Watermelon juice is good for you. It's just that I had too much. Kolkata does not do moderation. It's an all or nothing place.

In fact I can't get over the extreme contrasts. How can a luxury hotel like the Oberoi operate as it does within a mile or two of those alleys? Or within a few steps of the crowds and stalls and beggars you fall over immediately you step outside it? There were old messages for you and me at the desk – they must have come the day you left, I'd never checked – from that rather impressive chap – Mr Ahmad – who we talked to for a long time at the reception at Tagore House, do you remember. It's an invitation to drinks at his house – for tomorrow, so I might as well go. M.

I've had another bout of luxury. You would have loved it. The Ahmads live in an apartment block behind security gates with guards, and you can't move without a white-gloved servant popping up to open doors etc. Mrs A very welcoming, and attractive. Smashing modern apartment, high ceilings, all white, modern art on the walls, books, rugby memorabilia. He used to play at national level. Lots of whisky, and masses of delicious bits to eat passed around by the white-gloved ones. I think I took too many, I made them my dinner. There was an English couple there as well, she's with the British Council and he does something at the university. We talked about the cricket. The man had known a man, he said, called Ajay Chokrabarty, who actually turned down an offer to go and study cricket in England. Then we spoke about rugby, and about restoration of the colonial architecture, and about Harry Potter. Well, it certainly made a change of scene. They were very nice indeed and insisted on having me wafted back to the guesthouse with their car and driver.

No I haven't told Charlotte about the girl with the illness. I might, some time. But not now. M.

I now know where my little bald girlfriend lives. She lives on the pavement. During the day there are cardboard boxes and rolls of cloth and pans piled up against the walls of the buildings opposite the guesthouse. Staking claims. In the evening the families come back to their personal spaces. Last night coming home late, picking my way through the encampments, I saw her in her yellow dress stretched out on the pavement on her back fast asleep with three other kids, just a couple of feet from the screeches and honks and fumes – the traffic is non-stop. There were grown-ups huddled up near them. It may sound bad to you, but I can tell you that the way things are for children here I'm just glad that she has a family. I pass street children lying in piles in doorways, the big ones cuddling the little ones. What I really don't like, at night, are the packs of starving scabby dogs. Scary. M.

Ed, I've been back to that house and met someone else. Too long to tell you in an email, I'll write an attachment, you needn't even open it if you're busy. It's written as much for me as for you, if you can understand that. M.

Attachment:

This afternoon I went with Kumar back to the house where the girl with the illness lives, only this time we went upstairs. The stairs are rickety rotting wood, and running wet even though it hasn't rained. It was dark, or seemed dark after the glare out-side, and I kept slipping on the slimy steps, and I kicked over a tin can full of water. Someone cried out and came up behind me to put it back, it must be to catch the leak from a drain or a spring, there is no water on tap in the house. The smell is bad, as is the heat and airlessness, but I am kind of used to all that now and it doesn't bother me. On the way up I got sideways glimpses through open doorways into small dark spaces. Each one is home to some woman and some-times to children too. Like living in a lightless, airless cupboard. In one of them she was just lighting a paraffin lamp. It flared up and I saw her smiling face and a man's legs sprawling from off a bed. There were two pairs of children's sandals on the stairs, neatly lined up.

Kumar had told me as we were coming along that Jharna has the illness and has been very sick and hasn't been able to work for a while. She is in remission at the moment. He speaks of her with respect. He said he thought she would interest me, and that I could ask her anything I liked.

I didn't know what to expect.

We took off our shoes. We did *namaste.* Her room is tiny, a cell, but at least it has a bit of natural light from a small high window with no glass in it. No door, just a curtain. The only furniture is her bed, and that's just a shelf covered with cloths and cushions. There wouldn't be room for anything else. Her clothes and cloths are hanging from hooks on the scabby walls. A holy Hindu picture, a coloured print, pinned up near the window, curling at the edges. Jharna was sitting on the bed, doing nothing, her back straight, her legs tucked under her, her little brown feet just showing. She was wearing an orange and yellow cotton sari and long earrings. Her hair is neatly combed and twisted back off her face. She is thin and small, and beautiful. Difficult to tell her age. Not that young – about 28? She is very still, very serene. I think she was only fairly pleased to see Kumar.

Kumar squatted on the floor and they insisted that I sit up on the bed beside her in the place of honour. I am so big and clumsy, I couldn't tuck my legs up properly, and one dangling foot kicked over her cooking pans. She keeps then stacked in a pile on the floor at my end of the bed. It made a frightful clanging and crashing, very embarrassing.

You'd think it would be even more embarrassing to ask her about herself, but it wasn't, though it was a bit slow, because of the two-way translating. She comes from a village, and when she was still very young she was sent to live with an aunt here in Kolkata to work as a maid. Straight away the aunt put her to work going with men, taking the money for herself. Jharna ran away from the aunt, but in order to survive she had no choice other than going on working as a prostitute. She says no one will marry someone like her, prostitutes don't get married. The best a woman can hope for is that a regular client will take a liking to her, protect her, maybe move in with her. That happened to Jharna – he stayed around for four years and then buggered off. Those were the best four years of her life, she said. She hopes for nothing now. Women like her – they work, they get the illness, they die. That's what she said.

She shrugged, she smiled – such a smile. Although I understood nothing until Kumar translated, she said it all in an even, gentle voice, you could tell there was no self-pity or bitterness. Just acceptance. She was looking full at me with her great eyes, all the time. Then she called out to someone downstairs, and a young boy came up with three bottles of Coca Cola. I didn't really want any but thought I shouldn't reject her hospitality.

When we left I kicked the tin can again, and the water slopped all down the stairs. They were wet already anyway.

I think that Jharna is the most lovely and wonderful person I have ever met. I can't stop thinking about her.

So you did read it.

No, Ed, I haven't, I didn't. Not because of the illness. Not because of Charlotte either. But because Jharna is worth more than just that.

Kumar is going to Chennai the day after tomorrow on a project for his firm. He's pleased because his parents live in Chennai. I'm really going to miss him. M.

Today I went to the Indian Museum and had a good look at the Pali statues and all the Buddhas etc., in order to have something interesting to tell Charlotte apart from statistics. (Total population of India a thousand million. Mortality rate of children under five nearly 10 per cent.) And then went for a long walk on the Maidan to clear my head. For an hour, what with the green grass and Raj monuments, I could have been in Cheltenham, except that here people meet your eye and smile and want to get into conversation with you in English – a pair of law students, an old guy who has a brother in Birmingham, a middle-aged woman who turned out to be a journalist, and an intelligent boy of about eighteen who wanted a long, in-depth discussion about art. He gave me his mobile number and I might see him again. Then I went back to my foetid room and thought about Jharna. Maybe I can help her. Maybe she can help me, too, in spite of the life she's led. There's something spiritual about her. Spiritual. I've always thought that was the ultimate no-no word. A real give-away. Crystals, and New Age crap. But there's no other word for what I mean about her. It's not the romantics who are the spiritual people, it's those who have no illusions. Does that sound ridiculous? M.

No Ed, I am not going to make a fool of myself over Jharna. 'Risk-averse', remember? We went to see her again today. She's obviously very intelligent as well as beautiful. I'm beginning to think Kumar was a client, who became a friend. But he's not the man who stayed with her four years. She had a child with that man, Kumar says. That gave me a bit of a shock, though no reason why. Here's another attachment, for when you have time. M.

Attachment:

Yesterday I spent a long time wandering about in Howrah station after Kumar's train went. It covers a vast, murky acreage, and half of it seems derelict. It's noisy and hot and crowded beyond belief, same as the streets. Whole families sitting around on the ground with bits of food in cloths and all their bundles and belongings. They fill in time by having a kip.

Kumar had told me about the platform children, and it wasn't difficult to find them. They literally live and sleep on the station, in gangs. The thing is, that although they are filthy and ragged, they are really lively and look quite happy, and the big ones look after the little ones. They all cluster round you and pat and stroke you and hold your hands. Affectionate and wanting affection. (Wanting money and anything that you've got in your pockets, too.) The group I hung out with for a bit were all ages up to about fourteen. There are more boys than girls but the boss of this gang is a girl, weirdly pretty and graceful, like a gypsy princess or a dancer. One misshapen girl of about twelve was carrying a bare-bottomed baby. She called me Uncle and made me hold him – he stank, and he wasn't very well, his eyes were crusted and his nose was running. It was her baby, it had been born on the station platform. I know this from two young European women – one English, one Dutch – who came along and gave out paper and crayons and began playing with the children and setting them to draw and colour. This was going very well until a jam-packed train came in – and then the children dropped everything and stormed the train. That's how they live. They carry bags, push trolleys, and tear up and down the train scavenging for food, papers, bottles and anything at all left by the people getting off. It's bad at night, the women said, because the police are brutal to the children, and obviously they are prey to every kind of danger and abuse. But it's hard to get them to stay in the night shelter that's provided – because they don't like to be confined inside four walls, it seems unnatural to them. They are used to running wild, with no grown-ups in charge. There's a Loreto convent school which runs a teaching programme for the platform children, though the teachers can't make them attend – they call them the Rainbow Children, because they come and go. You'd say they were like little wild animals, except that there's this human intelligence shining out of them. Plus something I can't find the word for. Fearlessness, or spirit.

Then who should I run into but the clever boy I'd met on the Maidan – is that a coincidence, or what? I'm going to take him for a drink at the Tollygunge tomorrow. His name is Sunil.

I'm now getting up my courage to go and see Jharna, on my own.

Email not sent. Saved in 'Drafts' folder.

Well, now I am thoroughly churned up and even more obsessed. I passed a middle-aged man coming back up the alley on my way in. He looked seedy but self-important, like a civil servant. Couldn't help wondering whether he had been with Jharna. She must be working, else how can she survive? The women sitting in the alley recognise me now. I suppose they think I am a 'regular'.

The boy who brings the Coca Cola was in the doorway. I said, 'Jharna?' He shouted to someone inside the house, and a woman's voice shouted back. He nodded at me, and I went up.

She was sitting up on the bed as usual, and I did *namaste* and sat beside her as usual. But of course it was hopeless. I looked at her and I talked to her. I told her how lovely she was. I told her about home, about England. I told her I'd like to take her away from that horrible house, back to England, and make her safe and well and happy. I said anything that came into my head knowing that she could not understand a word. That's why I could say it. I held her hand and stroked it. She just looked at me, smiling, alert, like she was wondering what the next step was. With one hand she undid a button of my shirt, still smiling. I pushed her hand away. I wanted to get her to understand I'm not just another punter, that I am interested in the whole of her, the real her, and that I want to help her.

Except of course I am just the same as anyone else, I do want to fuck her. I want it more than anything in the world. I could scarcely get my breath when she touched me. But not yet, not now, not here.

Anyway suddenly this man came in, pushing the curtain aside, and stood foursquare in front of us. He had on a lungis and nothing else. He didn't look at Jharna. He started talking at me in a vehement way, it sounded as if he was asking questions. I shrugged and opened my hands to show him I didn't understand. He talked at me again, sounding angrier. Jharna just sat there, impassive, smiling slightly, maybe nervously. She pulled off an earring and put it back in her ear again. The man stood there with his arms folded. He wasn't going to go away. I got some money out of my pocket and put 100 rupees down on the bed. Neither of them looked at it or touched it. I pushed past him and down the stairs. Something scuttled down in front of me. A rat.

Apart from the humiliation of this, I am baffled because I had understood that the working girls were controlled by older women, not by men. I'll ask Sunil about it tomorrow. He's young but he knows his way around. M.

Hi, Ed. Remember that afternoon at the Tollygunge before you left? Watching the golfers? Strange being back there drinking Kingfishers without you and the boys, and strange being back in that tacky-smart 'exclusive' ex-colonial setting, after where I've been. They tell me that becoming a member is just as status-loaded as it was in the olden days when it was Europeans Only. Indians are just as snobbish as the Brits were. Sunil fitted in fine at the Tolly, in pressed shorts and a white shirt. I was all dingy and crumpled.

Going back there made me realise something. I was irritated by the Tolly chit system – a separate chit for everything you order, endless bits of paper and endless signatures, a mini-version of the strangulating petty bureaucracy that bedevils every single transaction, like when you and I were trying to negotiate the contract with the KMA. And then I thought about the whole of Kolkata with its 13 million people, the whole of West Bengal with its 80 million, the whole teeming subcontinent beyond that, with its dust and hunger, its inadequate infrastructure and unquantifiable lack of resources. The whole of India, in fact, in perpetual danger of collapsing into chaos.

So what you do is this: you construct small islands of orderliness in the middle of the chaos. It's a highly functional strategy. Hence the chit system and the bureaucracy. Hence the absolute neatness of Jharna's room and the perfection of her hair and fingernails. Hence the dignity of the people living on the streets, and the trouble they take to try and keep themselves and their children clean. The middle classes too – do you remember we noticed how many ads there are for soap on their TV? The pavement families scrub their kids at the open mains or a standpipe, there are pavement eateries and shoe-menders and pavement barbers. Everything happens in public. Privacy is a luxury they can't afford and have not learned to need.

Do you think this is all just sentimentality? M.

Christ, Ed, there was no need to give me such a bollocking. I know as well as you do that there are fantastic economic success stories here. I know as well as you do that there is a 'burgeoning new middle class' and how much 'Western governments and aid agencies contribute to child health and welfare'. You don't have to be so fucking condescending. I was just telling you how it looks from where I am standing. I suppose what I say about Jharna might seem sentimental. But what I feel about her is not sentimentality. I mean everything I said to her, more and more and definitely. I don't suppose you know what falling in love is like, I remember how you talk about women. You are gross sometimes, so just piss off. M.

Sorry about that. It was the bit about Jharna that got me on the raw. You may be right, though I don't think so. Sorry anyway. M.

Ed. Something amazing. Sunil has got a place to do technical drawing at some college in Liverpool, starting next year. And he started out as one of the platform children. Just proves my point, about their intelligence. Apparently there is an Englishman who takes children from the streets and stations and looks after them and educates them as far as they will go. He has a big old house where they live and are taught – a boarding school, though rather an odd one. He has to raise all the money for it. Sunil was there from age five. He calls the man who runs it 'Uncle', but then all friendly men are 'Uncle' here and all women are 'Auntie'. I'd really like to meet that Uncle.

I told Sunil something about Jharna, and he offered to come with me and translate. I said he was too young for that sort of thing. He said he knew the area. When I raised my eyebrows, he looked me in the eye and said his mother used to work there. She died. I just nodded, there was nothing to say. I suppose it would be all right to take him with me. M.

Email not sent. Saved in 'Drafts' folder:

We've been to see her a good many times now. Sunil is a better translator than Kumar, he gets on more naturally with Jharna, and is respectful at the same time. He has very good manners, and so does she. I tell him what I want to say or ask, and he turns to her and she looks at him – not at me, as she did when Kumar was there – and their voices flow in and out of each other, never a pause. This is difficult in one way, because they talk together for two or three minutes without a break before Sunil turns to me and speaks in English. Once or twice I've had to attract his attention, just to stop the flow and get at what they've been saying. And then when he translates, he says something quite short, it can't possibly cover everything she said.

But the good side is that while they are talking I can watch them uninterrupted. I think I see in Sunil's attentive face the sensitive and responsible man that he will become. And Jharna – she's like a lovely cat, she's incapable of an ungraceful move or gesture. Her hands and her posture are as expressive as her face. I look at her and look at her, trying to memorise every little thing about her, learning her by heart.

So what else have I learned about her? Her normal

charge to a client is 40 rupees. That's less than £1, though the exchange rate is meaningless. It's also exactly what I pay for an hour on the Internet in the place where I am now. Hard to know quite what to think about that economic parity. If the client looks rich, she might try asking 100 on the offchance, and let herself be bargained down. She prefers men who are complete strangers. It's low prestige among the women to take men they know, from around the area – and I guess they won't even pay the standard 40 rupees, either. Sometimes a regular will move in with a woman, and though they are glad of the protection they generally end up keeping him, and anyway he won't stay around for long.

That's what happened to her, as I knew from before. It reminded me to ask Sunil to find out about her child. Where was he, or she? Jharna talked to Sunil about this for a long time. All I got out of it at the end was that it's a boy, seven years old now, and living in the countryside 75 miles from the city in a Buddhist ashram which rescues children from the red-light areas – and from lives of crime and sexual abuse. Didn't she miss him? She shrugged. He was brought to see her every month or so. He was getting an education at the ashram. Also, it was better he was away. I thought she meant, for his sake, but she didn't. She meant it was difficult to work with a child hanging around just outside the room, it put the customers off. Not much sentimentality there . . . When I got Sunil to ask her whether she had good friends among the other women in the area, she said no. Because they are all in competition. 'People like me don't have friends.' Again, no bitterness, just acceptance, and the smile. M.

Hi, Ed. I'm not going to bang on to you about Jharna any more – but you did say you were interested in the red-light area 'sociologically'. So here's some more nuggets. M.

Attachment:

The man in the lungis came bursting into Jharna's room again today and started his ranting. He told Sunil he was Jharna's brother. He wanted to know what I was up to. Obviously not the usual thing. Maybe I was from the international police or from some interfering NGO. He needed to know, to protect his sister. Sunil calmed him down. I left some money again. Seemed the safest thing to do, I just hope Jharna gets to keep it.

It was only later that it dawned on me – of course he isn't Jharna's brother. What a fool I am. It's just a manner of speaking. (The aunt who turned little Jharna into a sex-worker wasn't really her aunt, either.) The man who sold me the lungis wasn't the brother of the man who guided me to the shop. And the brother in Birmingham whom the old man on the Maidan told me about is not really his brother. I need to ask someone about this. But I think 'brother' might mean 'mate'. And sometimes it means someone whom you respect or to whom you have an obligation for favours received – commercial, financial, sexual, whatever. What I think is, you don't mess with someone's brother round here.

When we were leaving I saw some little Tibetan girls huddled together at the end of the alley, all done up in tinselly frocks like for a children's party back home, but with lipstick and lots of eye make-up. Jailbait. Painful to see. Also kind of fascinating. I wanted to stop and talk to them with Sunil, but he grabbed my arm and hurried me past. He didn't speak their language, he said. Plus, we were being watched. The little girls are goldmines. He says they are trafficked from their home villages – bought or snatched – and a great deal can be charged for them here, they are more than ten times as expensive as the local women. Because they are so young, they can be marketed as virgins a good many times over. It would be good to be able to scoop them all up and take them to the ashram where Jharna's little boy lives. The Women's Committee, said Sumil, try and keep an eye on them.

I hadn't heard about the Women's Committee. Sunil pointed out a wide open doorway on the street off our alley, with a small front room crammed with plump middle-aged women sitting and chatting and watching the world go by. That's the Women's Committee. All ex-pros.

I asked Jharna today about the Women's Committee and gather that they got together in order to make the area safer. They make deals with the police to prevent working girls being harassed, and ban men who have been violent. They arrange for sick women or sick children to be taken to the hospital. They are apparently working with an NGO which subsidises them. According to Jharna, it's only the Women's Committee who are any help over anything. The aid-workers who come into the area from outside are useless, she says. 'They don't know us, and they don't know anyone else, and they don't stay.'

Then we went out! Jharna took us to meet a member of the Women's Committee in her room in the next-door house. This lady is fat and smiley, and has a skinny little niece kind of waiting on her – she was sent to fetch us the inevitable Cokes. I don't suppose she's really a niece. I'm learning. The room was a palace compared with the rooms in Jharna's house. Not much bigger, but crammed with stuff. The woman was reclining on a proper bed with a carved bedhead. There is a chair, which they made me sit on. Even a small television. I couldn't get a close look, and maybe it's just for show, or maybe she has miles of cable winding through the crumbling masonry and over the roofs, connected to the nearest building with electricity. She has an old Singer sewing-machine too, the sort you turn by hand. Maybe she would like to sew my lungis for me. Not! She has a mobile phone clamped to her wrist with elastic bands. In context, she is rich. Jharna seems in awe of her.

She's a fixer, if I ever saw one. I'm sure she and her colleagues really do help and protect the working girls, and control what goes on in a good way – but I'd guess that control is the operative word, and that there are kickbacks to be had from all kinds of interested parties. That would seem perfectly normal to anyone round here. It's beginning to seem normal to me too. What else can you do? People have to survive. I didn't like the lady very much though, so I may be wrong about her. As about much else that I am telling you. Kolkata is making me realise how oafish and unsubtle I am.

Then we went to the very top of the house where another friend of Jharna's lives on the roof. No, not a friend, Jharna doesn't have friends, remember. The last flight of stairs was so rickety that I thought the whole thing was going to splinter under my weight. We came out into the blazing sun where about a dozen people – all aunts, uncles, cousins, brothers, no doubt – were sitting on the concrete, all round the parapet edging the roof. There was a lean-to shack supported by the high building next door. We didn't meet the not-friend. She was behind the curtain in the shack with a customer. Maybe some of the men there were waiting their turn with her, like at the dentist or the barber. Sunil, Jharna and I did *namaste* to everyone and squatted down against the parapet too. I passed round my cigarettes. The aunts, uncles, cousins and brothers all took cigarettes and laughed a lot among themselves. I think they were laughing at me. This visit was not a great success.

Jharna was very tired afterwards, I don't think she goes out very often. Sunil helped her back on to her bed and she lay down. She is not looking well. Sunil had an appointment, he went off and left me with her. I stroked her arms and her back and talked to her about whatever came into my head. M.

OK Ed, I get the message. Time's up. I honestly hadn't realised I'd overshot the mark. Tell Her Upstairs that I've got myself on to the BA flight that gets into Heathrow at 14.00 on Friday, so I'll be back in the office on Monday morning. Is that good enough? M.

Email not sent: saved in 'Drafts' folder:

Ed, I've got to find a way of getting Jharna to England so that the illness can be treated. Do you think it would be easier to organise this from London? Otherwise I have to come back here very soon. So many of the women have the illness, and very little or nothing is done for them. I've done a bit of research. There are clinics, and 'programmes', but it's a matter of resources, logistics, everything. Going into hospital is the end of the line. It's just another slum to die in, if you don't die before you're taken there. I am determined to get her out of that hovel. I must start teaching her English. I bought an English/Bengali phrasebook this morning. I'm not even sure whether Bengali is her first language. We'll see. I want to give her life, and a life. The way she has given me life and a purpose. Before, I was sleep-walking. M.

Ed, I'm glad Charlotte was looking so well, she told me you all had a good time. But for God's sake, when you are next speaking to her, don't say anything about exactly when I'm coming back. She'd probably want to meet me off the plane or something and I don't want that. I've definitely decided to break it off with her. It would be disgusting to do it by email. Meanwhile my emails to her are just as disgusting, because I'm not being honest. I dare say she isn't fooled. Hard to tell, from what she writes to me. M.

OK, no problem, not your fault. I should have said earlier. I'll just have to tell her straight off, on the way back from Heathrow. Not so risk-averse after all?! M.

Email not sent. Saved in 'Drafts' folder.

I have discovered that Jharna can't read or write. This has knocked me sideways.

I took the phrase book up to her this morning, without Sunil, and showed it to her. It was to be the beginning of our direct communication, I thought. She's not any better, she was lying down and looks really ill. She took the book from me with polite interest, and turned the pages. She was holding it upside down. I put a ball-point in her hand and indicated that she should write her name in the book. She just laughed, and then coughed and coughed. There are black circles round her eyes.

What goes on in the head of a person who can't read or write? How do they know when they talk where one word begins and ends? How can they even think, if they can't put ideas into words and know what the words look like? How is this possible of my clever, articulate, lovely Jharna?

Then I thought of my sister's kids, who've all expressed themselves with amazing precision and originality by the age of three. Three-year-olds can't read or write. But we know that they will, it's just a matter of time.

If Sunil hadn't been taken off the station platform into that school, he probably wouldn't be able to read or write either. For that matter – if I had never been taught, neither would I. I wonder if there's time to get Sunil to introduce me to that English uncle who runs the school, he sounds an interesting bloke.

What else don't I know about Jharna? Almost everything. I've never even kissed her and yet, before I knew her, I never knew what loving someone was really like. But I must have no illusions about her. Does she know what love is? Has she been fooling me? Were the brother's visits pre-arranged between them so that she could make some money out of me in one way if not in another? Did she trot me round on those visits to show off some kind of profitable prize fool? Does she prefer Sunil to me anyway? I was thinking of finding the time before I leave to hire a car and take her to the ashram to see her son. Does she even care about him? I could care about him, a lot, because he is hers.

She's not well enough to go out, anyway. I'll go back this evening and see how she is. Perhaps something decisive will happen – something very good or very bad – to make everything clear to me so that I'll know what to do.

I haven't found anyone to sew my lungis yet. The little bald girl in the yellow dress hasn't been around for the last few days, I'm anxious about her. I suppose I ought to start thinking about packing. M.

[*Charlotte met the plane at Heathrow but he was not on it. He has not contacted the office.*]

The Hotel Calcutta

SIMON GARFIELD

1 I WAS SO HAPPY

My name is Sanjay, and I was born in Assam. I'm 23 now. I studied in school up to Class 8, but when I was 13 my father lost his job and I was forced to work to help the family. First I joined a plywood factory and then I worked in a garage changing tyres and mending punctures. In 1997 I got a call to say there was a new plywood factory setting up in Amtala, just outside Calcutta, and I worked there. It was my job to carry chemicals to the machines and boilers. The chemicals were very strong and bad for your health.

My brother ran away from home in 1992, ran away to Delhi. He broke a container at home, and my father got angry and hit him, and the next morning he wasn't there. He was about eight. He was away for two years and my mother and father had lost hope that he was alive but he came back two years later and we were so delighted to see him. In 1997 my sister was born with a handicap. She had club feet.

When I first came to Future Hope [a charity providing shelter and education to underprivileged children in Calcutta] I was having eating difficulties because of the chemicals. It was very interesting seeing all the children playing, because I didn't do that much when I was a child. When I came here I felt like a child again. I've been here for four years, learning technical skills and going to school classes and working for an electrical company.

I heard about a job at the new hotel about six months ago. Everyone said it was going to be a special place, and everybody wanted to work there. I had two interviews at the hotel. First I went with my application, and they asked me where I had worked before. The job was to work in the kitchens, so I was asked why I wanted to work there, and if there were other departments I wanted to work in also. I said that I want to be a chef, a good chef, and I had to start at the bottom. There aren't many people who could say they are a qualified chef, and I think there will always be work for me if I do that. If I am just a waiter – anybody can be a waiter and as a waiter I might not be in so much demand.

When I heard I got the job I couldn't believe it. I was so happy. I heard a few months ago. They said they like me and want to take me in, but I have to pass my exams first. Computers, mathematics, science, English. They are in October, and so I'm working hard. I will begin by peeling foods, the fruit and vegetables, and I will start in one restaurant and then move to another, and then slowly I will learn more skills. I don't know the salary at the moment but I think they will pay me well. My ambition is to be a chef in a most famous hotel, and I hope people will know of me.

2   WE LIKE TO USE THE TERM RESTOBIZ

My name is Ranvir Bhandari and I've been in the hotel business for 20 years. I was born in Calcutta in 1961 – all my formative years were here. The school offered a lot of extra-curricular activities and I played a lot of cricket and squash, elocution and debate. The idea was to be someone not just good at books, but also have a more complete exposure. My parents ensured that we travelled a lot, and as I grew up I realised that I just

enjoyed being around people, and I was very extrovert-
ed and gregarious. I realised I had to get into the
people business, although that didn't happen for a
while.

I studied to become a chartered accountant in
Calcutta. Midway I had an interview for the Oberoi
Centre for Learning and Development, and I was very
attracted by the brochure and the things people told
me. There were 12,000 of us being interviewed. There
were five rounds, and the final one was with Mr Oberoi
in Delhi, and they took twenty of us, and it made me
feel like the Prince of Wales.

Now I know the business I realise they were looking
for a great attitude, a great background, a good education, for someone who was good with people. So I
joined the two-year post-graduate course on hotel management, and you do everything in that period – from
being an innkeeper to being an entrepreneur. After the
course I transferred to the Oberoi Grand in Calcutta for
seven years, going from assistant manager to food and
beverages manager, and I took a sabbatical and went to
the Stamford in Singapore, at that time the tallest hotel
in the world. They have 22 kitchens and 18 restaurants,
so great learning for any food and beverage person.

In 2002 I jumped ship from the Oberoi group to ITC
and came back to Calcutta. People often have a very
negative perception of Calcutta as a place where nothing works. Many people who came here ten or twelve
years ago never returned, and Calcutta was not really
looked at as investor-friendly or a place to do good
business. So Calcutta was not marketed well. Suddenly
the new chief minister wanted to present a changing
face of West Bengal, and he wanted a showcase.
Kolkata has the largest intellectual prowess in the coun-

try, and there's no reason why it shouldn't rule the roost in the services sector and IT and retail. So I hope the Sonar Bangla will be at the centre of the Kolkatan Renaissance. Here is a hotel which is very modern, using cutting-edge technology, offering the world's best, yet seamlessly coexisting with the traditions of Bengal. It's a business resort. We like to use the term Restobiz.

Kolkatans are a very emotional people, the people here love water and many draw their livelihood from water. Fish is a major staple in the diet, they immerse their deities in water. When Kerry Hill, the architect and designer of this hotel, first came here he went around West Bengal for about six months and became inspired by water. And the old Calcuttan always enjoyed his country house, known as the *bagaanbari*, which had a lake and a great sense of space around it, allowing the Calcuttan to sit and create and read or just reminisce. It was also very well equipped for both leisure and work. This hotel develops that old bagaanbari concept.

For a start it gives you a great sense of space. The concept is that there's a great hub of activity in one place – seven restaurants, 22,000 square feet of convention facilities, a pub, everything, but once you're through you go through these walkways into a very quiet and private space and nobody disturbs you. We also created this spa and this chip-and-put golf course and the jogging track and tennis courts and yoga and aromatherapy and many forms of massage.

Previously people have said about Calcutta that things don't move, and even when they do they take a lifetime, so when this building went up in two years they didn't believe it. When we said that it would open on 31 December 2002 people said it can't be, but as it got closer people said 'Wow, maybe it can be.' And when we opened on time that was a big message. Locals have embraced it in hordes. Sonar Bangla means Golden Bengal.

The ITC, the Indian Tobacco Company, is headquartered in Kolkata. The company has diversified from tobacco into matches and timber and many leisure pursuits. Its plan was to make this a destination in itself. Most hotels are built on four or five acres and have rooms with 350 square feet. Ours is 16-and-a-half acres and our average room size is 400 square feet – so much more to offer. We have 240 rooms here, but that includes a CEO's wing, a vice-president's wing, and the executive wing, so you have a choice. If a company wants to bring in their top four layers they can separate them.

We're not fully on the market yet – it's a soft opening. We wanted to ensure that all three Ps – people, product and processes – were all in place before we start firing on all cylinders. I'm about to go to Bombay to market the hotel, to tell people that there will be no gap between promise and delivery. I'll be talking to heads of companies, the top professionals, big telecom people, the medical fraternity. I'm going to tell them to come to stay with me.

The advertising has just begun. This month [May 2003] there's the first national advertising in the newspapers. The photography of the hotel has just been taken, and the brochure is just being developed. We didn't want to photograph until the hotel was complete and the trees had grown a little bit. We had a launch party – the chairman of ITC had a party for the city at large, about 2,000 guests, and all the restaurants were open. Great publicity.

For any general manager to open his own hotel is a great opportunity and not everybody has it. Believe you me, it's wonderful to actually have your own toolkit when you open your hotel. It's like giving birth, and now I'm mothering the baby as I would wish to, teaching it the way I'd like it to walk. The team here have been recruited basically for attitude. They're all on a learning curve. We have very few levels in this hotel – only five levels from the lowest to the general manager, and we want to keep it tight because we want the reaction time to the guest to be very quick, we wanted decisions to be taken immediately. I just wanted graduates with great communication skills and a great willingness to serve. I selected them from all over India. I was with Oberoi for 18 years so a lot of them wanted to follow me, but many have come from all over, and we have some with experience and some fresh ones. We were inundated.

3 AFTER A WHILE WE HEARD RUMOURS ABOUT THIS PLACE

So I'm Chantelle Cropp. I'm from Sydney, schooled in the local public schools, grew up on the beach side. I was a dancer, and I danced for the Sydney Dance Company – classical ballet. But dancing doesn't really pay much money so it was time to look for a career and I became a certified practising accountant. But then I got married to a chef and moved overseas. I was in my last year at school when I met Matthew.

We moved to the Middle East in 1993 when I was 21 – Muscat in Oman, an Intercontinental Hotel. I was really just there as a spouse. Then another posting came up in Shanghai, and within a few weeks I had landed a job with the Australian Trade Commission doing finance and admin; here I became fluent in Mandarin. Then it was in Bangkok and I was working as the executive director of the Australian-Thai Chamber of Commerce. Then we moved to Bombay with ITC. We were there for two years, I did the spousing, I did a correspondence course, I did yoga and met up with the ladies group. It's Matthew's career I'm following, basically.

It can be very difficult, because you lose your identity and independence. But there's a goal of where we want to be financially. I think when we moved to Bombay we found thirteen other Australians. Here there are two – Matthew and myself. But we're working towards our goal and we love to discover new cultures and really get ingrained. When I moved to Kolkata I asked if there was an opportunity for me at the hotel and they said 'Sure'. Otherwise Kolkata is such a small city and there's not so much to do and the other option was to go back to Australia alone. We would do that six week thing – every six weeks one of us would travel to the other place. It's about 13–14 hours with a couple of stops on the way.

My uncle married an Indian lady, so I learnt a little bit in my teens about Indian culture. But I never thought I'd move to Kolkata. This movie with Patrick Swayze that was made at the Fairlawn Hotel – that was my vision of Kolkata. City of Something. Of Joy. Not exactly the most luxurious city on earth – I didn't want to go there, the poverty, the sickness, the dirt.

We were in Bombay at the Grand Maratha for two years. After a while we heard rumours about this place. 'Sonar Bangla is coming up, maybe Chef Cropp should go.' I was in Australia at the time, and he told me he was about to go into a meeting. Then he called back and said, 'It's Kolkata,' and I thought 'Oh God, I don't know about that for me at all.' But then again it's going somewhere different. We got here in August 2002, four months before it opened.

I hate to say it, but I really just asked for the job I have. With my background I wanted something that was quite high-profile. I didn't want to be reporting to junior managers and things like that. But it wasn't going to be easy. When I came here I didn't know the names of the important families, but the advantage is that I'm this Australian who is Ranvir Bhandari's secretary and the whole city knows about it and it brings in business in its own way.

I had to learn that Kolkata was a relationship-building city. It's all about old money and old families – a bit like Melbourne really – old groups that have been going for hundreds of years, company relationships and business partnerships. Learning that was a battle. You can't just walk in and say 'Hi, I'm Chantelle, how's it going?' It takes time. But I'd say that a lot of the families know who I am now. It's more than just a secretary. It goes from basic work like filing and telephone calls to complete management of heads of department, following up on what they're supposed to be doing, a lot of PR, a lot of guest relations involved, keeping guests happy and seeing that if there are any complaints that they're looked into and dealt with straight away. All the big families call me up for all their restaurant reservations, so I'm a table booker too. Hotels are all about PR really.

When we came here there was lots of rubble, and we couldn't live as we do now. You had to walk over cement and dirt. I started work in November and there was no air-conditioning and lots of grime.

But now we have the unique spa and I love the West View restaurant. It's really quite classy. I love going out and looking at the water lilies. The management want this to be a seven-star deluxe hotel, an ambition in itself. This hotel wants to be the Rolls Royce, not the Ambassador you see on every street. It's all about how you feel when you walk around, a learned thing, something that must be groomed and developed. I would say that this hotel is definitely on its way. And that's really sad for us, because we always leave just as it gets really good.

4   I NEVER USED TO GO BEYOND PARK CIRCUS

My name is Ravi Krishnan and I was born in Calcutta way back in 1964. My father was working here as a chartered accountant. The school I went to – St Xavier's – is even today considered to be one of the finest institutions, and growing up here was great fun for me. The quality of academia I always thought was considerably higher than many of the other cities. Calcutta has always had a tremendous sporting heritage – football, hockey, cricket – and I was staying in the south of Calcutta next to the lakes where rowing was big and I used to be a member of the rowing club.

In those days people mostly spoke of Calcutta being hugely congested, with all this poverty, and we had a huge power problem. There were hours and hours of load shedding, and we were the butt of ridicule throughout the country. In a day of 24 hours we would only get power for 12 hours. The infrastructure was mismanaged. In the early 1980s I was aware that the other cities were progressing fast, and Calcutta was really lagging behind. Not much happening in the city, and the youth started getting into lots of activities that were not beneficial, and very politicised.

I began as a management trainee and I've spent most of my hotel career in food and beverage all over India. I went to Cornell University in the US for six weeks on the general manager's programme. That was wonderful – you got to meet up with your counterparts from all over the world, and it was great exchanging notes, very enlightening. Then I stayed in London for three or four days and got to see the Savoy – the Grill Room and the rest. I was always a big P.G. Wodehouse fan. I saw the Dorchester and then the Waldorf Astoria in New York.

The moment I came back from Cornell I was moved back to Kolkata as the resident manager to set up this hotel in September 2002, when the hotel was still a project site. The teething problems here ... many unknown problems – how does one handle the water and horticulture? – and getting used to the layout is very different. The architecture is not very functional – there are challenges to cleaning all this glass, a problem we're still grappling with. This hotel is in an area which used to have a lot of leather tanneries, so there used to be a smell permeating into the open areas, and a fair amount of work has been done to clean that up. Then we had to do the first time-and-motion studies for room service: we had to find how long it would take from the kitchen to all the rooms, through all the narrow corridors below the hotel. One day we had a huge thunderstorm measuring about 120 kilometres per hour, and that made us realise how open the hotel was – all this water inside. A guest got stranded between his room and the central walkways which were unnavigable. So we had to call back the architect to say we needed one area totally reinforced so the guests could get to the restaurants.

But the kind of affection that the opening of this hotel has created in Kolkata has far outdone all these small niggling things. The whole city has been talking about it and has taken to it. Four months on it's become a destination.

When I was growing up I hardly knew of this area. I just knew there was something called the Bypass. We used to live and party and dance – everything on the other side of town. I never used to go beyond Park Circus. I just couldn't picture anything lovely in this part of the city because this is where the garbage dumps are. Or were. The underbelly of Calcutta. But this is now the new face of our city – its hasn't transformed itself from an ugly duckling to a swan quite yet, but the progression is happening. And people have come to realise that actually this hotel is not very far away, just six kilometres from the middle of town. The new generation in Kolkata is changing too – they are now in tandem with what's going on with the rest of the country, no longer a decade behind.

As far as food and beverage is concerned, 90 per cent is local Kolkatans, and 10 per cent is people who stay in the rooms. I think it will take at least a year for the hotel to establish itself completely and for the whole country to be talking about us. Now all the rooms are open for sale, and there's only one restaurant we're waiting for, the Pan-Asian, and then we'll only have the chip-and-put golf to come. The landscaping is done, and now we're waiting for it all to mature. I'd like to think that during the season we'll be as busy as we'd like to be. The season here begins in October until February, after the rains are done, and I would imagine we will be very busy then. We're pretty gung-ho about everything we've done so far, pretty gung-ho.

5   HAZELNUTS ON THE 24TH SHELF

I grew up wanting to be a pilot. Then I enjoyed learning to cook with my grandmother. Then I had the opportunity to go into a hotel so I tried it, I enjoyed it, I excelled, and I aspired to being an executive chef. I gave myself a goal of 35 which I achieved at 27.

The nomadic life has its ups and downs. You can't compare living in India with living in Sydney, but that's the challenge. Working in Australia should be an 8 or 10 hour a day job. Here it's 16, 18 or 20 if required. We went abroad because we saw doors opening, and we took opportunities that we wouldn't have got until years later if we had stayed in Australia. I've done two openings now. Chantelle and I developed our business minds at an early age, and we'll continue to travel until we have children and go home. We want to put our children through Australian schools.

The image I had of India was the Taj Mahal. *Around The World in 80 Days*. Mother Teresa. That's about it. I could have just stayed in Bombay, because there's another hotel opening up there soon. But I was called into a meeting, and the vice president said he was going to ask me a question and I said 'Yes'. And he said, 'Well Chef Cropp, I haven't asked you yet,' but I said, 'Yes. You want me to go to Kolkata.' After all, this is the flag-ship for the hotel group.

When we came here in August the kitchen had been designed but there were a lot of small changes to make in terms of floor plans. There were all the pots and pans and utensils to get, some local, some imported, and we had to sort out all the procedures and policies, and the staff recruitment was a lengthy process. I'm in charge of all the restaurants, even the Indian ones.

Most of my staff speak English, some better English

than us Australians. They are very educated people. But opening a hotel is a very stressful business, and it is hard implementing things sometimes. People are overloaded with work. It's tomorrowland. It's hard to complete jobs and put things to one side – always focusing on fifty things. If I don't order butter for the storeroom it just won't be ordered. Things are slowly getting in line, but it can still be frustrating – getting people who haven't had international experience to see what I want to achieve.

The menus were also very challenging, in terms of imported ingredients versus local ingredients. If the locals can produce goods as well as imported ones then I have no problem. But if they can't, and we're marketing ourselves as a seven-star deluxe hotel, then you need to buy these things. Yes they're costly, but we reflect that in the selling price. And you have a financial controller who wants to know what Dijon mustard is, and why we need to buy so much of it. Why we need so many imported black and green olives.

A small issue the other day with Human Resources. Most of my managers are coming from other ITC properties and I want to know how many pending days leave they have. I got caught with this in Bangkok where I had 156 chefs and they were owed something like 3,000 days in annual leave. 'Oh we don't give that information.' Why not? 'It's confidential.' So I had to approach it in a different way and go higher up.

I have 110 chefs under me at present and about 150 people in all, and there will be 186 if I'm lucky, for the seven restaurants plus bars and lounges. We haven't really promoted the F&B yet – which is a good idea. Let's get everything in place first and then boast about it. It will take a good twelve months, and if other hotels are judging us before then it's very unprofessional.

I've just finished sorting out the deli shop. The variety we're offering, the pricing structure, getting the pastry chef, training the staff. My work's pretty much done – I'm just waiting for the refrigerators to arrive. I'm now focusing on banqueting. We have a portfolio of 200 menus. I'm working out a selling matrix – I'd like to sell at this price, but I can go down to this price if need be. Then there's the Pan-Asian restaurant to open, then I get a holiday, then I'll come back and open up the Spa restaurant. A lot of starches, pulses, low-fat and low-sodium items. But the work is never done. We're not in the cooking business, we're in the teaching business. We have to teach and educate the guests as to what we want them to eat, about ingredients they may not be accustomed to, which they may or may not like. It's about how you sell it to them.

Also, it's all about staff motivation. We've developed this two-year programme which this young man you mentioned will go through, a complete theoretical and practical course with mid-term and annual exams. There will be outside trips to the vegetable, fruit, fish and meat markets. It's a case of organisation – having all the nuts in one place, the rice and pulses all together in the storeroom. That was a good twenty-four-hour job. There were hazelnuts on the first shelf and hazelnuts on the 24th shelf, so that obviously needed sorting.

The local staff who work under me – the younger ones look at it as a fantastic opportunity. The older ones look at it as a threat. I've got one guy with me here now who was chef at a 40-room property. We have conflicts, but pretty much I have to tell him who he is and who I am and put him in his place. After that there have been no issues. You have the old world and the new world, and you can't change the old world. The new guys are very good. They're very anxious, they're very ambitious, they know knowledge is money and power – very switched on.

We seem to be getting quite a good crowd from outside. But you don't have as many tourists here as you do in Mumbai or Delhi. Hotels in India are expensive versus the salary cost. In Bangkok you can get a five-star hotel for $75 a night, but here in India the minimum is about $150. That's just how it is. It's a huge investment – for this property you're looking at $40 million. I said I want a beautiful pastry trolley, I want a beautiful flambé trolley – they're $5,000 each. I want beautiful outdoor barbecues imported – no problem. I think after Bombay they have the confidence to say, 'Let's give him what he wants.'

6 THE REST OF THE ROADS ARE ALL OH MY GOD

They put me in one of their executive suites – ground floor by the pool and spa, an ultra-tasteful brown and beige spread, with dark woods and furniture covered in silks and a huge sunken television. There was marble and a bar area and a walk-in shower that looked onto a leafy courtyard, and lying on the bed surveying the scene was like being wrapped up in *World of Interiors* magazine. A big slab of chilled chocolate on a table was inscribed 'Welcome, Mr Garfield!' and next to it were publications featuring the Bollywood goddess Aishwarya Rai and news of the Calcuttan renaissance, not least the forthcoming shopping centre with the latest hi-tech stuff from Japan. But it was clear that the new Kolkata was already here in this hotel; everything was serene and odourless, and there was broadband too. The only anomaly was by the window, a terrifying black massage chair from America that shook you up like Buzz Aldrin on re-entry.

They treated me well, sometimes overwhelmingly. It was impossible to sit down in one of the lobbies without little cakes appearing on expensive trolleys from all angles. The staff hovered around the waterfalls and bamboo groves and canopied walkways, eager to impress that they weren't going to stop at seven stars if eight stars were attainable by legal means. Whatever their post, they were certain they had landed the best job in town.

I was informed that the kitchen consultant was from Germany and the disco designer was from Ireland. I was handed many details about the Dum Pukht restaurant, a majestic place with an entire wall made from onyx and a floor flown in from Italy. The menu had four culinary styles, including one favoured by the Jolly Nabobs of the East India Company. Each style had its own chef, and the hotel marketing department believed that some of their creations 'may well go down in history'. If not, the menu might: if you go to the Dum Pukht, for the love of God make sure you get an early reservation. There are more than fifty dishes with very long explanations, and your waiter will have historical footnotes to most of them. A kebab is not a kebab, not when it comes with pomegranate sauce and a swirl of coriander cream sprinkled with mace on mudkipuffed rice. Not when you're eating something frequently enjoyed by the enduring symbol of the English-educated professional middle-class urbane intellectual Kolkatan known as the Bhadralok. I ate a delicious meal there one evening (small pieces of lamb marinated with green papaya and spices, served with luchi; paneer cubes sautéed and then cooked in a silky puree of tomatoes and fenugreek, with a touch of cream; a baked pudding of khoya mixed with ground almonds and saffron, strewn with raisins and nuts and served with a delicate brandy sauce) and my dry cleaner has since examined the shirt I was wearing and says there are no chemicals on earth that are ready for it.

On my third day I was handed papers about the ITC group. The company had been in the hotels business for almost thirty years. It now has 46 properties, but none of them is quite like the Sonar Bangla. None of them, for example, has an area called Dublin, which the casual visitor might casually refer to as an Irish theme pub, a description which would annoy its creators very much. According to one hotel 'communiqué', the area is based on the 'Third Place' principle hotly favoured by sociologists and readers of *Wallpaper* magazine, the notion of a hangout that is neither home nor work, but one where like-minded individuals may gather in a non-threatening environment. The pub was split into several sections. There was Point Dublin, described as 'the reception of revelry'. There was Dubliner's lounge, 'a pilgrimage of privacy'. The Diplomatic Enclave was the 'seat of the stately', while the Alumni Square is where 'the old school ties tie up . . . steeped in nostalgia . . . memories on the rocks'. Finally there was Ladies Only, 'an enclosure where claws can be sharpened and people can be bitched out over some bourbon'. One evening I came away from Dublin to the strains of a live local string quartet playing 'The Theme from Love Story' and 'My Favourite Things', and passed a sign announcing a special feast for the Ambassador of Bulgaria.

Not everyone in town loved ITC and its opulent creations the way its employees seemed to. Some charities still see the company principally as a cancer empire. You mention the company's record of investing in technology for less-privileged children, of giving something back to its city, and it's dismissed as window dressing, public relations.

After staying at the Sonar Bangla for a few days I wanted to experience how it used to be for the tourist before ITC cleaned up the tannery stench, and how it still is for many. So I checked into another hotel, slap in the middle of all the usual Kolkatan madness – all the limbless dogs and general putrid nakedness. I told Ravi Krishnan of my intentions and his tone implied I might be making a tactical error. 'It's a backpackers' hotel,' he said. 'Very traditional'. My room had a signed picture of a famous actress in it. The late-eighteenth-century building seemed to be on the verge of collapsing beneath the weight of its faded glory. Every inch of external wall was covered in greenery, and every inch of hallway by a painting or photograph of old Calcutta and old-style Calcuttans whooping it up with gin. The furniture was old, and not always in a charming way. I promised the owner that I wouldn't say anything bad about the place, but all promises were broken when a giant rat crawled up the air-conditioning cable in my room at three in the morning.

There were no such incidents at the Sonar Bangla, but it was early days. The place lacked only one thing apart from rats and its chip-and-put golf: a history. It was so far apart from what Calcutta was used to, and from what visitors expected, that it was yet to develop the character that comes only from mass habitation, from people leaving their imprints on the sofas. When that time comes (and it may be happening by the time

148

you're reading this), then all the talk of elegance and waterlilies will come not from the staff but from paying customers, and the hotel will probably do more than any other single building to wrest the image of the city from the clutches of Mother Teresa. It is pure new Kolkata.

On my first night I met a girl called Debolina who made me feel like James Bond. She worked as a customer relations expert in one of the restaurants, and at the end of my meal she made a crepe suzette with two types of sugar and a running commentary. The next day she took me to her house in another new part of Kolkata. She said of course I must see the Victoria Memorial and the Writers' Building and the Howrah Bridge and all the other great old and famous things in the city, but we were now off to Salt Lake, a township that's come up nicely in two decades, where she and her family have built their own modern home.

'It's called Salt Lake because previously there were fish ponds all around,' she said. 'A lot of sand was put in, and it was levelled. Now we have all the cabbages and all the fresh vegetables growing here.' We travelled along the Eastern Metropolitan Bypass, a link road between the airport and edge of town that carried a billboard advertisement for a mobile phone company every fifty yards. The amazing thing was, Westerners could actually imagine driving along this road, something it was impossible to do anywhere else in the city. As Debolina had it, 'This road is actually very nice, very smooth, but the rest of the roads are all Oh My God.'

We passed engineering and management colleges, and the office of the Geological Survey of India, and then Nicco Park and Aquatica, the theme parks where Debolina's younger brother begged to go every day of the holidays. 'This is now the area where all the business and residential buildings are coming up,' she said as we entered a leafy suburb that benefited greatly from central planning. Everything was in an ordered place like a town plan in a children's book – the hospital, the school, the shops, the recreational area; again, not like the Calcutta in our heads.

Debolina gave me a tour of her fine house, with wood from Assam and lilac walls and the goddess of learning, Sariswati, in one of the bedrooms. Then we had some delicate food her mother had prepared, and on the way back to the hotel she pointed with pride to several gleaming buildings with familiar brandings high up on their glass: Siemens, Infiniti, Philips, Price Waterhouse Coopers. Three years ago this place had absolutely nothing, Debolina said. It was like jungle.

7 OVERSATISFIED

My name is Debolina Mukherjee, and I was born here in Calcutta. I'm Bengali. I'm from a middle-class family. My dad worked as an engineer and my mum is a senior accountant, both on the railways. After I was born my father was transferred to Assam, so we all went there when I was one. I was in the Holy Child School, a beautiful missionary school at the top of a hill. My mum is still working, but my dad has been travelling too much so he has taken voluntary retirement. He's at home starting his own business. My brother Ankur is in Calcutta Boys School. He's 11 and his ambition is to go to England to play county cricket. When he gets home we start fighting and my mum is fed up with it.

In Calcutta I completed my schooling, and when I was in class 11 my brother was born. My dad was posted to France, and at that time we faced some difficulties because my mum found it hard to balance professional and home life. The Bengali culture is full of traditions and fastings, so there were all these things to uphold, but she managed it well. My mum is also a classical singer, and she wanted me to learn Rabindra Sangeet, the Bengali songs, the songs of Rabindranath Tagore. But I was more inclined towards dance, and I was good at it, and if ever there was a function I would always be called. I was really good at all the academic subjects apart from maths. I was more into biology and chemistry and history. My parents wanted me to take the sciences further when I got older, but I needed better maths. So I shifted to commerce. I was pretty good at sports also – I was the badminton champion for three years. I'm 22 now.

This is the second hotel I've worked in. In fact, it's my second job. I did my graduation in English honours, and I was also doing a PR correspondence course with Delhi University. They told me there was a vacancy at the Oberoi Grand in Calcutta. I really never thought of working in hotels but I thought I'd give it a try – it was my first interview ever. I passed the first round and the second interview was with Mr Ranvir Bhandari. I got through that as well, but I still had my final year of graduation, a morning course. He asked me whether I would be interested to work there if something could be worked out. My experience with hotels up until then was going to them with my parents and just eating there. I said 'Yes, sir, I would like to work here.' So he shifted me to a department which opened in the evening – an F&B outlet that just opened for dinner. It was authentic north Indian cuisine. Kebabs and tandoori food. I was a little scared at first, but because it was Indian I didn't face much of a difficulty. I'd say 60 per cent would be local clientele, and 40 per cent were tourists and business travellers from across the globe. One guest was from London, and there are a lot of Indian restaurants over there. But he said he wanted to try the difference between English Indian and Indian Indian, so I suggested the kind of food he might like, and he liked it very much. After six months he came back with a group of friends.

So I started working there and quite liked it – every day talking to new people about their lives. I was interested to learn how first-time visitors liked Calcutta. I liked trying to solve a guest's problems, and then seeing them afterwards and they're happy.

This was in 2000. I was there until I came here. I completed my graduation. I was there for almost two years, and then Mr Bhandari shifted to the Sonar Bangla. I was very scared when I first met him, but he made me feel so relaxed, and I came to rely on him and I still listen to his advice.

When I heard he was leaving I approached him and said, 'Sir, I am very depressed.' He said, 'This is how the professional life goes.'

I said, 'Sir, can I also move with you and join the new hotel?'

He said, 'Yes, why not?'

So I applied and came over. I was interviewed by the assistant F&B manager. Right now he's looking after the banquets. Then I had another interview in front of a panel, with people from head office. I got through and originally wanted to be in some public relations post, but Mr Bhandari told me that because I knew the Kolkatan clientele well by their names and faces I should go to a F&B outlet, and then when people come and recognise me they will feel good about it. He said that after that I can move on to wherever I would like. So I am a guest service co-ordinator, a GSC now. My outlet is mostly for dinner. I start my work from three in the afternoon and end at about 12.30 a.m. At the beginning it was very tiring being on the feet all the time, but now we are used to it. Then I use the car facility of the hotel to come home – the security here is very good. My job is to ensure that the whole operation goes smoothly for the guest and my subordinates as well. When the guests come here they should have a great time and when they go out the door they should be oversatisfied.

My parents have not eaten at the hotel yet. We employees are not supposed to have family in, and my mum is very touchy about it. But I have just spoken about this with my boss and he says it shouldn't be a problem: I just have to take a small permission from Mr Bhandari. In fact I told my mum and she was quite happy. She said, 'Let's plan out, and we'll definitely be there one day.' My mum is a travel freak and loves to visit places, but we always go together if we can, and she doesn't want to eat at the hotel with me working there. She wants to go all together.

I must honestly say that this hotel is completely different from the rest. Whenever I enter I always feel there is a sea beach close by. People like to feel a hotel is like the perfect home – relaxing, beautiful, warm. Our interior designer is from Singapore. Even the water lilies are imported from Thailand. In the other hotels you know you are in Kolkata, but here I quite forget where I am.

Before people come here they say, 'Kolkata doesn't have anything, I don't want to go there.' But when they see the place the city grows on you. My friends who have left to go to Mumbai or Delhi they all say, 'Why don't you leave to join us,' but I always tell them 'No, I'm very happy being here, I just love this place.'

Reality Orientation

IRVINE WELSH

1 THE BASE OF THE SPINE

I open my eyes and my pulse quickens and the fear rises within me as the contents of the room pull into focus. In a panic I try to snap my ragged eyelids shut but the onset of a despairing sickness of realisation signals to me that somehow the room's contents will not vanish from my sight. The gold-leaf mirror remains in front of my face, showing me a chillingly distorted self: my features, wracked with anxiety and terror, seem to be almost melting. I can hear the strains of a ghastly parody of an old song, the words of which I cannot quite make out. All I can do is try to screw my eyes shut, but this will not banish what I see: it only serves to blur the objects in room, rendering them amorphous and pulsating.

With a supreme effort of will, I manage to look away from the large mirror. Yet I feel my head being lifted up from under my chin, trying to force me to engage with an image which seems to be rising to meet me. As I attempt to turn my head I feel a warm breath on my neck . . . and now something is pressing into the base of my spine, like a finger, no, like a screw; working its way through the skin, into the bone and cartilage and now bending upwards through the marrow of my vertebrae. My breathing is irregular and this intrusive entity now feels like a steel rod inside me. I sense that my spine is cracking open under the weight of this cold, foreign body, but my head is still being raised and the sinew and tendons in my neck strain as all my energy goes into keeping my head down because I am unable to cover my lidless eyes as my arms are leaden by my

side and I know that I cannot face what waits in that
mirror ...
  Fight ... fight ...

... I fight into consciousness like a drowning woman
cast into a torrid sea might battle for breath. My dry
throat rasps as I spring bolt upright in a sweat-saturated
bed. I fill my burning lungs with air and feverishly try to
take in the contents of the darkened room.

My location seems familiar. My identity, though, I only
have a flimsy concept of, outside of those nightmares.

After a few, stupefied seconds, I see it on the table by
my bedside, that large black folder that contains the lifeline to at least some of my past. I pick it up with
trembling hands and read the cover:

REALITY ORIENTATION
Mrs Kalyani Chakraborty
Northwestern University
Evanston, Illinois

I rise slowly and take the book in my arms. I move over
to the mirror on my dresser and study my image. Then
I open the ring binder and see a picture of myself with
accompanying notes.

If you do not have memory, you do not have a past.
You are not a person. The lifeline to my own humanity
and therefore to all humanity, is contained in that
book.

2   THE ARCHITECT'S WIFE
The book is telling me that I am Kaliana Chakraborty,
wife of Sanjay Chakraborty, who is a most successful

Kolkata architect. As I see Sanjay's picture opposite my own, I am overwhelmed with a great emotion, a surge of what could only be described as pure love.

Yet, as to the details of our life, or as to where my husband is now, I am uncertain. My hand still shakes as I turn the pages of my biography.

I am 25 years old. I grew up in Calcutta, where I have lived for most of my adult life. Sanjay and I emigrated to the United States of America after I started to show signs of being stricken by the disease that necessitated the keeping of this record.

As my lassitude, depression and memory loss grew more pronounced, we decided that we needed to drastically change our lives. At the time Calcutta, with its blistering, suffocating heat, seemed to our troubled minds to have cursed us. So we moved to America where Sanjay finished his Master's degree in architecture and commenced employment in a thriving practice in Chicago.

Yet even in my new environment, my health continued to deteriorate. We saw various specialists before my terrible ailment was diagnosed, along with the frightening revelation that nothing could save me from its remorseless development.

After a few years we returned to India, to Calcutta. Chicago was too cold for me in the winter, so cold that I could not leave our house, the top apartment of a duplex on one of the interminable long, flat, straight streets of that city. I turn a ring-bound leaf and in plastic holders I see a series of pictures of our old dwelling, marked: 2441 Oklahoma Street, Chicago.

Now I recall a beautiful avenue in the summer: lush and green, with rows of trees and emerald grass sidings by the pavements. In the winter, everything just died. It was dark and barren, as empty and gloomy as our broken spirits.

Now my husband has gone somewhere. I must find out where. I miss him more than I can ever express. I know that I drew so much strength from Sanjay: in his absence I feel more hollow and weak than ever.

I keep turning the pages and memories start to flood back, almost too overwhelming. There are photos of Sanjay and I, my friend Gita and her husband Moni. One picture is of an old man and it is marked: Colonel Colqhoun; another of a smiling, elderly woman dubbed Poppy.

My friends.

There is a knock at the door. Sanjay! I pull on my robe and open it and a man stands before me. But he is gloomy and sullen, this surely cannot be my Sanjay. He wears the uniform of a driver.

We look at each other in silence before he says, – The car is ready, memsahib.

– Yes . . .

– Memsahib said she wanted to have a light breakfast at the big hotel and then to train in its fitness suite, he informs me.

– Yes, of course. I will be down presently.

The servant nods and departs. I run to the folder and examine some more photographs. There is one of him, this man Gupta, our servant.

The breakfast room at the hotel and the gymnasium were familiar to me. I seemed to know what machines to use, and for how long. I remember that Gupta's driving is intolerably bad, or rather he reminds me on our way home. One bump on Chowringhee results in my head hitting the roof of the vehicle at some force. I rub my crown and look at him with a sense of violation.

I recall that Gupta is a man to whom it is very diffi-cult to say anything. While he always obeys an instruction without question, his only acknowledge-ment of the request comes in the form of a grunt or a nod. He is even more taciturn when he drives, often appearing oblivious to any other presence. Sometimes I am made to feel that it is *he* who is the master and I the servant. He sits slouched back languishing in the seat, his round shoulders rolling, his eyes dreamy and specu-lative, thinking about anything other than his task at hand. Gupta and his deeply lined, prune-like face: yes, they are always by my side whether I like it or not.

As we prepare to turn onto another road my heart races to my mouth as a bus speeds towards us and col-lision is only narrowly avoided by some swerving, then a breaking action on the part of the vehicle's driver. The driver's horn can be heard above the cacophony on the road. Astonishingly Gupta remains silent, acknowledges neither the shouting driver nor my incredulous stare.

Fortunately the traffic becomes so bad that it slows down to a crawl, allowing my shredded nerves to calm somewhat. I am very edgy as I had another bad night of only fitful sleep and exhaustion's smoky grit throbs in my eyeballs. I tiredly acknowledge the new doorman as we enter the gates of my apartments. Dismissing Gupta, I go into my home where a young boy wearing a white servant uniform with gold braiding is waiting for me. I recollect that he is called Rashid. On my request, he pours me a gin and tonic.

Gin and tonic.

I clutch my file to my chest, holding it like a lifebelt.

I remember that my good friend Colonel Colqhoun, such a dear, sweet old man, brought me several bottles of the tonic water back from England! I can never quite understand why it is so hard to obtain tonic water in this country: after all, the quinine is good for malaria, so one would have thought it would be popular here.

But things do not always happen as they should.

Reclining onto the sofa in the lounge of my apartment, I let the cool air from the overhead fan give relief to my burning, aching limbs. This is the largest room onto which all the others open. Our entire apartment is floored with marble, and covered with rugs. The lounge leads to an open-plan kitchen, a large dining room, a bathroom and three bedrooms, one of which, our master bedroom, has its own en-suite bathing and toileting facilities. This main room also opens out onto a balcony. Like the rest of the apartment, this space is full of large houseplants, which grow most prolifically. I have a much admired marble fireplace, over which hangs a portrait painting by one of India's foremost young artists, Prakesh Jagjeet.

I myself am the subject of the portrait that Sanjay commissioned about five years ago. When I look at myself in the picture, an initial air of contentment always gives way to more intense scrutiny. My nose is thin, but more hooked than I would like. I have full lips and large, brown eyes but the dark shadows under them are not represented in the portrait. Perhaps I am somewhat harsh on myself, as this may be a feature exaggerated by the malady of my disease and my recent sleeplessness.

In the painting I am wearing a turquoise sari and some gold and ruby earrings with a necklace and a few bangles. My hair is braided into two long pleats and my expression is one that I would describe as serene. Sanjay always says that the portrait captures me excellently, although I suspect that it is a little too beautiful and that the artist, like my husband, is a born flatterer.

I look across at the picture of Sanjay on the oak chest behind the couch. His hair is parted on the left and his eyes seem to dance in a knowing intensity. His lips are frozen in a thin smile. He looks so handsome and clever. How I miss him and long for his return. I am most troubled and insecure without his comforting presence.

Later, the young servant Rashid appears and serves me up some samosas he has made, along with a selection of vegetable dishes. I only pick at them: it is now too late to eat alone. It is *always* too late to eat alone yet *never* too late to dine in company.

My notebook informs me that it has only just turned a month since I returned from Chicago: Kolkata still awaits my rediscovery and I am hungry to remake its acquaintance. I realise that I am already anticipating the party at Poppy's tomorrow. I take another drink but it makes me slightly dizzy, forcing me to retire to my bedroom.

3   THE DISEASE

I never go to bed until I am at the point of exhaustion. The night holds nothing but dread and fretting for me, especially in Sanjay's absence. When conscious, I worry about my condition; whether or not my disease is in remission, a sleeping tiger, or whether the beast is crouching, ready to pounce and rip more of my life from me. I scrutinise all my actions, even my thoughts, looking into them for evidence of the chaos it must wreak.

Now even sleep offers no respite. When I drift off into its realms I invariably find myself back in the torment of the Red Room. How I dread my involuntary sojourns to that most sinister and despicable place, which, until recently, I could not recall visiting since my childhood. It seems now that the short remainder of my life will offer me little respite from woe and anguish.

My comfort comes from my Reality Orientation book. Through its pages I learn again, I wonder for how many times, about the terrible condition from which I suffer. But worse still are the omissions, for a small ring binder cannot contain the story of somebody's life.

My husband. Where is he?

When I met my Sanjay I was somebody without a past. I found then, as I do now, it so perplexing and arduous to simply recall the ordinary, everyday events that other people effortlessly connect to form the pattern of their lives. I had only a scant and elusive concept of where I had come from and how I had got to the point I was now at.

I can recall that at first Sanjay did not mind my reticence, jokingly referring to me as 'his mystery woman'. Soon though, my growing depression and erratic behaviour put a terrible strain on our love. I tried to treat my listlessness and memory loss as well as I could here in Bengal, but nothing seemed to help. Then we moved to Chicago, where I attended the Northwestern Hospital and was eventually diagnosed as suffering from Pick's Disease.

It is rare for someone to be given this diagnosis so young as it usually affects individuals between forty and sixty years of age. Pick's Disease is a form of dementia characterised by a slow and progressive deterioration of social skills and changes in personality, along with a general impairment of intellect, memory and language. Symptoms differ between individuals but in my case include memory loss, emotional dullness, a loss of judgement and a difficulty in thinking and concentrating. I often 'hear' things that are said to me which are outrageous and offensive but are seemingly uttered totally out of context, usually denigrating my behaviour or my character. This can lead to embarrassment in social situations.

There is no cure for this disease and although it is different in individuals its progression cannot be slowed down. Death, usually through infection, can occur within two years, but people can go on for more than ten years, albeit with impaired capacity. Pick's Disease is often thought to occur due to a build-up of an abnormal form of the protein tau. The American specialists, after examination of my brain scan results, said that I showed slight abnormalities in the frontal and temporal lobes. These test findings and my general behaviour formed the evidence for their diagnosis.

Sanjay could not accept this. He would walk around our apartment in a daze, declaring that he would engage other specialists and seek out different forms of treatment. I was somehow more resigned to my fate. I wanted to go back home to Calcutta.

Now death's shadow hangs over me, which I do not fear. What worries me is that there will be enfeeblement, helplessness, that I will go on for years unable to sense my decline, my lunacy, and oblivious to all my indignities.

I must have Sanjay back soon. We have told nobody about my condition, but I fear that before long it will become too apparent to conceal.

In my bed my thoughts burn through my head until exhaustion tugs me into the domain of jagged sleep.

4 THE STAIRWELL

*I am in bed, but the room is different. On the wall I see
the head of an elephant. It grins at me, then winks in a
carnal, disturbing manner. Then, to my intense discomfort and great alarm, I realise that something is in the
bed beside me. For a few heartbeats I gain a temporary
elation as I think . . . no, it cannot be Sanjay . . .*

*Now I can hear horrible noises and I feel a wild
thrashing next to me. I cannot bear to turn so I spring
from the bed and exit the room in a terrible state of fear,
a sound of inhuman laughter ringing in my ears . . . I
approach the railless stairwell with its worn steps, and I
gingerly negotiate them, all the time aware that with one
slip I could fall into the black oblivion of the well
below . . . I proceed with caution, yet haste because I
know that I am being followed. I feel the hot breath on
my neck again . . . then fingers tickle me, groping me,
grappling my rib cage . . . the sick shriek of a banshee
trumpets in my ears . . . I sense that I am naked from the
waist down . . . the stairwell is crumbling and I am
going to fall, but then I see a door in the wall and I open
it and slam it behind me and in here everything is
bright, still, and all is now quiet.*

*I am back in the Red Room. But the terrible noise has
started again, now stronger than ever . . .*

I awoke, at once hot and cold in the empty bed, with
sweat pasting my nightgown to my skin. The same
inhuman howling has followed me into this world and I
am briefly stricken with terror. My thumping heartbeat
steadies as the realisation grows that it is only the wild
dogs outside; those ugly, mongrel creatures that I am
normally moved to curse. This time they have provided

me with deliverance from my torment by waking me with their frightful baying.

Once again my bedroom takes a while to come into focus, and when it does so, it remains somehow incomplete and diminished. While my dreams are becoming more real and vivid, my conscious world fuzzes and blurs all around me. How long, I fretfully wonder, horribly aware of my hideous curse, until they cross over?

I lay for a while in a battered semi-doze as the morning light, sickly and weak, starts to come up. A horn blares, insistent and close above the rest of the growing traffic sounds outside, and I rise and throw on a robe and open the shutters. The searing light is blinding as it rushes in. I sweep back strands of sweaty hair from my face and try to focus my eyes. Across the street and beyond the courtyard I see the old ruined church that was built by the British. Looking down, I spy Gupta's silver-grey shorn head. His face no longer looks so wizened, but is animated in a mould of intent. I might even call it boyish, as it hints at a man who in his youth might have been considered handsome and perhaps even carefree . . .

. . . like Sanjay. I seem to remember a letter, an official Government letter. Saying that he had been called away. Some sort of business.

There is a knock on the door. It is Rashid and I bid him to enter.

Rashid is a small, thin young boy with an eager smile. He sustained a bad injury from a fall as a child and walks with a pronounced limp. It is good that here I can have servants, they are sorely needed as it is impossible to do even the most basic household tasks in this heat. That was one thing I disliked about Chicago: having to do everything for one's self.

– Pardon, memsahib, but Guptada is waiting with the car, he urges in his high squeaky tones, the voice of a little boy really.

– Good. Kindly inform him that I will be down presently.

– Yes, memsahib, he cheeps as he departs, his face sad and worried. He does not want to cross Gupta, or even be the bearer of bad news to him. I suspect that Gupta bullies Rashid.

Despite Rashid's doubtful look, I remain unmoved. Gupta can wait; the tail must never be allowed to wag the dog.

I dress at leisure, deciding to wear a red sari with a red and black pashmina. Red always suits me, as it brings to my bearing a certain levity, some might even say gaiety. Or at least it did until this illness took over my life. My melancholy is exacerbated by Sanjay's departure on the Government business he is probably bound to be secret about. In his absence, my spirit cannot be anchored in my flesh alone. Without his arms around me it wanders the world, rootless and restless. And now my dreams of that terrible room, red, vivid, decadent and frightening, have returned to plague me for the first time since my girlhood. No amount of fine dressing can abate these torments, but to lose one's sense of propriety and style is to surrender one's life. This disease may claim me, but I will never help it to do so through my own passivity.

In the small study I check my email on the computer for any news from Sanjay, but there is nothing. My cellphone shows no missed calls and only one text, from Gita Patel, who is reminding me about tonight's party at Poppy's. I see that Rashid has left the post, just one item of mail. I pick up the mahogany-handled dagger that we use as a letter-opener and urgently slice it open, but it is only a notice of a fund-raising event for a charity I am involved with.

I leave the apartment and head down the marble staircase. I can tolerate this time of the year when everything is *relatively* cool before the furnace of the summer builds and the monsoon threatens to sweep the city away. Without it though, Kolkata would die in the heat and squalor, crumbling into dust in its own filth. Even Chicago winters have not stemmed my dread of a Kolkata summer.

Small triumphs: Gupta looks impassive rather than irascible as he opens the door and I climb into the car. I must search for a new outfit for tonight's party and I feel that today's purchases will be most extravagant. Why not? Soon I will have no judgement for fabric or colour, and even those simple pleasures will be eroded.

We take off in the noise and stench of the traffic, heading down the Chowringee towards Park Street, a thoroughfare regarded by many as a centre of vice but only really a place of harmless indulgences. I forced myself to stay awake a large portion of last night, in order to try and stave off the torments and horrors of my dreams and that strange Red Room. As a result, I now find myself dozing in the heat. I focus on the car in front of me in order to retain activity in my senses. It is a standard black and yellow taxi but there is a man in one of the back passenger seats.

There is something about the back of his neck that galls me; it looks scabbed over. Now his head is about to turn towards me. An uneasy tumult rises in my breast and I am forced to look away. Then Gupta suddenly stops the car, thrusting me forward. I look over at him in rising panic but I see that he has only halted as we have reached our destination.

Somewhat shakily, I get out of the car and emerge onto the crowded street. I see some silks arranged in the adjacent shop window and they lift my spirits quite discernibly.

5   POPPY'S HOTEL

Tonight I have elected to dress Western style and I am wearing a long, white skirt with a black, glittering top. We have arrived at Poppy's early. I sit in the car outside the hotel as I send Gupta in to take Polaroid pictures of all the rooms in the building.

I have thought extensively about these dreams and I think I know their dreaded meaning.

If I ever walk into the Red Room in my conscious life, I walk into the place of my death. I have a deep fear, a superstition, an irrational but nonetheless overwhelming belief, that somehow my condition and this Red Room are inextricably linked. Yes, that strange room, at once both familiar and alien, yet resisting any definition, is surely the place where I will meet my end in this world. For the Red Room is my port of passage from this place to the next.

How I know this is as big a mystery to me as the room itself, its specific nature and the more detailed secrets it holds. For all I know I may already be crazy, the madwoman that the Chicago specialists say I will surely become. In the ravages of those tortured nights I have often been moved to question my hold on my sanity. Yet I am certain that if I encounter the Red Room I encounter death: I am more certain of this than anything in my life. Therefore I must have the rooms in each building I enter recorded, so that I will never accidentally walk into that dreaded chamber.

The car grows stiflingly hot. I feel sick as the traffic fumes waft in, mingling with the human stench coming up from the gutters and sewers. We are close to the bustling market and the bustee-lined streets of the poor. My memory does not function well but in the odd phantom sensations of recall that the French call *déjà vu*, I sense that I once knew those streets. As a result I am as uncomfortable around here as only someone in such circumstances could be, where everything manages to be both foreign and familiar at the same time.

After a painfully long wait, Gupta returns with the pictures of the rooms. – Did you get all of them? I ask him, looking over the glossy images.

Gupta shrugs blankly.

– All of them? I urge in mounting anxiety, as I turn over each photograph, all the time bracing myself for the impact of encountering an image of the Red Room.

– I used all the film in the camera, he tells me, so evidently unconcerned in the face of my extreme vexation.

– But did you manage to get all the rooms? I implore, still inspecting the series of images, those empty rooms, which ought to be innocuous but are somehow still oddly threatening in their starkness. My gaze whips up again to meet Gupta's.

Again he casually shrugs, then he turns and his eyes dance in his head for a second or two, as if something across the street has caught their attention. Then he looks back to me and says in a somewhat grand and arrogant tone, – It may be that I missed a couple.

I stare straight at him, now apoplectic in my rage. The traffic noises seem to have mysteriously stopped. All is now silent. The prints shake in my trembling hands. I force myself to listen, to will *some* sound into my ears, and I am relieved, when, after a couple of heartbeats, I register the long scream of a child. The sweat from my hands stains the photos. I flick awkwardly through the last of the pictures. There is no Red Room in any of them. My heartbeat starts to steady. I look back at Gupta.

My servant stares evenly at me. – I looked in all the rooms. There were two rooms too many for the number of exposures left on this film.

Once more I look through the pictures that he has taken. No, there is nothing here that even approximates to the Red Room. But I still cannot go into the Hotel. – Those two rooms you missed, can you describe them to me?

He looks flustered, evasive even. – I beg your pardon, I . . . he begins, – Memsahib, people in the hotel saw what I was doing . . . they questioned me . . . what could I say?

My anger can no longer be curtailed. Does this idiot believe that the derision of a few oafs matters more than my safety? – Describe the rooms you missed! I command. – The decor, the furniture . . . the colours! What colours were the walls in the rooms?

Guptah raises his eyebrows in shock at my outburst, but it has the desired effect as he furnishes me with the descriptions. – One, as I recall, was green, the other, if I remember correctly, was blue . . . there was a mustard – coloured settee with matching cushions and a television set.

– Are you absolutely sure of the colours?

– I cannot be absolutely sure, I ...

– Check again! I command him, and the wretch glances at me coldly before heading away to do my bidding, albeit with great reluctance.

Gupta came from a high caste, but I am the one who

has the money. This is something I will never let him forget. Because that is what happens, that is what you must do to the underminers and the abusers, you must show them that the hurt they try to give to you is but a pittance in comparison to the damage that you will visit upon them. You will do this through trickery, seduction, subterfuge and, if called for, that bluntest instrument of the thug and goondah, naked violence.

He returns about ten minutes later. Now I have satisfied myself that the Red Room is not located in Poppy's Hotel. I walk past the doorman through the arched gates and across the gardens to join my hosts on the patio.

The hotel is an old three-storey colonial building. It is painted pink and green, the two most beautiful and natural of colours. Plants and flowers grow on the terrace and from the balconies in pots and in hanging baskets, while vines twist sensually through the wrought-iron railings.

An Anglo-Indian family has owned the place for four generations. Poppy is the current proprietor, an old friend of ours from our first spell in Calcutta. She greets me warmly and expansively. – Kalyani, my darling, she booms, kissing me once on each cheek. Poppy is one summer short of eighty but could pass for sixty. Her second husband, David, is eight years her junior and currently in England undergoing a hip replacement operation. – The poor darling is doing quite well, but that's the tragedy of men, my angel. The poor dears simply aren't built to last, she says ruefully, rubbing my shoulders as she leads me to a chair.

We are seated around a series of tables, which are laid out with food. Attentive servants bring drinks for the guests. I look out to see if I can see Gita Patel, but the only people so far present are acquaintances. So many people seem to have gone from Kolkata during my period of absence in America, or gone from my recollection, at any rate. They dance in my memory like ghosts: faces and laughter and voices that I cannot quite put names to.

I am hoping that Gita, or Colonel Angus Colqhoun, or someone else I know well will arrive soon. Some other faces from my book. While the hotel is an oasis in this part of Kolkata, it is hardly a tranquil one. The noise of the traffic and the bustle of the streets are still highly audible in the background, and insects whir around our ears.

Poppy comes into her own in the hostess role, and tonight she is on particularly good form; laughing, joking and drinking, loudly yet eloquently recalling all the great poets, writers and actors from England and America who have stayed under her roof. She is one of life's natural performers, who can effortlessly enrich any social gathering, simply by being who she is. On more than a few occasions she raises her glass and exclaims a self-evident truth, – I just love people!

At one point I notice that a strange, roly-poly man, white, Western, and wearing mustard slacks with a beige shirt, has been staring at me for some time. I find this rudeness rather unnerving. Then, when I look back at him, he suddenly breaks into a queer little trot and heads straight towards me, quickly closing the distance between us. – Forgive me, Mrs Chakraborty, he says in an accent which sounds between American and Australian. – We met before.

I can recollect nothing of this.

– I am Dr Marcus Goss, recently arrived here from London via Sydney.

I am put out of kilter by his forwardness, but determined not to give him the satisfaction of showing it.

– As a permanent resident? I ask coolly, hoping that his reply is in the negative.

– One hopes so. I have established a practice here, he informs me, evidently looking for some sort of response. Dr Goss has shoulder-length brown hair and a round, sweaty head. It strikes me that he is not as old as I thought; his face is fleshy but not thickset and he cannot yet be forty. Although he is out of condition and overweight, his eyes are piercing, confident, one might even say flirty. They hint that a handsome man may have stood behind them quite recently, before going to seed. And you can see Goss's vice; he wears it quite literally, as his shirt is stained with food. He holds, indiscreetly close to his chest, a plate absolutely heaped with victuals.

– Well, Dr Goss, I have heard this statement many times over from gentlemen like yourself who arrive in our city at this time of the year. When the temperature rises to 120 degrees and is only alleviated by the floods that the monsoon brings in its wake, then, miraculously, such gentlemen are nowhere to be found.

– No, Goss says with a hint of mischief. By his bearing he evidently feels more endearing than he is. – I am in this for the long haul, he contends, champing on a pastry.

I nod courteously, noticing that Gita Patel has arrived. She is dressed in a beige sari and from this angle and distance, although she is still so small and doll-like, it appears as if she has gained some weight. For a second I wonder whether she is pregnant. Surely though, if this was so, she would have told me, her best friend. Her arrival gives me the opportunity to excuse myself and I am happy to get away from Dr Goss, his sweaty presence, his food-stained shirt, and those dreadful polyester trousers.

Gita and myself are soon in discussion of our favourite topics, bridge and clothes, as the drinks continue to flow freely. I love that wondrous look of awe and astonishment in her eyes. It can make the most commonplace events seem intriguing, scandalous even.

I have taken to consuming pink gins, which my friend Colonel Colqhoun, who has still yet to arrive, always drinks in such prodigious quantities. As the dusk begins to creep in, a servant augments the lighting with tasteful candles. Once again, above the buzz of chatter, I hear Poppy announce that she loves people.

Dr Goss (I did not see the abominable man on my shoulder) leans into me, whispering coldly, – There may not be that many of them where she is headed. An old woman who has never had faith should be more sober in her habits . . . just as an insurance policy, perhaps?

I am appalled and irritated at his nonsense, and all the more so when I realise that his foolishness is intrinsic and not drink induced, for it seems that he has been on nothing stronger than fruit juice all evening. – Her faith is in the human race and it's that faith she will celebrate until her last day, I tell him.

– Yes, we all need some sort of faith. This city seems to exist on faith alone. Look at the cult of Mother Teresa. I wish somebody would think about that – the city and Mother Teresa. And what do we do as the city crumbles around us? Goss asks in a manner that assures me that he has the answer to his own question, – We attend parties.

– And we pray, I whisper, thinking of Sanjay and my

condition, before setting off on a steady course to the opposite end of the patio.

Gita is talking to some young English businessman who chucks his brandy around in a glass. I do believe she has mesmerised him. I fancy that he might be related to Colonel Colquhoun as I hear him explain to her, – . . . Yes, of old Scots-Ulster stock. From the plantations in Ireland, where they were obviously crown loyalists, to America, where they changed over to support the colonists. Yes, Angus's great grandfather was even in the American Government. But the wife took the family back to England and his father went to India. His branch of the Colqhouns have been here ever since, bar some schooling in England.

Now a woman whom I cannot recall but sense that I have met before is asking me about America. I try to talk to her but I grow edgy and distracted, scratching my leg and ankle. I do believe that a mosquito has bitten me.

I hear Poppy remark in mock exasperation, – That old rascal Colonel Colqhoun promised me that he would be here by eight and I had the staff prepare the fish kebabs the way he likes them. And where is the old rogue? Probably gin-sodden at the Calcutta Club even as we speak!

Then a quite astonishing thing happens. I see that one man, who is sitting at the table, is looking very uncomfortable. I had recognised him as a Bengali politician called Burman, whom I met briefly some years ago. He is clasping his throat and coughing in a laboured way as his eyes start to roll in his head and he struggles to his feet, gasping for breath. There is real terror on his face, which is soon mirrored by the expressions on the guests around him. – He's choking! somebody shouts.

Then someone asks, almost casually, – Oh, is it a fishbone? But nobody moves except Dr Goss. This ungainly slug of a man is the one who is the quickest and most decisive. He hits Neru on his back, and the politician coughs and then splutters up some vomit, but his throat is free of the offending bone.

Neru hacks, gasps and swallows: wheezing gratitude at the doctor through his tears. Goss, sweaty and bovine, seems as depleted by the effort as the politician and is breathing almost as heavily as the man whose life he has possibly just saved.

Then I hear a familiar voice behind me which barks, – Looks like I've missed all the blasted fun! Colonel Colqhoun, still straight-backed, but with his big old head drooping, straining his neck, heads to Poppy, kissing her on each cheek. – Evening m'dear. Got a little bit held up.

Poppy gives the Colonel a mildly chastising look, but it is overlaid with great affection. I dance over and kiss him on his cheek. – Wonderful to see you Angus, I tell him excitedly.

– Charming . . . absolutely charming . . . he replies in a throaty gasp.

I leave him to catch up with Poppy, and emboldened by the alcohol, pull Gita Patel away from the blonde-haired Englishman. We are soon back to talking about the things that delight us, while the Englishman approaches Colonel Colqhoun. As engrossed with Gita as I am, my blood runs cold when I hear this young Englishman ask Angus, – So you've never heard of the Red Room?

My heart almost stops and I know that Gita is talking, I see her mouth move, but I cannot hear what she is saying. Then doubt fills her eyes and she suddenly stops, – Kalyani, is everything okay?

– . . . Yes . . . I hesitate, – I believe that this gin has gone to my head. Excuse me, I say, heading to the toilet but circling round and collaring Colonel Colqhoun who is waving at a servant for another gin.

– What was it you were talking about? With that young man, I ask, looking across to the Englishman, who is now talking to someone else, another white man of a similar age.

– Oh, the young chap wanted to know about Calcutta, Angus says, somewhat distractedly.

– Did I hear him say something about a Red Room? What is it?

– Oh! Colonel Colqhoun's bloodhound eyes go large. – The Red Room was supposed to be this place where all sorts of things of ill repute went on.

– Where? I mean, where is it?

– That's the point my darling, it wasn't anywhere. It didn't exist. It was one of those old Calcutta myths.

– But where did it come from?

– Who can say? he says offhandedly, then, as if noting the disappointment etched onto my face, cheerfully expands, – This is a city that cherishes its myths more than most. At dinner parties and in its finest clubs we sit around espousing them or mocking them but we are never less than fascinated by them.

– But you must tell me . . .

– Kalyani my darling, I would never repeat old mess tales to a young lady. Well, not at this level of intoxication anyway, he winks, and saunters off in search of another waiter, brandishing his empty glass. I go to seek out the young Englishman, but it seems that he and his friend have gone.

I see Goss, oddly self-effacing, still brushing off all the attention from the politician and his friends. When I go to pay tribute to his decisiveness and resourcefulness he pulls me aside and thrusts a card into my hand and says, – To remind you, he begins, then hesitates, – I mean, if you ever need my counsel . . .

It reads:

> *Marcus W. Goss*
> *Psychotherapist*

The words frighten me, almost as much as the knowing expression on Goss's big, banal face. – What makes you think that I could require your counsel? I snap, in panic, my voice sounding high and fey.

There is a sudden chiming in my ears. Over the hubbub and noise I hear him say something insulting like, – You are common street trash. Remember that.

I throw the glass of gin into his face.

To my horror Goss stands his ground, looking outraged and flustered as he protests and tries to explain himself. – Why the hell did she do that? He asks the aghast onlookers. Then he turns to me – I only told you that you have important friends who care about your well-being. I said you should always remember that!

The mortifying thing is that I can tell from his shocked reaction that he is not lying. Now people are gathering around me, crowding me out. It is so hot. I cannot cope with their concern. – Forgive me, Doctor, there was a strange ringing in my ears and I picked you up wrong. It was just that . . . I was sure that you insulted me.

– Why would I want to do that? We were just having a–

In my distress, I can think of no good reason. I know I have to leave this place right now. I raise a hand to silence him. – I am sorry but I am so tired, I must go home.

As I go, I hear Goss urging me, – Please come and see me again Mrs Chakaborty. We *have* met before!

I head to the car, oblivious to the various enquiries as to my well-being and the odd plea for me to remain. Colonel Colqhoun urges Gita to go with me but I tell her, – Just walk me to the car. Gupta is waiting.

And he is, leaning on the vehicle's bonnet, reading some xeroxed pamphlet. He seems slightly panicked to see us, and crudely stuffs the paper into his trouser pocket. He opens the door and I climb in as Gita urges, – Come and see me tomorrow.

We have met before.

I nod wearily and we depart snaking and inching into the relentless flow of Kolkata traffic, Gupta's silence on the drive alternately comforting and disturbing.

What did Goss mean? Why did he not say where and under what circumstances we had met before?

6 GITA PATEL

It was with some trepidation that I arrived at Gita's house the following day. I was worried as to what the reaction would be at my terrible outburst. In the event, Gita acts as if nothing has happened, which I find very unnerving. She pours us some tea into thin china bowls, one of which she cups in her fingers, so long for such a petite woman. Her nails are painted a very daring purple. It goes with the pattern on the bowls, and of course, with the blouse she is wearing.

Gita's apartment is beautifully furnished. A tiger skin hung on the wall dominates the lounge. The natural wooden furnishings and finishings, the colours of the walls and the plants clustered in pots tastefully blend to suggest the very foliage and fauna the magnificent beast originated from.

I missed Gita more than anyone else when we were over in Chicago. On one occasion she came to visit us. I recall taking her to the Art Institute and to the top of the John Hamcock building, where we drank champagne. One night we spent with Sanjay at the Green Mill jazz club. She and I always had plenty to say to each other but now we are awkward and tense.

Eventually I decide that I must shatter the ice that seems to have formed in the space between us. – My exhibition last night was unforgivable.

She looks at me for a while, then starts to giggle. – Oh Kalyani, his face!

We have met before . . .

Despite my disgrace, I, too, cannot help but to laugh. When I am with her it does not take us long to become the younger women that we once were. It is as if adulthood is just a veneer to be torn away by our delight in each other's company.

Gita crosses her legs and lights a cigarette. I have never learned to smoke the way she does, to hold a cigarette like a Western woman. She smoothes down her turquoise trousers. – Have you had any thoughts as to what you will do now that you are back, I mean, when you get settled?

– No . . . I . . .

Her eyes grow big and sorrowful. – It will be so hard for a while, without Sanjay.

– It will not be long. He'll be back soon.

Gita looks strangely at me, as if she expects me to say something else, then she gets up and excuses herself. – I must go to the bathroom.

Of course, Gita always loved Sanjay. I could always tell. Even now, after all those years, her heart still pines for him.

When she comes back into the room, Gita Patel looks at me, and with a big smile says, – Oh Kalyani, it is so good that you have returned to Kolkata!

7   DR GOSS

The voices are all around me, shrieking, taunting, 'We are coming Kalyani!' What do you do? You hide away, under the bed again!

And yes, I scramble under the bed and I feel like I am climbing into my own tomb, that the weight of the world is on me, suffocating me, burying me alive. Then I turn and look out from my vantage point and I see a girl on the floor, with her long black hair and her big eyes. Now her head is slowly turning towards me. And I see her face as she looks into my eyes. She is in such pain and I want to ask her what is wrong but she makes an imploring, silencing gesture, a shhh pout with her mouth and I fall silent . . .

Last night's dream. To my troubled and disturbed mind, it seems more vivid and real than the events of the last two days. But it is the aggregate of both that has led me to Dr Marcus Goss's door.

I am very embarrassed at being here and I still don't know why I have come. Is it to apologise to Goss in person, or is it because I collapsed in Middleton Street after having just been to take tea at Gita's house?

Gupta saw me fall and came to my aid. On his urgings I went to a physician, knowing that this doctor would be unable to find anything wrong with me. At home I stared for a long passage of time at my face in the mirror. I tried to imagine inside the skin, skull and brain: to contemplate the cruel misconfigurations and the slight deformities that are shaping my life. I attempted to visualise the accursed toxins that were rushing in, as implacable as a dark tide.

As the day progressed, Goss's card seemed to burn a hole in my bag. My inexplicable collapse in the street and my breakdown the previous day had embarrassed me as much as last night's dreams had tormented me. After agonising for a few hours, I was moved to call Goss's office and make an appointment. A woman took my details and said that I could be seen at any time. I opted for as soon as possible.

On reaching the office I was greeted by a very good-looking young Indian woman, recognising her voice as that of the one who took my appointment details on the phone. – Dr Goss will see you soon, she informs me.

And it is only really a short time before Goss does appear, poking his head around the door and summoning me into his office. As I step in behind him I am surprised at how dark it is.

– Forgive the darkness, Goss says by way of an explanation, – I took a bad migraine. I'm rather prone to them unfortunately, but I feel better now.

– No problem, I say, although with some trepidation as it is very dark. I can barely make out the objects in the room.

– I'm glad you came.

– I just wanted to apologise, I explain tentatively,

– for my behaviour the other evening at Poppy's.

Goss does not respond to my apology, nor does he even acknowledge it. – A psychotherapist in Kolkata, he smiles, walking over to the window and pulling the curtains open and looking at the street scene outside. – Is that your man downstairs? He asks, turning and regarding me now with a gentle curiosity.

As the sun streams in, I see that Dr Goss's office is painted in a relaxing sky blue. A great painting with representations of street children adjourns the space behind his large, ornate, leather-topped desk. It disturbs me; they are packed in rows along the platform of a railway station, like sardines in a tin. Their faces have a resigned serenity that is almost spectral. I look and see that the signature of the artist is familiar. It is Prakesh Jagjeet who painted my portrait . . . surely he does not know this Dr Goss . . .

– The man outside? Goss asks again, nodding to the window.

I go across to the window. Gupta idly leans against the car and contemplates a group of ragged men who stand outside a bazaar. – I'm sorry . . . yes it is ...

– A terrible indulgence, is it not?

I do not like to be made to feel guilty about my wealth. I have a sense that I know, more than Goss ever could, that the real crime, the real shame, is poverty. The doctor seems over fond of this sort of self-righteous behaviour. – I take no shame from my privileges. Is it not strange that a man who indulges the well-to-do with his supposed abilities should then try to make them feel guilty for being able to afford to participate in his circus? I ask, moving across the room and lighting a cigarette. – What kind of game are you playing, Doctor?

– You misunderstand me, Goss says easily, proffering a glass ashtray from his desk and bidding me to sit down. – I mean that the city of Kolkata should certainly have more pressing problems than the mental well-being of a small number of its idle rich, he explains as he glances at the picture on his wall.

I am still amazed at his attitude, though I have composed myself somewhat. And I suppose that you need not be a Bengali communist to see the veracity of Goss's argument. I am aware that psychotherapy is a Western fashion, which even the wealthiest here find too ludicrous to indulge in, or so they claim. When you feel the summer heat and you are soaked just walking out the door and to the car, the simple management of everyday life takes precedence over any deeper issues to be resolved. This is what I have always believed. That is, until this terrible condition crashed into my life and that Red Room reappeared, in all its vivid ferocity.

Goss looks quizzically at me. Then he says coolly, – You were here once before, two weeks ago. I asked you to come back the following week but you didn't show up. My secretary left a message on your answerphone at home but you didn't get back to us. You really don't remember at all, do you? He asks, quite fascinated.

– What did we speak of?

– Your memory problems . . . in strictest client confidentiality, of course. You told me that you had a terrible problem whereby you could experience almost total memory wipe and needed prompts and in some cases complete re-education as to your own past.

– Yes . . . I feel as if my life is being stolen from me . . .

A horrible silence grows between us and soon becomes an unbearable void, which I must fill. There is so much silence in my days now, and I can bear it no more.

– I have been having dreams. Disturbing dreams. About a strange room, I explain. I have resolved that I will say nothing more of my Pick's Disease. Despite the knowledge that Goss can do nothing for my condition, I somehow feel that I may gain some peace and serenity through talking to him.

– Tell me about them, he urges, crouching forward in the seat. – Sit down and tell me about this room.

8 PURI

The irony hits me with some force. I am sitting in a unaccustomed room with a man I feel I have only briefly met, feel little empathy towards and whom I abused terribly on our first encounter, or at least the first one I can recall. This is the man I am now about to confide in, to expose the contents of my troubled and diseased mind to.

Now it seems as if the world has just stopped, leaving only this peculiar man and myself, sitting back and contemplating each other, breathing in shallow synchronicity. It is this pool of serenity within the great festering garden of noise, into which I will empty my thoughts.

– To describe the room, well it is obviously red. Even on the occasions when it appears to have no colour, on waking up I sense it overwhelmingly as red. It has a large gold-leaf-framed mirror. There is usually a large chair there. Sometimes this chair is turned away from me, but when I look at the back of it I am aware that someone is sitting in it.

Often I see their shadow or hear a dull, mirthless laugh coming from behind it.

– Yes, somebody is in this chair. I do not know if it is the same person, or force or entity of evil which comes behind me in the mirror.

I pause and hesitate, looking across at Goss sitting in

his chair. His face is ruddy; it is as if he has been doing exercises or making love. Both seem such unlikely activities for this man.

– When did you first dream of this Red Room?

I consider this for only a few seconds. – As a young child. I would put the start of the dreams back to the time when my father left us; my mother, my sister Gitanjali and myself.

I gasp, almost shattered by an eruption of elation, purely due to this simple recollection. Tasneem. Mother. Father. I had forgotten!

Goss is silent and I sense that he will remain so. Excited by the tantalising images that dance in my head, I take his stillness as a prompt and continue. – Our home was the seaside town of Puri, on the Indian Ocean . . . I pant luxuriantly as I now swear that I can smell the sea in my nostrils. I close my eyes and continue. – . . . It is a resort that entertains many visitors, mainly from Kolkata, but also from all over India and even further afield. My memories of life in this town are vague . . . but I recall being covered in a swarm of lady-birds, yes . . . I sniff deeply again, indulging myself further, – . . . I remember the smell of the sea, and tales of the unsuspecting bathers that its treacherous under-currents took away . . . I exhale deeply, as a leathery face comes into my mind. – My father drove a rickshaw! I recollect that we were blissfully happy . . . I open my eyes excitedly.

Though still obviously engaged, Goss's expression does not change. His skin has now gone paler, but one patch on his cheek remains blotched and red.

I am remembering! – It seemed though, that my father, in order to save his poor legs, had borrowed from moneylenders so that he could buy a new motorised rickshaw. It cost a lot of money, and being motorised, its licence was also much more expensive. I remember very little about my father. My mother said that he was a good man but a weak one. In this case, it seemed that my father had outstretched his meagre finances. He defaulted on the payments and then one day he just fled, never to be seen again. Mother was so devastated. At first she led us to believe that he was dead, I blurt out my words, looking over at the doctor who again urges my continuance.

I continue to speak in celerity: almost ranting, fearful lest this precious well of memory evaporates before I can verbalise it. – The moneylenders could not find him either, so they harassed my mother, forcing us to flee to Calcutta. Through some obscure family connection, we found accommodation in an old, semi-ruined colonial tenement building of many rooms. Our one was at the top of a dark stairway, to which it led from a wet court-yard, I explain, and I can smell the dankness, the fetid stink . . .

I recall paddling through stagnant water to go to and from our room . . .

– There was no balustrade on part of the stair, which made it dangerous to ascend and descend, particularly in the night. Our room was very small, it held my mother's double bed, where she, my sister and I all slept.

It contained two stools and had some shelving with pots, pans and clothes, which were also draped from a frame surrounding the bed, and hung from the wooden shutters by the window . . .

– Our building was in a narrow alley surrounded by others like it on either side.

It was a fetid, stinking hole, where packs of stray

dogs would fight and snarl at each other for scraps or lie in the shade asleep . . .

– Children would play and hawkers would manoeuvre their wares in barrows down its lengths, onto the main roads it bisected. We had some friends, two young boys Benji and Ranjit, who stayed in the lane, and Rita, a little girl who lived opposite.

I remember Benji, his spiky hair and his mischievous, sparkling eyes. Like Ranjit, tall, quiet and resourceful, he was always so respectful of Gitanjali's great beauty. They would do anything she asked and followed her like the dogs trotted after their masters . . .

– So, Goss says, – a very different proposition from the opulence of this Red Room.

For a second I consider whether Goss is implying that the Red Room is a fantasy I have constructed in order to deny my earlier poverty. Certainly, while my memory is still incomplete, I sense that I have always been circumspect about my background, and in the past have probably taken pains to conceal it from friends. After all, this is a city dominated by class and caste considerations, though they now seem so trivial to me.

Content that there seems to be no sign of any such assumption on his part, I am delighted to continue.

– Yes, in its squalor the room in which I grew up was a great contrast to the Red Room. Yet it was shortly after this, when I was about eight years old, that I started having the dreams. I was not aware in any detail of the contents of the Red Room at this stage of my dreaming, although I did have a sense of it as an opulent place. It was only later, when I reached my teenage years, that a picture of the room began to form. Slowly, over time, it took overt shape, always showing me more of the mysteries it held, but never everything.

I grew to know its red walls – red, not rose, terracotta or anything else – the gold leaf mirror and the chairs with the velvet cushions. Overall though, the impression of this room is inconclusive. It is neither an obvious living room, nor a bedroom, although there was often what looked like a chaise longue and what sometimes appeared to be a mattress on the floor. The room subtly shifts its contents although the walls, mirror and chair seem constantly present.

Despite my growing familiarity with it over the years, I never felt safe in the Red Room. I believed that something or someone else was in there with me, watching me, just out of the range of my vision.

Often I found myself standing frozen, unable to turn through my paralysing fear. I knew that I had to look in the mirror, to see what was behind me, but could never bear to move my gaze from the comfort of the wall. I could hear the heavy breathing, feel the hot breath on my neck and I would invariably wake up in a state of terror . . .

– What do you feel that this Red Room signifies? Goss asks.

– There are two things that I am convinced of. I know that the room is real and that I will see it some day. I also believe that I will encounter death there, that to visit this place will also be the end of my life in this world.

Dr Goss's voice seems to come out of nowhere. – We have to stop, he says.

I look around and I see that the sun has gone down. I feel disorientated and tired, yet more unburdened than I have been for such a long time. I am shaking, and yes, it is with fear, but I am also experiencing a strange exaltation.

9 DIGESTIVE ACCOMPANIMENT

Dr Goss has listened to my tale with great patience. I am more than happy to write a cheque for the fee he has requested. I look at my name as it is printed on each of the cheques in the book, and sign with a flourish, feeling myself to actually *be* that person. It is that sensation, that unfamiliar but most welcome recognition of personal integration: it makes me feel almost giddy with optimism.

As I make to leave he asks me, in a conversational manner, what I am planning to do tonight. I smile at him, marvelling at how quickly our perception of people can alter, and I tell him that I will go to my ballroom dancing. I feel that Sanjay would want me to continue participating in this pastime of ours. I will eat a late supper around midnight.

The doctor looks somewhat disapproving. – That is very late. It is little wonder you are having nightmares, he says.

Dr Goss is a newcomer to Kolkata and evidently does not understand the way people in mannered society here choose to socialise. – All my friends . . . I begin, but am interrupted.

– Do you take any digestive accompaniments, in the sense of medication . . . like flatulence powders?

– No! I . . . I begin, thinking, perhaps somewhat perversely, that I am being mocked.

Again Goss cuts me off, with a sweep of his hand, indicating to me that his line of questioning is serious.

– Forgive me, but you really should not eat so late, he says.

I nod in slow recognition. I have to concede that there have been so many times where I felt that I have eaten and drunk far too much before retiring. Can one expect not to have nightmares in such circumstances? I look to the painting on the wall. When its artist painted the portrait of me, he told me that the surrealists ate raw meat and cheeses in order to elicit more dreams.

– Come and see me again on Friday, he requests.

– I shall do so, I say, rising and feeling drained and giddy but still oddly ablaze to have rediscovered the part of myself I have just shared with him. – Thank you, Doctor.

His words about late suppers ring in my ear. But this is Kolkata. I will go out dancing and dining tonight with Gita and Moni Patel. I will dress in my red sari and with a choice of jewellery, be both beautiful and elegant. I prefer vivid colours; red and bright green being the ones which suit my skin tone best. I wear a lot of gold, and I am not above wearing Western clothes like jeans and a blouse. I took a fancy to such garments in Chicago, frequenting the stores on the Miracle Mile, much to poor Sanjay's dismay.

My session with Dr Goss seems to have freed up so much space in my usually crowded head. As I catch the scent of the blooms in the garden adjacent to the car park, I even smile at Gupta as he opens the car door for me.

10 OMNI

In terrible distress, I lie prone on the floor, captive and completely powerless as fingers of steel tickle and grope me. I cannot see anything and am unable to ascertain the identity of my assailant. Then, just as the nauseating violation of my torment grows unbearable, I realise that it is not me who is suffering this fate, but my sister Tasneem. Now I am watching her struggling, from my refuge under the bed, my body as cold as a corpse's on the stone floor.

Someone is on top of Tasneem; it is a man, but I do not know his identity. A hairy arm is visible, the strong fingers at the end of it pulling and ripping at her clothes. In abject defeat, she turns her face away from her oppressor to see me looking out at her from my vantage point and she shakes her head and mouths an urgent ssshh!

ssssshhh . . . sssssshhh . . .

I fight into consciousness, that terrible hissing sound leaking out of my ears. I spring for the notepad I keep on the mahogany bedside table. I now have two sections in my journal: one for my half-forgotten real life and another for my dreams. Goss suggested that, on my awakening, I should try to record my nocturnal trips. It is so difficult, as the dreams seem to fall through your mind like sands through fingers, and the details that appear to be the most pertinent are often the hardest to hold on to. My condition and my circumstances, however, have given me a certain education in this procedure and I scribble prodigiously.

The one thing I noticed was that the nightmare shifted, as they tend to do, from first to third person so that you become both a direct victim of torment, then a witness to your own self being persecuted. As a result of this new point of observation the person being terrorised is no longer you, but you are aware that you must escape so that you will not suffer their fate. So the nightmare is cyclical, it starts over again.

While I am the victim, it seems as if my sister is . . .

But are these not simply dreams, made into games by a Western head-doctor, who, for all I know, may be nothing more than a charlatan. What can such nonsense tell us?

Yet I checked my answer machine. Judging by the number of messages on it, I had not done this for a while, usually operating with my cellphone, which I now cannot seem to find. And Goss is correct, there was a message from his secretary, asking me to call back.

When I rise I go to the Omni Hotel's fitness club, in order to work out on the treadmill and the Stairmaster. Although I am tired I must work hard to keep myself fit and ensure that those late dinners do not start to show on my frame. What will Sanjay think when, if on his return, he is to be greeted by a fat wife?

The fitness club is practically empty. One young, white man who has masses of muscles lifts some free weights. His arms bulge and his skin colour turns from its normal milky to a reddy-pink. Two well-manicured Indian women walk next to each other on matching treadmills.

I head to the Stairmaster climbing machine and set it on level eight. As my strides establish a rhythm, I recall the office in the downtown Chicago tower block where Sanjay worked. There was a gym on one level, the 22nd floor, which many of the staff employed in the building used during their lunch break. The Stairmaster was always popular, yet the employees never used the block's real stairs, only the elevators. People would take it to the 22nd floor then climb roughly the same amount on this machine in the gym at lunchtime!

I climb until I feel the burn in my calf and thigh muscles, and can do no more. I return home sore and exhausted, but in the more satisfactory way that brisk exercise can engender, and watch an afternoon film on the television. It is Bengali cinema, rather than Bollywood, which is my preference. Sonya, the heroine, played by the great actress Anjana Mukherjee, has been forced to leave her village to seek her lover who has gone to Calcutta to find work. At first I am captivated but after a while the film starts to disturb me. Soon I find it hard to focus and drift off into an afternoon nap.

There is a ringing in my ears and I am in the court-yard of our old home. I am being followed. I can hear the footsteps behind me. Somebody is coming down the stair. I run to the exit of the building, my feet splashing in the water which seems so thick, like treacle . . . I am aware that I am no longer a young girl, but my present age. That notion seems to give me strength and I come out of the stair and almost collide with two white men, their faces wild and distorted, and one asks me in a strange, sing-song voice, – Where is the Red Room?

I wake up with a heart-shuddering start, feeling a hand on me, on my shoulder. I see Gupta's face staring into mine. Startled, I sit bolt upright. – You! What are you doing! How dare you touch me . . .

Gupta stands his ground, his urgent, nacreous eyes scrutinising my very essence. – I beg your pardon madam. You were having a bad dream. The noises you made were very distressed so I thought that I should wake you up. How are you?

I feel a tightening in my chest, and I start to cry in halting sobs, and find myself throwing my arms around Gupta. – Hold me, I say, – just hold me.

His arms go around me. He is strong and I like the smell of him, the smell of a man.

Sanjay . . .

My nails dig into his back through his shirt. There is a sinking feeling of great mutual comfort, and then I can feel his body stiffen and tense. A shock of recognition spears my heart and I almost choke in disgust and self-loathing.

I release my grip and move away. – Please go, I say, in a voice too low and broken for this to come over as the decisive command it most certainly is.

Gupta stands up, looking at me all the time. At first he seems reluctant to go, and his face is so kind I almost beg him to stay. Then, although his mouth remains set, his eyes seem to change, frosting over, serpent-like, mocking me. – As you wish, he spits in ridicule.

I run through to my bedroom and lock the door.

11   THE GOLF CLUB

I have been invited along to the Tollygunge Club where the men, their men, are playing golf. I took a taxi down here, as I could not face Gupta after yesterday's embarrassing encounter.

I sit with Gita and a woman called Elisabeth Kingsley, in the outdoor Will's Sports Pavilion Bar. We drink lime sodas as a group of the men hit balls down the fairway towards the first hole. There is some sort of tournament taking place and many of the participants have completed their round and are now drinking heavily.

I watch those wealthy men: young and old, Indian and British, Hindu, Muslim, Sikh and Christian, with their wines and champagnes and beers. All from different religious and cultural backgrounds, yet they all seem to be the same kind of unbeliever. I would say that their common God was money, but then, why should they not believe in their designated religion if fortune has endorsed their lives by smiling so beatifically upon them?

Two young Englishmen, somewhat the worse for drink, have taken their shirts off to sun bathe their pink skins and are approached by a brown-coated steward.

– Excuse me sir, he snaps urgently, looking to our table for any signs of offence taken, – that is not allowed. The swimming pool is over there, he points to the building behind them.

One of the Englishmen is familiar. I know him by sight from Poppy's party. It is the one with the floppy, blond fringe, which I find oddly affecting. The one who spoke of the Red Room. – Might one not plead anarchy, the desire to precipitate chaos, as a mitigating factor for one's behaviour? he asks in that facetious, mock earnest way regularly deployed by the British as humour.

– No sir, only the swimming pool, the steward repeats, his eyes bulging in concern, his hands shaking.

– Good God, we really did a job on them, the blond man laughs, pulling on his shirt as his friend follows suit. – Turned a whole country into a pack of arseholes. Then he raises his voice, in order to make it audible to the other tables. – Walk outside those fucking walls and half the poor bastards in this city are starving to death in the streets around here. There's a load of them living inside the perimeter walls of this damn club, for pity sakes! One would think that they'd have a little bit more to concern themselves with!

– C'mon Teddy, drink up, the other man says with a burr I take to be Scottish or Irish, and they down their drinks and depart, presumably for the swimming pool.

– What a horrid young man, the tall Englishwoman named Elisabeth Kingsley remarks in a kind of *faux* outrage, which she customarily deploys on such occasions.

– Just a very drunk one, Gita Patel explains, – and he didn't even recognise me from the conversation we had the other night at Poppy's party.

– I do not remember those men from Poppy's, I lie.

Gita looks doubtfully at me and then expands: – I think that they must have arrived shortly after you left, Kalyani. Oh, he was a perfect sweetheart then. An architect, working on a couple of restoration projects.

An architect. Like Sanjay. Also, a man who was seeking something that I too wanted to know about. It was probably just bizarre coincidence as there was no real way that the Red Room of his imagination could be the same place as the one in my nightmares. Nonetheless, I feel compelled to investigate, fighting down a shudder of fear that naggingly hints at my further dissolution into cretinism.

I excuse myself, making for the indoor pool at the back of this bar. With the air-conditioning on it is rather cold in here, and I am relieved to get outside to the rear and the open-air pool. It is practically empty: a young white boy in yellow swimming trunks splashes in the water, watched keenly by his father, a fat man whom the sun has burned lobster red.

The two men I have assumed to be British are sitting at the cocktail bar drinking and talking. They have their still-shirted backs to me as I signal to the barman for a drink. As he prepares my lemonade I hear the blond Englishman say to his friend, – Yes, every treacherous and barbarous act from Ulster to the Caribbean to Bengal, these rogues have been involved . . .

I usually find it difficult to approach strangers, but the urgency imposed by my condition and my jogged memories through my session with Dr Goss have encouraged a certain social disinhibition. – Did you ever find the Red Room? I interrupt them, addressing my question to the blond man.

The Englishman turns round and regards me for a second, then looks highly embarrassed. – Forgive me,

Miss, I've behaved terribly, far too much drink in this sun . . .

– No, please do not worry about that. My name is *Mrs* Chakraborty. The Red Room, have you found it yet?

– I, eh . . . no, he stammers. Now his discomfort has been multiplied tenfold.

– Please do not be concerned, I implore. As anxious as I am to learn about the Red Room, I am feeling uneasy, conscious of the fact that I have embarrassed this man. I am still a respectable woman and Sanjay's wife and propriety makes me eager to save the Englishman from further chagrin. – This is not perhaps the time, I say, and I pull out a pen from my bag and scrawl my name and number out on a piece of note-paper, which I hand to him. – If you ever find the Red Room, please let me know. It is very important.

I head back to my company and the sun, leaving them somewhat astonished and myself more curious than ever. Although things in the Pavilion Bar are agree-able enough, I find myself growing more solicitous with many questions and bizarre speculations jostling around in my crowded, fevered mind. Where is my Sanjay? What did I say to Dr Goss when I first met him? What does that Red Room and those horrible dreams signify?

I am also feeling the onset of melancholy as I realise that I am the only woman whose husband is not pre-sent, not that Sanjay was ever one for golf. Now I am remembering that he used to say that 'golf is a game for men with too much time on their hands and too little going on in their heads'.

Oh Sanjay, if only I could remember the important things about you, not just the foolish ones!

I wait for a while until the warm sun has receded over the back of the jungle, which towers over this golf course and sporting club, always threatening to overrun it. It takes so much work just to stop nature from reclaiming this place, especially during the wet season. Bored, troubled and restless, I decide to do a very radical thing. Without announcing my departure, I discreetly take my leave and walk down the driveway towards the gates that lead out onto the street.

Yes, I will walk out of here and head down the street and take the metro train into Park Street Station. Then I will go into Flury's and have a pastry and some coffee like Sanjay and I often used to do.

When I get outside onto the busy road, I see that there is a large hole in the brick wall that borders the club. People come in and out of it, like wasps going to and from a nest. The Englishman is right: people live in a hole in the perimeter wall of this club. I walk by, feeling oddly perturbed that this is the first time that I have noticed this. Or maybe I had simply forgotten about it.

But the strange lives we live: I have resided in Calcutta for many years but this is the first time I have ever ridden the metro. Many times I have been tempted but I always believed that heading down those steps would be like a descent into some sort of hell. Yet here in the cool station with its spacious concourse, platforms and big trains, it is more agreeable than the elevated train in Chicago or the crowded London underground. Yes, we went to that city for Sanjay's father's funeral . . .

I find myself alighting before Park Street, at Kalighat, near the Temple. I do not know why I got off here. I am close to the refuge run by the late Mother Teresa. I walk slowly, watching as touts harass tourists, offering their services as guides. I shudder as a toothless, laughing fool tugs on the sleeve of my sari, beckoning me into

the arena where the live goats and buffalo are sacrificed. What simpletons would wish to witness the
slaughter of an animal?

I pull away and beat a hasty retreat, my head heavy
and legs weary in the heat, realising that I am winding
into the back streets, yet somehow disinclined to stop
and turn around. But to my increasing apprehension
the faces of market traders and shoppers are becoming
those of whores and pimps. An insidious unease, rising
so slowly, eventually hits a point at where I cannot bear
it any longer. It stops me in my tracks. I glance around.

Some whores are looking me up and down, most of
them Nepalese harlots who have come here to escape
their own poverty. For twenty rupees those filthy sluts
will sell their bodies, will have vile men who could
have been anywhere committing the act which should
be engaged in only in marriage.

People cook in battered pots on makeshift fires by
the side of the road and in the mouths of the ruined old
buildings built by the white settlers. A greasy, fetid
smell rises from the pots and stoves and merges with
the filthy exhaust fumes from the cars and that of the
excrement from animals and humans. I am almost choking in its rank odour.

But these streets are now so familiar to me. Here I
would play with Gitanjali, and little Rita, so deaf in one
ear that you had to turn her head to you when you
addressed her. I remembered that Benji, the smiling
one, and tall Ranjit mysteriously vanished one day, with
their family. I missed them terribly, but nothing was said
and the grown-ups discouraged you from asking about
their fate.

Ahead I see the mouth of my old alleyway and head
down it, instantly passing from blinding sun into hot,

rank darkness. As my eyes adjust, I see that while I know this place, the people here are all strangers. They stare at me unselfconsciously, the way poor people do. This country is so different from America. Here, you can have no private life. It strikes me how accustomed I have become to such a life, after only four years.

To avoid their gazes I move through a doorway, finding myself back again in that decrepit slum I was once so intimate with. The old place inside is so run-down and filthy water seeps into my shoes. Then my heart sinks as I see a familiar staircase. It has no balustrade. A little girl stands at the top of it. Her stare is cold and judging and it chills me. I think so much that it is little Rita, and I want to shout her name, but that would be stupid! Rita would be a young woman now . . .

A spasm of panic rises in me and I turn and head back out into the alleyway, breaking into a trot and almost knocking over a cursing old woman. A dog barks and I hear voices behind me as I hurry down the narrow lane, too fearful to look back. Ahead I can see the opening onto the main street, with its sunlight, cars, rickshaws and pedestrians. I pray I will make it before the evil that I now sense in here will pursue and engulf me.

As I burst into the sunlight of the busy street, the image of a terrible face flashes into my head and I instantly realise that I know what this evil is.

12 THE GOONDA

I am in Dr Goss's office again. This time there are very few preliminaries between us, the only major one concerning my medical condition. I have decided to take him into my confidence with regard to my illness and he listens sympathetically as I explain the nature of Pick's Disease to him.

– It is not a condition I am acquainted with, he says, then correcting himself adds, – I mean, I know of it, but it is very rare, especially in persons of your relative youth. Did you get a second opinion on this diagnosis?

– This was from the Northwestern Memorial Hospital in Chicago, which is part of the Northwestern University in Evanston, Illinois. It is one of the top schools in America. How could I be wrongly diagnosed in such a place?

Goss looks doubtful, struggles for air as he distastefully digs the end of his pen into his own gums. – I'm not suggesting that you were, only that you may want to get another viewpoint. Do you feel as if your condition is progressively deteriorating?

I do not know about this. All I do know is that I need to talk. – I cannot tell. I will seek further medical counsel. But there are some other things I have been thinking about, remembering, if you will. Might I continue?

The doctor nods in eager acquiescence.

I talk and talk, unable to stop and no longer worrying about where all this will take me. – At first I was not aware of what my mother did to support us. It was only when he, the goonda, began to appear that for the first time in my life I started to know real fear.

– This man was a gangster?

I nod slowly, trying to picture him in my own mind's eye. The image I conjure up is all too vivid and I shudder in chilling recognition but force myself to carry on. – He was a tall man, with dark hair and a dark beard. His eyes blazed with a terrible madness, and they had that unmistakable focus and glint of evil and cruelty. He was badly disfigured with three scars on one of his cheeks. They ran so deep it was as if some nerves underneath had been severed, giving one side of the face a frozen, shrunken aspect. Yet it was a far from ugly face . . . I pause, suddenly unable to continue . . .

– You make him sound unappealing. Yet you say he wasn't? Dr Goss interjects, aware of my hesitation.

His intervention seems to lift the paralysis from my chest. – On the contrary, there was a terrible mesmerising beauty in it, I explain, as I recall the way the goonda looked at people. – His face could ignite in a smile so intoxicating that many women and men longed to bask in the patronage of its all too fleeting glow . . .

Goss nods at me as if he understands that kind of power. I wonder, in his vanity, does he entertain the ridiculous fantasy that he shares it? But I quickly break off my guilty speculations and continue with my story.

That was how the goonda pulled them in . . .

– Then the smile was gone, as welcome but as transient as a cool breeze in the stifling, humid summer heat. And it was always replaced by this certain expression . . . it was a look which made you believe in evil, in its purest and simplest form.

The stare from Goss indicates his Western, liberal view that such absolutes are childish.

– The goonda's spite knew no bounds. Mister Duborcy, a kindly man from across the lane, had contracted a mild leprosy. The goonda instantly started a hate campaign against him, saying that he had to be banished. People feared both leprosy and the goonda, so Mr Duborcy was forced out and into the leper community, which lived in a squalid bustee at the back of our houses.

I would bring him food and watch his condition deteriorate.

– The lepers were the only people the goonda feared. He would cross the road to avoid them.

I pause for what could only be a few seconds, yet into which the whole of time itself seems to collapse. I suddenly think of Devon Avenue in the north of Chicago, where the brash and gaudy trinket wealth of Indian peasants made good is so ostentatiously displayed. Finally, I hear Goss's throaty voice, so disembodied that it seems at first to come from another world. – What did this gangster character have to do with your mother and sister?

I feel myself answering a horrible truth I have so long denied in a tone of strange, detached nonchalance. – The Goondah would come to the small room that we shared. When he came Mother would send Tasneem and me to play with our friend Rita who lived across the lane.

– He was . . . your mother and he were . . .

– Yes, I suddenly blurt out, feeling the tears well up and roll down my face. My voice goes small. – I believe so, I sob. – I think she needed to . . . with other men. But I think that he found them for her.

My tears are flowing now. Goss hands me a handkerchief. I take it, but only to dab at my cheeks. – Then there was one time he came and my mother was not home so I hid under the bed. Tasneem could not get away in time.

– What happened to your sister? Goss asked me.

– I do not know, I tell him, – He took her away. They left and I never saw her again.

13 THE RACECOURSE

Colonel Angus Colqhoun has invited me to spend the day with him at the Kolkata Racetrack. Gupta, as is his custom, is sullen as he drives me to the Colonel's residence where we meet up with Gita and change cars, climbing into the Colonel's large vehicle.

The traffic is heavy and we miss the first race, an occurrence that causes Angus, a deeply superstitious man, some obvious distress. – I always bloody well win on the first race . . . the whole day's gone to pot already and it hasn't even damn well started . . . Madam Chakraborty, Missus Patel, he nods apologetically, – pardon one's French. Can't you sort something out Ashish, he complains to his driver, but the spark has been spent and his rage descends into a vague muttering that in turn dissolves into a drunken smirk at some passing thought, as his heavy old shoulders shake uncontrollably.

We take the wrought-iron elevator up to the Stewards box. The sky is clear and blue and we are fortunately shaded from the punishing sun. From our spectating point we have an excellent view of the track and the ornate, yellow grandstand towering over it. Colonel Colqhoun is now animated as he introduces everybody to everyone else, even though some present will have met each other one hundred times before. He commandeers Gita and me to sit on either side of him. – An old man's indulgence . . . he wheezes as he quaffs down a pink gin, – is to have a pretty lady on either side of him at the dinner table . . . another pink gin my man, he crisply snaps at a waiter, – and the same for the ladies!

Gita and I make signs of mock exasperation at each other and fallacious protests at Angus, which he completely ignores, busying himself with the form card.

I look across the racetrack at the wonderful Victoria Memorial, its grand white dome shimmering in the heat. Colonel Colqhoun catches my eye. – Of course, they built it for Queen Victoria but the Empress of India didn't deign to grace it with her presence. The bloody French . . . well, it's not often I've a good word to say for them but they had the right idea with that crowd . . . he makes a chopping movement across his neck.

– You did accept the OBE though, so it's rather rich to play the republican now, I tease, watching Gita giggle and raise her hand to her mouth.

His OBE! How do I remember this?

– Of course I did. It would have been appalling manners to have refused, he balks in mock outrage. Then, as is the way with the Colonel, another tale quickly springs to mind before the residue from the current one has been processed. – I recall the one time we took some Americans up here into Stewards. They asked me about that wonderful building with the great white dome. I told them, 'Why, that's our clubhouse of course.' Being Yanks and therefore rather naïve, they absolutely believed me.

I had heard this story at least three times before, as had Gita, but we never ceased to appreciate its telling.

We are served tomato soup and then head into the great dining hall for the buffet. – When I die, Colonel Colqhoun bellows at nobody in particular as he heads back to the table with a well-stacked plate, – stick me on a blessed pyre. Who the hell would want a Christian burial? he asks, sitting down then guzzling back a pink gin and signalling for another in almost one fluid gesture. – None of that sending my ashes down the bloody Ganges though. That cesspool is just about the only place on God's earth where I could catch something I don't already have . . . and a chap must retain at least some degree of modesty, even in death, don't you agree Mrs Patel?

– I am sure you know a lot more about the modesty

of men than me Colonel, Gita says demurely.

– I should bloody well hope not! Colonel Colqhoun bellows, laughing loudly and we all join in, oblivious to the slightly disapproving stares around the table.

I look over to my left, watching the new bridge standing in its incongruently modern splendour. Below us to the front of the boards and the finishing line, a bank of blistering red and yellow marigolds reverberate in the heat and my tired, semi-drunk eyes.

Colonel Colqhoun orders more pink gin and I murmur in drunken acquiescence, gently scolding and profusely thanking him for his most terrible and generous indulgence. He looks at me with red, lively eyes.

– Pleasure ma'am . . . pleashhuhh ...

No one except Gita seems to win anything on the next three races. I see a group of women follow the track, stamping down the divots the horses kick up. Knowing nothing about horses I follow Gita's advice, consistently backing the jockey described on the board as 'C.Alford'. I am therefore delighted that I am winning by a small amount at the end of race six.

The last race is held up by twenty minutes. Apparently stewards were called to investigate an unsavoury incident in the paddock. – What's happened? I feel my voice rising in a fright that surprises me. At that moment a large, black and silver crow flies onto the corner of the table and snatches a piece of nan bread from my plate.

– Just a bloody crow, Colonel Colqhoun says, as the creature flies off and swoops over the grandstand, – scavenging blighter.

– No, in the paddock . . . I reply weakly, feeling suddenly dizzy as I try to focus on the bloodhound eyes in Colonel Colqhoun's head.

– Nothing for you to worry your pretty little head

about, my darling. Asheed! he shouts, then smirks to the company, – I think we've got one filly over here who's just had her last race of the day!

And I feel Guptah and Asheed leading me away, Colonel Colqhoun's soft tone in the background saying something like, – Poor girl, it must have been terrible with poor old Sanjay . . . lovely chap . . .

I want to turn and shout: what do you know? What do any of you know? Why do you lie to me and patronise me so? Are you all evil? Are you all mad?

I remember being taken into the back of the car and drifting into a sleep and when I wake up I am in the Red Room.

14 HOTTER

The noise in my ears: morphing into the monstrous clarity of his speech. The heat of his breath on my neck and his dirty, tender words: sweeter and more loathsome than ever before. I see my face in the mirror and I shake my head and my hair flies and with great strength of will I force myself into a new place. I am in my youth again and I am back in the fetid slum with Gitanjali.

We are in the alleyway but he is following us and I have her by the hand as we run in terror.

I hear him shout something, some ugly curse, then his laugh lashes out like a whip and echoes down the narrow street. I keep running ahead and I see them out of the corner of my eye, in the shadows, beckoning me to them. My mother always told me keep away, keep away from them . . . they are diseased . . . they are death . . .

Sanjay . . . where are you my love?

15   GITANJALI

The heat in the city is becoming unbearable. The frozen Chicago winters that I used to curse so emphatically, which my poor, dear Sanjay would bear with such patient grace, I would gladly take them now. Yes, I believe that I would even savour that flesh-stripping cold over this suffocating heat. I can hardly breathe, yet the calendar tells me that our hottest spell has yet to begin in earnest.

Poor Dr Goss is looking even more uncomfortable than I feel. His voice has developed a terrible dry rasp, which the bottle of water by his side cannot moisten. – When was the last time you saw your sister? he abruptly asks me, and I immediately feel as debilitated in this furnace as he looks. I begin to speak, slowly, falteringly, but my words soon gain a terrible velocity. – The last time . . . was when I was alone and hiding under the bed. I saw her face, Gitanjali's . . . I was only a few feet away and I wanted to reach her but she went 'no'. I initially thought, as he did, this man on top of her, that this 'no' was for him, but it was directed at me, her younger sister.

– This man was raping her and she was protecting you from the same fate, Goss says coldly, but he knows what he is doing, for I need to hear his words. I have buried so much, denied so much to myself . . .

– When the goonda had finished his terrible deed, he told her to get up and come with him.

As they left, I saw the back of my sister's head, but I never saw her face again . . . not al–

– . . . I followed them out of the building and into the alley where I shouted but she would not turn round. He registered my scream, however, and he pushed Tasneem into a waiting car at the bottom of the lane. I saw two hands emerge from the car and pull her inside, then the goonda turned and ran back up the alley in pursuit of me . . .

He knew he could catch me any time, he was toying with me, saying that he was going to take me somewhere nice . . .

– . . . I was so frightened . . . I ran in terror, almost into the arms of Mr Duborcy and his friends.

I stop again, wiping the water from my cheeks.

– Go on, Goss gently urges.

– I screamed for a second or two, as Duborcy's face was alarming.

It was eaten away to the point that there was no nose, just a gaping hole ...

– The top jaw was gone, replaced by a channel that led from that gorge where the nose once sat, to a large, toothless and lipless cavern where his mouth used to be. He could no longer speak, but in his gentle eyes I saw that in front of me was still, after everything, this kind and decent man. . . .

I was comforted and strengthened by his presence . .

.

– . . . I turned to face the goonda, Mr Duborcy's withered hand on my chest. His other claw swept the hair from my face as the scar-faced thug came cautiously towards us.

– What happened? Goss asks, perhaps for the first time seeming to be so obviously led by curiosity rather than professional concern.

– The goonda looked at me, then at the lepers, with silent fear and bitter distaste. He spat, then muttered a curse before turning and running back down towards the car. He climbed in and they drove off. The windows were dirty and I could not see into the car, make out neither my sister nor the other person who was with them, probably restraining her.

I waited to make sure that the goonda had departed, then I left my leper friends and went to find my mother. I searched everywhere, but she too was gone.

Dr Goss looks at me, seems genuinely sad. – My oh my . . .

– I never saw her again.

– What did you do?

I hear a voice of pain coming from within me. It is not my voice, it is the voice of the little girl I once was, alone and frightened. – I cried and wandered the street, begging our neighbours for help. People shunned me, told me to go, they were in such fear of the goonda, I gasp breathlessly. My face is a brittle mask that feels like it is going to crack open. I can see the dread of it in Goss's eyes.

He nods for me to continue.

– But Mr Duborcy was still alive, and with all the others whom I had been told to avoid. I went to them, went to their hovel, finding protection amidst their decomposing, rotting limbs. And I was safe there, because I knew he would not follow me, knew he would not touch me if he believed me to be one of them; cursed, diseased, fouler in some way than he could ever be, yet never so foul in the soul . . .

Dr Goss seems as breathless as I am. – I think we need to continue. I want to hear everything. But I have another appointment. Would you be able to come back in an hour?

– Yes, I tell him, then head outside into the sun. I too am in need of a break. I have a fan, which I take from my bag. After a few waves though, the effort of fanning in this heat becomes so wearisome and makes me perspire so much that the exercise is counterproductive.

Gupta, parked a little down the street, sees me approach and opens the door of the car. – Where to?

– Wait here. I need to walk for a while.

– But . . .

– I need to walk, I tell him, heading off in brisk, peremptory movements.

I head through the avenues of north Kolkata, past the Raj buildings, as the worn streets narrow out. Old colonial mansions, once owned by a single family, now house scores of them as they crumble in the dry heat. A tree grows prolifically out of the side of one house, its roots twisting into the plaster and brickwork. Seeds carry on the wind, fall into cracks and grow relentlessly in the heat and monsoon rains. Did the British think that the jungle would not eventually claim back its own, take back the city they hacked from it?

Before I know it, I have wandered into the zone that is all Muslim. The people here gather the rubbish in boxes, and sell their rugs in the markets. I have never walked these streets before. But unlike other cities in India, there is no tension here between Hindu and Muslim, and I walk without harassment.

At a vendors I stop for some sugared tea.

I am fifteen minutes late in getting back to Dr Goss's office as I had wandered further than I had intended. I am anxious that I will not be able to see him, that he will have gone home, but he is still there, sweating profusely, and scarcely seems to have noticed my lateness. Indeed, the doctor himself looks rather anxious, even somewhat disturbed. His hands are visibly trembling as he holds a sheath of papers.

– Are you all right? I ask him.

– One sees and hears terrible things . . . I . . . he

begins, then seems to pull himself together, – . . . I'm sorry. It is this heat, this climate. It is absolutely unbearable at times. One can hardly breathe, he says, shaking his head. – Please, please, continue. You were talking about your life on the streets, he remarks, glancing over to the painting of the street children hanging on his wall.

– I could not stay with the lepers indefinitely. I needed to find my family. One day I set off, walking the streets of Calcutta. Soon I was lost, alone and forlorn, but I met some abandoned children who saw my plight and I went with them to the railway station to sleep. Their leader was a boy called Naza. He was good, strong and knew the streets. Through him I met up again with Benji and Ranjit, the friends from our neighbourhood. I was so delighted to see them, Benji with his big, happy grin, and the tall, serene Ranjit. They too had lost their mother and gone with the street children. They were broken-hearted when I told them of the terrible fate that had befallen Gitanjali and they vowed to help me find out what had become of her.

My friends on the street taught me how to survive. We would huddle together on the cold railway platforms, laughing and joking until exhaustion took us into a broken half-sleep from which we would rise in the morning to beg for change from passers-by or scraps of food from merchants.

Goss nods and wheezes. I continue, talking for what seems a timeless period, it could have been minutes or hours, telling him about the good people who would come and help us. They were charity workers, and they gave us clothes and food. Nazar, the leader of our group, told us how to distinguish them from the evil ones, like the goonda. I saw him once, hanging around, talking to young children. We stayed together in large groups for protection, and we often had dogs with us.

I tell the Doctor how the police would come and drive us out of the station in the middle of the night, sometimes hitting us with their batons.

I am drained after these confessions. The Doctor says nothing for a while. Assured that I am spent, he lets me rest and brings me some tea.

The tea is refreshing and invigorating. I close my eyes and I see Sanjay, and a tear slips from me and rolls down my cheek.

I hear Dr Goss's voice asking me, – Are you all right?

– Yes, I tell him, dabbing at my cheek with a tissue. – I would like to continue.

Goss sanctions my request with a curt nod of his head.

– One day I was in the street with some of the others, down by the market, when I saw the goonda's car.

– This was how long after the abduction? My psychotherapist groans, breathing laboriously.

– It would only be a few weeks or so later, although I cannot be sure. Time has no meaning when you are sleeping rough on the streets. Anyway, I followed the car; this was easy as it was held up in the traffic and moved slowly. It only went a short distance, stopping outside a big, opulent, well-maintained building.

– Can you remember anything about this building?

– No . . . I cannot . . .

– Try, Goss urges.

I think about this place, and I seem to recall large gates. – I have a feeling that there were gates, yes, big gates . . . and grounds . . . the first time though, I did not go in. No, I merely walked around this building, looking at all the entrances and exits. It was only the following day that I plucked up the courage to go inside.

– Yes . . . what did you find?

Fear paralyses me, my train of thought shuddering to a halt like a vehicle run off the road. What did I find? Can I be sure? Was it all not just an absurd fiction formed by the dreams, fantasy and speculations of a frightened young girl who has grown into an immature, crazy and ill woman? But no, it does now seem so real to me, so terribly clear.

– I found the Red Room, I tell Dr Goss, as I see that horrible place, coming into focus, almost forming around me. I have to look to remind myself that I am still in his office. Then I compose myself, breathing slowly and deeply. – I went through a door and up some steps into a large hall. There were lots of rooms within the hall, flimsily partitioned rooms, each seeming to contain a different sort of treasure, the nature of which I could not understand. Then I heard familiar voices and followed them.

I climbed up a small, marble staircase to the rear of the building where I saw the goonda standing outside this room with another man. I sensed that they were preparing to leave and I hid around a corner and waited for them to depart. I could hear their laughter, their shoes on the stairs as they descended. I tracked back and went into the room. Walking down a narrow passageway there was another door. I opened it. It was the Red Room. There was a table on which my sister Gitanjali lay. I thought she was asleep. I spoke to her, called her name. There was no response, so I touched her hand and it was cold. There were marks on her neck. She was . . . she was dead, I tell Goss, unable to believe my own thoughts and words, convinced that my twisted, diseased mind was tricking me. A weight of nausea settled within me. I have the phantom feeling I had back then, of time elongating, stretching itself past its habitual span, one meagre second seeming eternal.

Now Goss also appears struck dumb with terror. He clears his throat. – My God . . . What the hell did you do?

– I ran out of the room, down the staircase and out of the building. I went to tell the police, but they thought I was just a crazy child and it took me so long to convince them. When we got back to the place, her body was gone. The police, who beat me and left me in the street, called me a liar and street vermin.

– Where was this place, this building which housed the Red Room?

– I cannot say . . . I do not remember, I respond weakly, as the pain comes flooding back through every cell in my body. My pulse races and for a few seconds I think that I am going to pass out. But it subsides, as my knotted stomach begins to unravel. Goss is breathing heavily, the rhythmic wheeze coming from his body sounding almost like a snore.

– A few days later some street children said that a young girl's body had washed up in the Hooghly. This is not uncommon, but somehow I had no doubts that this was my sister. I suspect that my mother suffered the same fate, and probably many more like her. I went back to the railway station, where I lay down on the cold platform with the other children and the dogs, looked up to the station roof and wondered if any God ever saw my plight.

16 PYRE

It has grown dark. Shadows fall across the room but the stifling heat will not abate, nor does the Doctor's breathless groan. His decline in the growing heat seems so coterminous with my story that I entertain a horrible sense that it is my tale that is destroying Goss, corroding him from the inside. Yet we are both compelled towards my finishing of it. – In the morning we went to see the body. It was hard to identify it as Tasneem's. The river had turned the corpse white and the dogs that found her had done their terrible work. But my friends and I took her down to the ghats.

Two men from the Dom supervised the ritual. I washed her down with a trembling hand under the instruction of Ranjeet who remained pious and impassive throughout the act. Then we took her close to the river where Ranjeet muttered some request, asking the river to cleanse one of its own. After this we lay her on the wooden stretcher and carried her up the bank to the pyre the others were building. There were so many other funerals taking place at the same time. Many of the mourners were dressed in white and I lamented that I only had a white shawl to see my sister off in. They put some incense sticks around her body and I stood back to watch the smoke gently rise from her.

Just a few feet away two other bodies blazed on separate pyres, and the heat from them was discomforting. In spite of the burning incense to mask it, the smell of flesh being consumed by fire was nauseating to me. I began to cry softly, thinking of Gitanjali as a small girl, although she was two years my senior. I cannot be sure through the grief and fogged memory, but I recall that Benji, now so uncharacteristically remorseful, and Ranjit and one other young man from our part of town had their penises exposed. Each of them had a single white ribbon tied to their genitalia. It was the first male organs I had seen and I still do not know to this day what this meant. I would like to think that it meant that they all loved her, or even that they believed her to be a virgin . . . I hesitate, – which I know not to be true.

Goss says nothing, but I know because I was there when the goonda took her. And she bore this in silence, simply in order to protect me.

Now there is more silence. There is always more silence. And that, I think, was why I really returned to Kolkata, this town which hates silence so much, as much as I do.

To fill this mute void I tell Goss the rest of my story. How the Christian missionaries took me off the streets, and I became a housekeeper in a family of wealthy merchants, where Sanjay was a nephew. We loved each other at first sight. The family disapproved but we married. Then we moved to America. Then . . .

. . . then I think that I have said enough, and I rise to make my departure, leaving Dr Goss breathing heavily in his armchair.

Goss does not even attempt to rise to show me out. Instead he just groans slowly, – Madame, I must tell you that we will not be able to continue those sessions next week . . . I have been advised by my physician to return to England for the good of my health . . . I'm hoping to come back later in the year . . . it seems, though, that you were right . . . I underestimated the heat . . .

– You have not seen anything yet, Dr Goss, I say gravely as I leave my money for the session on his desk table and wish him well.

17 INVESTIGATIONS

My apartment is like a tomb in Sanjay's continued absence. I do not feel at ease here. I water the house-plants, noting that they were drying out, all the time wondering where young Rashid has gone.

The only person who seems to be around is Gupta, as sullen and as dangerous as Sanjay was decent and loyal. In a rage last night I dismissed him from my service yet he turned up the next morning, ready for work as if nothing had passed between us.

And I wondered whether or not this was a dream, as I found myself too ashamed to raise any mention of it, as if in acknowledgement that my fevered, demented mind was finally succumbing to lunacy. But I tell him to get the car ready, as we are going on a drive.

– Where to, Memsahib?

– I will tell you, I reply with a cold grace, as I slip the paper-opening dagger from the office into my bag.

18 KALYANI'S DEATH

I knew what I would encounter in the room, and I knew that it would be my death. A girl from Puri, a street girl, was never meant to achieve my position in Kolkata society. The missionaries had intervened, toyed with my fate. My destiny has been warped and distorted by their intervention. The gods had messed up and by taking Sanjay from me had embarked on the first big step of righting that wrong.

Because my beloved Sanjay has gone and is not coming back.

I know the building. You get wonderful views of it from the racecourse. It is a museum, the one that Queen Victoria never saw. When we get there, Gupta parks outside.

The ornate, bronze gates are open and I walk through the sprawling grounds with its lakes, trees and flowering plants, down the approach that leads to the regal statue of the old, long-dead British queen, seated on her throne.

I see the bronze angel on the top of the memorial's glistening, white dome and take the wide stairs up to the front door, which leads to the central hall. Inside, the hall rises for about fifty feet, with a balcony halfway up running around the perimeter. It is a museum, and it is about to close.

As people file out of the building, I frantically search through the galleries for the door. I feel frustrated after a while, almost believing that it is just a dream, or only the sad confusion of an enfeebled mind. Then I see this rosewood piano and writing desk, and behind them, half-obscured, stands the door, so cold and ordinary.

I pull the handle and open it, slipping inside, out of the crowds of departing tourists. I ascend the marble staircase, to one of the private rooms that the visitors never see. It is located at a bend near the top of the stairs. Its door gives no indication of what lies inside; it could be a broom cupboard. Instead it is a place the wealthy patrons of our Kolkata society have always used for their after-hours activities.

A fierce prickle of dread and alarm courses the length of my spine as I turn the handle and pull the door open. I walk along a narrow corridor to another door. I feel a strong flush rising in me as my blood comes up to my cheeks. I open it and step into the Red Room.

As I enter, closing the door behind me, I face a thin curtain. I can see through the light that somebody is on the other side. I pull it aside, seeing a man, sitting in a swivel chair with his back to me. He is gasping desperately, making strange, animal noises. He swivels the chair around. A young girl sits in his lap. Her hand is inside his trousers.

– Mrs Chakraborty . . . the man rasps in shock, his brow furrowed and febrile. – What in the blazes are you doing in here . . . this is no place for . . .

It is Colonel Angus Colqhoun.

– So the room does exist, I say, looking around its features; the chaise longue, the mirror, the mattress on the floor. – It is no myth. This foul brothel! And where is he, the murderer who brings you your street girls!

– I know nothing about that . . . old Angus Colqhoun says, hanging his head in shame and pushing the young Nepalese girl from his lap. He stands up shakily and zips himself and exits from the room. She walks behind him with her jacket and trousers under her arm.

I turn away, to look into the mirror at my distorted face and cry.

It is then that I realise, in my horror, that as Colqhoun has left, someone else has entered the room behind him. I hear some gruff words exchanged and the interloper closing the door. I cannot turn around and cannot look into the mirror as sickly fluids churn in disorder within me, my hair prickling at my scalp. I clutch my handbag firmly.

– You came back to me, Kalyani, back to the room. After more than fifteen years, he says, his breath hot on the back of my neck. – Still so lovely . . . I read all about you in the newspaper, how well you'd done. And then, about your poor husband. Ah so sad, he says, then I tremble as I feel his arms around me. – Let me comfort you, my darling, I could always do that, do you remember?

And yes, I do remember, because he did take me to

the Red Room once. When my mother had to take Gitanjali to the hospital and I was back in our place alone, awaiting her return. And I remember the things they did, the strange and horrible things, both he and the kind old man in the chair did to me. I remember running down the steps, running down that marble staircase . . .

And once again his rough, callused hands are against me, rubbing up and down on my bare arms, then the back of my legs. I take a step forward and reach into my bag for the dagger and . . .

The clock on the wall ticks . . .

I can feel the blade's cold steel . . .

. . . The clock strikes on the hour, a low baritone sound.

I see his face in the mirror. It is older than before but the scars have not faded. I realise that in spite of all my Western affectations I am an Indian woman after all. I do not fear death and he has already inflicted all the pain on me that he can. I slip the knife from my bag and I turn quickly as he says my name again and his cruel eyes light up, making him look like somebody else. In them I briefly see all the other possibilities for him, perhaps had his life not been lived on those brutal, unforgiving streets.

But it's too late for him as shock replaces lust and horror replaces yearning, because I stick the knife in him once, it goes in with such surprising ease, then I pull it out and do it again, still meeting no resistance. There is a lot of blood and he rallies somewhat on my third thrust, grabbing my wrist and throwing me onto the bed. As I fall back the blade spins from my grasp. He looks at his wounds, touches the blood and glares at me in brute accusation.

He sneers something horrible like, – You dirty, filthy little street whore, but he is silenced as there is someone else in the room now, somebody standing behind him, a man who fells him with a single blow to the head.

As the pimp crashes to the ground, his assailant and my saviour is revealed. I wished so much it had been Sanjay, but it is Gupta who urgently asks me, – Is Memsahib all right?

And I think of Sanjay, and the words of the sad, bewildered young American boy in the courtroom, who said, – He just stepped off the sidewalk in front of me, and all my hurt bursts open like a sore, the poison spreading through my body.

Sanjay had come out of a design exhibition at the Merchandise Mart, a huge grey building on Well Street, just north of the Chicago River. He never stood a chance as the young man in the car tore down the street. They said he was showing off to his girlfriend, racing the elevated train, which hurtled past above them. He had been drinking alcohol, my own terrible solvent.

I never had a chance to say goodbye. Never an opportunity to tell Sanjay how much I loved him, to express my gratitude for how he saved me and gave me a second chance in life.

Now I am once more damned.

I hear Guptah repeat, – Is memsahib all right?

There is no disease, no dementing illness. My head is clear, I am not stricken. But I will never be right, because a terrible vengeance will be mine and I know that I have only just begun to claim it.

Going
Underground

SAM MILLER

THE film director Satyajit Ray once told me to ignore people who said Calcutta was a dying city. 'Visit the Metro,' he said. 'It's better than the London Underground.' I did what he told me and have never forgotten it. The Calcutta system was then the only Metro in India; it was clean and fast, so different from the place overhead, the city of woes and infamous troubles. I departed the city and now, 15 years later, am returning to discover whether Ray's gentle optimism was anything greater than hope.

The entrances to Rabindra Sadan metro station are now in permanent shadow; up above, carving its way through central Kolkata, is a new 2.5 kilometre-long four-lane flyover. Metro passengers are informed they are entering a different world, and that a very different behaviour is expected of them. Written in block capitals on the walls of the entrance to the stations are forbidding signs in Bengali, Hindi and English. 'SITTING, GOSSIPING ON METRO STAIRCASE IS STRICTLY PROHIBITED' and further down the stairs: 'TIME SPENDING IS PROHIBITED IN METRO PREMISES'. The platform itself is as clean and uncluttered as I remembered it. One entire wall is covered in copies of the jottings of Tagore, all in his own hand. Strange doodles of frightened horned monsters, as if caught doing something embarrassing, are displayed next to his poems and aphorisms: 'The rose is a great deal more than a blushing apology for its thorns', 'I am able to love my God because he gives me the freedom to deny him.'

The platforms are empty of all but passengers, except for check-your-weight, tell-your-fortune machines. For one rupee, I receive a little printed card that told me I was 'glamorous, magnetic, proud and confident' – and over-weight. Suspended from the roof, at intervals of ten metres, were television screens, in front of which large groups of passengers had gathered. Charlie Chaplin's *Night in the Show* (1915) was being watched by a large group of amused Kolkatans.

Fifteen years ago I was arrested at Rabindra Sadan Station. After Satyajit Ray told me to visit the Metro, I dutifully sought directions to the station nearest to his house. I planned to use those final words of his in the radio programme I was making, and segue them with sounds of a train pulling into a station. I must have made a strange sight, a headphone-wearing Westerner by himself on a Calcutta metro platform with a microphone pointed at the oncoming train. Within seconds I had been detained and led away by two grim-faced policemen to a small, unventilated room in the metro station complex. I was accused of breaking a byelaw relating to the filming of sensitive locations without permission. Announcing that I had no camera, and was therefore innocent, I got up to leave. One of the police-men blocked the door. I tried another tack. 'Satyajit Ray told me I must come here.' That was received with a doubting sneer. 'Let me prove it,' I said, getting out my tape-recorder. I played them the end of the interview with Ray – and they listened awestruck. To these two Calcutta policemen, Ray was a demigod. They asked me about his health and whether he would ever direct a film again – they had forgotten my crime, but continued to interrogate me for more than an hour about Ray, teaching me how to pronounce Satyajit Ray (Shottojeet

Rye) correctly and pressing me to eat some snacks.

Here again in 2004, I climbed aboard the first train to Dum Dum, the northern terminus. Compared with the streets and the buses, the metro trains were quiet. For once, Kolkatans did not seem to want to talk to each other. The doors between the carriages were open, and I could walk the length of the train. I scanned the advertisements, which appeared to be themed – home loans and constipation pills in one carriage; perfumes and air-fresheners in the next. I got my camera out to take a picture of one advertisement – a particularly constipated-looking man holding a bottle of 'Belly Tone – a herbal Laxative'. A man got up from the seat opposite and, just as the shutter clicked, told me in the most officious of voices to stop. 'No photographs allowed,' he said. 'These are the regulations.'

*

'The opportunities here are mind-boggling,' Pulak Chamaria told me as we surveyed Salt Lake City, Sector 5, from the rooftop of his company's flagship building, the newly constructed Infinity Complex. Salt Lake is a satellite town of Kolkata; so close to the airport and with such good amenities, Pulak informed me, that you never need to enter the city. The Infinity Complex is a building with a brain – 'a live demonstration of the IT-empowered workspace', according to one of the brochures. Pulak, who is in his mid-twenties, is a property-developer, though he smiles roguishly when I call him that, and insists on being called an IT infrastructure-provider. He left Calcutta at the age of ten, living in Dubai and Singapore before returning recently to join his father's business. He believes that before long Kolkata will be India's IT hub. Kolkata has everything, he says, except a positive image. 'Why did people not invest in Calcutta? One: because of power cuts. Now, Kolkata has too much electricity. Two: because of the unions. Now the Communist government has declared the IT sector an essential service – and that means our staff can work 24 hours a day, 365 days a year. Labour costs are lower than in the rest of country, education is taken more seriously. Kolkata has a great future.'

Pulak took me to the BNK call centre inside the Infinity Complex. Here, in a huge, open-plan office, more than two hundred English-speaking twenty-somethings spend their nights answering routine calls for a wide range of American and British companies. On small notice boards at each desk was a piece of paper saying 'Smile, it increases your face value' and different handwritten scripts for different callers – how to deal with complaints about medical insurance from California or problems with telephone bills from the UK. The call-centre workers have adopted Westernised names; Anirban Basu had become Simon Daunt; Suvarnananda Rao had become Bart Nelson. Callers should not be able to guess they are in India – and certainly not Kolkata.

Call centres are big business in India, though not, yet, in Kolkata. BNK is both Kolkata's largest and – and at the age of three – its oldest call centre. It recruits only graduates, an equal mix of men and women, and is run by Brigadier Suresh Menon, 36 years an infantryman. At first, he told me, Kolkata parents were reluctant to allow their children to work through the nights – but a few tea parties, to show them the work environment, changed all that. 'Now', he added proudly, 'we've even had a few marriages between call-centre workers, with the parents' permission of course.' All his recruits have to be computer literate, have a good telephone manner, and 'whatever else, they mustn't have MTI'. Brigadier Menon said MTI as if it were a killer disease. 'MTI?' I asked. 'Mother-tongue influence. All recruits must have neutral accents in English, you should not be able to tell what their mother tongue is.' As part of their three-week induction course, the new recruits are then sent off to one of two in-house voice trainers – to learn how to put on either an English or an American accent. Brigadier Menon tells me that Kolkata is the best place in the country for neutrally accented English, and because of that, as well as the low labour costs and relaxed labour laws, the city will eventually become the call-centre capital of India.

Brigadier Menon's vision of Kolkata's future is shared by Pulak Chamaria. He points out that, next to the existing glass-and-steel Infinity Complex, a second, even taller building is under construction, named 'Tower 2'. Pulak tells me half the space is already taken. He shows me the sketches for Infinity's biggest project yet, a series of Smart Towers, 'a multi-purpose, multi-structure infotech park complex' which will overlook 'a large, picturesque and placid water body'. I was later to learn that the 'water body' was not just an ordinary lake.

*

'Those Infinity people I could happily stab,' an old Calcutta friend told me as we toured the city. Like much else that is said in Kolkata, the remark betrayed his emotions not his intentions. For my friend, the Infinity people had come to represent all that is bad about property development; it is one aspect of the new life that large parts of old Calcutta are slowly disappearing. Many of Kolkata's finest buildings, often containing long-term tenants paying miniscule rents, stand on the city's most valuable land, though some have been burnt to the ground in mysterious fires. Families who have occupied large houses for several generations often find the financial benefits of selling just too attractive. And throughout the city shopping malls, business centres, fast food chains and computer training schools are being built. Yet at the heart of Kolkata, the former second city of the British Empire, you can still find beautiful and historically important nineteenth- and early twentieth-century buildings, some of them in a state of almost unimaginable decay. The Nawab of Murshidabad's old mansion on Park Street appears only to be held together by the trees that are growing through and around its walls. The roof of Howrah town hall collapsed recently in the middle of the night, a few hours before one thousand people were due to meet there.

The lakes and fisheries that ring the east of the city are now being reclaimed for development. Gunter Grass famously compared Calcutta to a pile of shit dropped by God, and was condemned for doing so, but the more light-hearted might be moved to consider the key role that shit plays in the ecology of the city. The lakes are fed by canals of sewage, their noxious contents neutralised by the effects of the sun and the passage of time. The fish then feed on the algae produced by the sewage. The fisheries, which employ thousands of people, provide Kolkata households with the Bengali staple food as well as treating quite breathtaking quantities of human sewage. The lakes do not smell, and the fish, everyone says, taste even nicer. Many of the lakes have already disappeared, such is the pressure for land to develop, and more are doing so all the time. There is, however, perhaps a small reason for hope – at least so long as organisations like Infinity continue to refer to the enormous sewage-fed fishpond close to the site of the Smart Tower complex as a 'large, picturesque and placid body of water'.

The shopping malls, the bowling alley, the amusements parks, the cinema multiplex: one might wonder if Kolkata is in the process of becoming everywhere else. I stayed in the same hotel as fifteen years ago; redeveloped, it now has a pub called 'Big Ben' which comes complete with a red telephone box, a copy of the *Daily Sketch* from the day after Edward VIII's abdication, and a custard advertisement, 'The National Dish! Since 1837, clever British housewives have prized the wonderful flavour of Birds Custard'. The only thing lacking was customers, in contrast to the city's hippest night-club, Tantra on Park Street, which, by 1.30 a.m. on Saturday evening, is packed with several hundred clubbers, many of whom, the night I arrived, were from Kolkata's large Chinese community, out celebrating their new year. Lots of self-conscious young people were glowering at each other; others were being entertained by a bartender who juggled cocktail shakers, first-time smokers were as usual puffing too frequently to look as cool as they hoped, and dancers desperately pretended to ignore each other. There is a display cupboard with crockery signed by famous visitors: Melanie Griffiths, Ricky Martin, and Bollywood stars Aishwarya Rai and Hrithik Roshan. At Tantra I spotted just two women wearing Indian-style clothes;

they didn't look comfortable, one of them anxiously grasping a mobile phone as if waiting for the call that would allow her to escape back to her normal life. Upstairs, overlooking the main bar and the dance-floor, was a more exclusive area, for the Kolkata élite – with malt whiskies and Cuban cigars on offer. In this group, I met an event manager desperate to return to Mumbai; a young IT professional from Bangalore who told me that Kolkata was not a city of joy but a city of sorrow; and, most unexpectedly, a senior police officer who came up and introduced himself to me.

'You want to know about Kolkata?' he said. 'I will tell you. It is the only place in India where you can still have a decent conversation about Pablo Neruda or Akira Kurosawa.' He began writing notes in my notebook, listing key facts that I clearly needed to know. 'One: In this city, there are more massage parlours than in Pattaya or Bangkok or Hong Kong. Two: In the Presidency Jail, all teenage inmates have sexually transmitted diseases – they are abused by older inmates, and the law stops us from providing them with condoms. Three: Have you been to Victoria Memorial between 7 p.m. and 8 p.m.? No? Go there and you will see many couples copulating in the grounds. Same at Minto Park – they have nowhere else to go. Four: Kolkata is the only city in the world where you can buy a meal, a full meal for less than $1.' And so on, until he'd filled five pages of the notebook. It was by then two o'clock in the morning, and the DJ was playing hip-hop and trance. I turned to the officer, more than bemused, and said that I'd never met a policeman quite like him before. 'Yes, there aren't many like me. Most of them are just interested in their career prospects, and sit at home with their wives. They wouldn't be seen dead in a nightclub.'

Sleeping on the roadside close to Park Street Metro were small-time traders, beggars and pavement dwellers. A man disfigured by leprosy waved a finger-less hand through the open window of my taxi. In his other two-fingered hand he held a tin mug. I did not give him any money. I remembered visiting a leprosy clinic here. On my arrival a young doctor was berating a terribly deformed patient of his – which I took, understandably enough, to show a lack of compassion. When he had calmed down, I asked him why he was so upset with his patient. He explained to me that leprosy was a curable disease, which, if treated early, had only minor symptoms. However, he said, some of his patients knew that the more they were deformed – the more money they could make, especially from foreigners. He was furious, he said, because a patient he had helped cure had deliberately re-infected himself so as to earn more money. He then introduced me to a nine-year-old leprosy patient called Basanti, whose sparkling eyes contrasted so strongly with her twisted fingers. She had no future, he told me – she would either end up in an institution or take to begging. I somehow had the idea that I would spot her again the other day – 24 now, yet still out on the streets of Kolkata – and I searched for her in the eyes of every female beggar that I encountered.

I was photographing a tree growing horizontally out of a block of flats, when a man in his thirties wearing a bright red shirt interrupted me. He had one eye firmly and permanently closed. He asked if he could help me. I said that I was fine and I didn't need any help. He asked me why I was taking a photo of a petrol pump. I said that I wasn't and pointed to the tree, its roots twisted round the balustrades of the balcony. I decided to ignore him; his English was implausibly good. He didn't like me ignoring him and became more persistent. As I tried to leave, he stood in front of me. 'I only want a job', he said. Suddenly. I began to doubt my belief that he was a con-man. He did not speak for two or three seconds and then said, 'My daughter died two days ago.' I couldn't open my mouth. My composure broke and I slunk away. I had just read, on the plane journey to Kolkata, this most painful of poems by Tagore, whose words and message were now resounding in my ears.

> No sign of my servant this morning
> The door stood unlatched   my bath-water was unfetched
>   The rascal didn't turn up last night.
> Where my clean clothes were   I had no clue
>   Nor where my meal was coming from.
> Time passed, the clock ticking   I sat, irritation pricking –
>   I would really tell him off, I would.
> At last quite late he came   greeted me in the same way
>   As usual, palms pressed meekly together.
> I was seized by a fit   I cried, 'Go, get out,
>   I do not want to see your face!'
> He heard me like a dunce   as if stunned for once
>   He searched my face in surprise.
> Then he said, 'Last night– '   he choked, 'at midnight –
>   My little girl she died.'
> So saying, in haste   cloth on shoulder he went to face
>   His daily chores alone.
> And, as on any other day,   he cleaned, polished, scrubbed away.
>   Left not a single task undone.

I cannot be sure if my one-eyed, red-shirted man had really lost his daughter, but I sensed immediately afterwards that I had handled our encounter badly. I felt shame. Looking back, there is little I could have done for him, except given him the benefit of the doubt.

Kolkata is an emotionally exacting city. It is hard not to get involved. The city makes exceptional and continuous demands on one's senses: on the eyes – its colours, the street life of ordinary people, the urban decay; the smells, almost overpowering in rainy season, of rotting vegetation, of sewers, of leather factories, of street cooking; then the taste of Bengali sweets, of (sewage-fed) fish, and the strange, saccharine taste of the air; the sounds of cars, of street-sellers, of manual typewriters, of crows, of people quarrelling and of children playing; and of course, the touch, the touch of other people, and of the occasional goat or cow. You can't exist in Kolkata if you can't stand being jostled and squashed. Public and private transport works on the principle that there is always room for one more person. The seats on the metro, for instance, form one continuous bench, and I was repeatedly urged to push up for someone new.

I bumped into an old journalist colleague of mine outside Tollygunge metro station. As we squeezed ourselves onto the train seats he too expressed his admiration for what had become his main means of travel, even though he could afford a car and a driver. But he then went on to say that, as with so much development and modernity, the metro had some unforeseen drawbacks. He described how the television screens, which were now showing Charlie Chaplin, had in 2002 shown the football World Cup. Crowds grew around the screen at one station – and in the excitement that followed a Brazil goal one commuter was pushed into the path of a train and died. And these were not the only deaths, my friend went on. People used to commit suicide in Calcutta by throwing themselves from the towering Ochterlony monument. But now, he said, with a wise look on his face, the efficient Metro has taken its place. I was silenced once more by this city of ironies, as Satyajit Ray's Metro smashed through the darkness to reach the core of Kolkata.

Waking Up from Your Father's Dreams

MICHAEL ATHERTON

WHEN he looked back on his life, which he did with greater frequency since the diagnosis, Ajay Chokrabarty was quite certain that it was the letter that arrived the day after his seventeenth birthday that changed everything. It was in an envelope much like the one that stared back at him now, from the silver-plated breakfast tray that Mrs Mukherjee, his housekeeper of twenty years, had placed before him: slim and white and cool to touch, embossed with spidery black-ink lettering and adorned with an English stamp. Ajay recalled his father's absurd pride in the stamp. For years later, whenever relatives or guests came to their small village house, his father would point, with a mixture of ceremony and solemnity, to the place on the wall where he had fixed it, despite its being a reminder of the moment that shattered his dream.

Ajay turned to his writing desk, to a framed portrait of his father, and was surprised, as always, to find how little they resembled each other. Only last week Ajay had asked his sister how she remembered him as a young man. He had given the impression, she said, that he was tall and graceful because he walked around with his chin tilted upwards as if he were constantly looking towards the horizon. She said that he spoke softly, so that people had to lean towards him to hear his words, and that he had a strange habit of elongating his vowels so that his sentences lasted longer than they ought, which gave an impression that he said more than he ever did. This combination – his bearing and the way people bowed deferentially towards him – gave him an air of nobility.

His father, on the other hand, was a short, nervous man with a pinched face and he was a chatterbox. When a cigarette or bidi wasn't dangling from his thin lips he was always talking about cricket. It was the only thing that his father seemed passionate about – his only release from the daily grind of the clerk's office in Dalhousie Square. Scorecards from every Test match he had attended at Eden Gardens were pasted into a red-fronted, black-edged scrapbook, which, along with an MCC coaching manual, were the only books in the house.

The morning the letter arrived Ajay remembered that his father had seemed especially irritable. The reply to the application for Ajay's cricket scholarship to the MCC ground staff in England was long overdue, and the postman, who came to the village on Wednesdays and Saturdays, was late. His father paced between the two rooms of the house, one hand unconsciously fingering a matchbox until he had mashed it to a pulp, the thumb and forefinger of his other hand combing the sides of his moustache. Each time he reached the front door he scanned the dirt track road, down which the postman, in his neat khaki uniform, would come.

Ajay remembered watching his father bitterly from the bed in the front room in which he and his sister slept. The room doubled up as a kitchen and his mother was sat on her haunches supervising the milk, tea and sugar boiling in a pan. She set out the breakfast before them: paratha bread, muri, vegetables and aloo curry. His father sipped the tea from a glass thimble, scolded his mother for its sweetness, and tipped the remains into the courtyard.

The back room was where his father and mother, and more lately their grandmother, slept. He could see the sleeping figure of his grandmother, her white hair wrapped tightly in a bun, her chest rising and falling gently. Above, a clothesline stretched across the room, sagging under the pressure of the saris, dresses and pyjamas that hung there. The green-brick walls were filled with old copies of the *Sunday Telegraph*. It was the only paper they received all week – 'because the English is so simple and easy to understand', his father said. Alongside the cuttings were framed portraits of the gods – Durga, Kali, Shiva, Hanuman and Krishna – just about his father's only concession to his mother.

As he looked at the portrait of his father, and recalled the house in the village of Kusumba where he grew up, Ajay realised that he was unconsciously rubbing the back of his right calf and that he had an uncomfortable feeling in the pit of his stomach. He frowned at the memory. He stood and walked over to the bookcase. He ran his fingers across the spines of the books and admired his wife's etchings that filled the walls of their flat. Looking out from the balcony he could just make out the green expanse of the maidan through the early morning mist. He called Mrs Mukherjee and asked her to send for his driver.

Shisha Pal, his driver, was a trim-looking Punjabi whose family had moved to Calcutta 25 years ago in search of work. The sleeves of his freshly ironed shirt were rolled up as if he was ready for work, and the hair on his bare arms was flecked with grey, betraying his age. Ajay had never seen Shisha Pal get flustered by the maniacal driving on the roads of Kolkata.

'Let's go to the maidan, please Shisha.'

'Yes, sir.'

The white Ambassador deftly negotiated the back streets of Ballygunge. The pavements were mostly empty of the sleeping by now and crowds huddled around the teashops, warming themselves with a hot drink and each other's company. At Chowringhee, Shisha turned right and then they crawled anti-clock-wise around the sides of the maidan, constantly fighting the clogged traffic. Despite his 60 years in Calcutta, Ajay had never come to terms with the hooting of the car horns; they were a permanent assault. When they reached the corner of the Red Road and the Fort William, Ajay asked Shisha Pal to stop and he got out of the car.

Ajay had forgotten that it was Id al-Fitr, the celebra-tion of the end of Ramadhan, and therefore a national holiday. He marvelled, now, at the Muslims who were streaming across the maidan in their thousands: the men in brilliant white kurtas and the women in their pretty pastel-coloured saris.

It was just before eight in the morning. The mon-soons had stopped a month earlier, so that the maidan had already started to lose its green freshness and the seasonal alopecia had already begun to appear. Over the next six months it would spread until the rains restored growth again. Clouds of dust rose from the ground as the Muslims swept across the maidan; the air was still thick and the combination gave the scene an impressionist, sepia quality.

Ajay guessed that the Muslims would have been gath-ering along the Red Road since seven. Small numbers huddled now around the water pumps that lined the edge of the road. They sat on their haunches, washing themselves thoroughly: first, the backs of their necks, then their faces, cleaning their teeth with their forefingers and blowing black snot from their nostrils. Then, they cupped the water in the palms of their hands and let it run down their bare arms. Finally, they finished with their feet, making sure the space between each toe was not forgotten. When cleansed, they joined the massed ranks, layered with military precision, facing towards Mecca.

Loudspeakers had been strapped to the lamp posts and, as eight o'clock approached, the Imam's urgings became more and more frenetic. On the hour there was silence, apart from the crackling from the loudspeakers. Then came the prayer.

'Allah Akbar!' It began.

In unison the Muslims cupped their hands to their ears, fingers pointing towards the sky, and they began to flick their earlobes with their thumbs.

'Allah Akbar!'

This time they stood, heads bowed and hands clasped in front of their bodies.

'Allah Akbar!'

They leaned forward into a prostrate position, their bodies at a 45-degree angle to the ground, and then they stood again. Ajay's eyes focused on one little boy who impatiently tugged the corner of his father's kurta. Then, he lifted his father's hat and glasses and tried them on. Others hissed at him to be quiet but the father's reaction was more measured: he placed his hand on the boy's shoulder until he was calmed.

'Allah Akbar!'

This time the Muslims knelt down in the full praying position. The pressure of the father's hand on the boy's shoulder increased gently until the boy, also, was kneeling in prayer. From his position Ajay could see all the way down the Red Road. He estimated that there were over 100,000 Muslims stretched along the prayer mat that ran the length of the road. Only a few small children, and the odd photographer, stood.

'Allah Akbar!'

The Muslims sat now, their bodies at a slight angle, one leg bent, the other leg straightened, hands cupped as if they were carefully holding a wounded bird, and they were rocking and moaning. The Imam's prayer was a beautiful one, delivered in rich, mellifluous tones in stark contrast to his earlier urgings. At around 8.30 the Muslims began to drift away and Ajay removed the handkerchief that he had placed on his head as a mark of respect.

He sat on a bench with his back to the Victoria Memorial and looked out over the maidan. Because of the holiday there were hundreds of cricket matches being played – not a patch of turf unoccupied. He was always amazed how the matches co-existed side by side, with often only twenty yards separating them. There were no boundary markings and yet the umpires knew instinctively when to signal a four or a six, and there never seemed to be any injuries. The players themselves umpired the matches and he had never yet seen a decision disputed.

The match nearest to him was being played on a completely bare pitch within the shade of three huge trees. The players wore ragtag outfits – some in whites, others in colours. The cricket itself was of a decent standard – bustling medium pacers and hard-hitting batsmen. Best of all, their passion for the game was obvious; every run and wicket was celebrated with joyous high-fives and whoops of delight.

It had been many years since Ajay had seen a Test

match at Eden Gardens – the match-fixing scandal and stories of sledging had diminished his desire to go there again. Only this morning he was disgusted to read a story in the *Times of India* about an Indian player, Abhijit Kale, who had allegedly tried to bribe two Indian selectors, and a Hyderabad cricketer who said that a selector demanded Rs50 lakh for an India 'A' tour berth. Still, he liked to come to the maidan occasionally. Here, he felt, the true spirit of cricket could be found, something that had been lost in the short distance between the maidan and Eden Gardens.

A ball rolled over towards him.

'Uncle! Uncle! Throw the ball back please.'

Ajay bent down stiffly, his kurta flapping in the dust, and he held the ball, which was still hard to touch but was no longer red in colour. It felt strange to him now, as strange as it had once felt natural. His hands, which had once been hard and callused as a result of the fielding practice his father had forced upon him, were now smooth and soft. Regretfully, he realised that the boys were out of range for him and he called them over.

'Where are you from?' he asked them.

'Uncle, we've come from Nimtala.' Ajay smiled. Nimtallah was many kilometres away and he knew that the boys would have been up before sunrise to make sure that they claimed a pitch.

'Who is your favourite player?'

'Sachin!' they cried.

'Who is the best team at the moment?'

'The Australians, Uncle. They play like warriors!'

All over the maidan, such scenes were being played out. Boys imagining themselves to be Sachin, or Saurav or Rahul, and their patch of turf to be Eden Gardens, or Sydney or Lord's.

It was here, not twenty yards from where they stood, that his father had introduced him to the game when he was five years old. Looking around, not much had changed: the floodlights of Eden Gardens, which he could see shimmering in the distance, were a recent addition, as was the superstructure of the Vidyasagar Bridge to his left. The statues, which when he first came were of British lords – Kitchener, Curzon and Northbrook – had been replaced by Ghandi, Nehru and Roy. What would his father have thought of that? Otherwise things were much the same: horses and herds of goats roaming the sides; villagers carrying trays of chickaloo on their heads, weaving in between the cricket games and city folk selling their bangles.

Ajay wandered over to the narrow, stony path where his father first knocked in the three pieces of wood to signal the fact that his cricketing education had formally begun. Every Sunday morning they would come to the same place with his sister. His father would lift his face to the sky, breathe in the cloying air, announce that The Maidan was the 'lungs of Calcutta' and then practice would begin. Ajay remembered his first instructions:

'Pick the bat up like you would an axe,' his father said, 'with the "v" between your thumbs and forefingers pointing down the back of the bat handle.' His father then stood behind him as he lifted the bat. It had been cut by his uncle in the village but was too heavy and too long, and so he had to hold it right at the bottom of the handle. Then his father leaned over from behind, covered Ajay's hands with his own and taught him the stance.

'It's a sideways game, Ajay,' he said, removing one hand to point to where an imaginary bowler would come from, 'a sideways game – always remember that.'

His father started off throwing a soft ball, made up of old scraps of scrunched-up paper stuck together with sticky tape. He would stand, four or five yards away, bringing the ball to his ear and throwing, left-handed. Until he grew stronger, Ajay remembered that he could barely lift the bat and he dragged it along the floor like a sweeping brush. Occasionally, he would connect and send the ball flying over mid-wicket and he recalled the feelings of exhilaration and pride, holding his pose (the bat behind his head, looking far into the distance and grinning) for any would-be photographers. His father was rarely happy though.

'You must play straight, Ajay, you must play straight, otherwise you will never make a cricketer!' And his father would roll up his sleeves, take the bat from him, take a step forward and bring the bat down vertically into the forward defensive position, head down looking over the ball, so that Ajay could see the bald patch that was beginning to develop around the crown of his father's head.

The sessions lasted two or three hours, often until his hands were blistered and bleeding from rubbing against the harsh wooden handle of the bat and until his sister jumped up and down in frustration and pleaded to go home. At the end of the sessions, Ajay was allowed to ride a pony the length of the maidan as a treat. It always made him want to come back for more.

Eventually, they graduated from a soft ball to a hard ball. His father would stand a little further away – ten or twelve yards – but to compensate, his throwing and his criticisms became more fierce. The unevenness of the pitch meant that the bounce was never predictable and he was often hit. He wore no pads and his shins were covered in bruises. The first time he got hit on the body was on the point of the shoulder. He bit his lip hard to fight back the tears that began to sting his eyes and he got ready to face the next ball. The first time he got hit in the face, just above the left eye, the pain was too much: he threw down his bat and rushed into the arms of his father, sobbing.

After that, Ajay couldn't help but retreat from the ball. Just as his father raised his left arm to throw it, Ajay's right leg would, unconsciously and instinctively, begin to make little steps to square-leg. His father would become enraged. 'I'll teach you to behave like a coward!' he shouted one time and he grabbed Ajay's bat, bent him over his thigh and repeatedly slapped his right calf with the face of the bat until it was red and swollen. His father may have been a bully, but he wasn't a brutal man and it was the only beating Ajay could ever remember. He stopped retreating after that, but the fear remained and he knew that he would always be a coward when it came to physical dangers.

Ajay walked back to Shisha Pal and was happy for the company.

'Let us go, Shisha.'

'Home, sir?'

'No. There are a couple more places I would like to visit again.'

He directed Shisha around the maidan, until they began to pass the sports clubs on their left. He asked Shisha to stop in between the War and East Bengal Clubs. Ajay got out and walked down the narrow path that separated the two, until he came to an opening, where around a hundred boys were practising in three turf and three artificial nets. On his left was a tin shed that doubled-up as a pavilion, and on his right were two trees over which was draped some tattered cricket netting that created an artificial menagerie in which birds flapped about. This was the home of the Bourn Vita Cricket Academy. It was where his father had sent him three times a week before school, between the ages of nine and fifteen, long before it had acquired its current sponsored status.

Ajay smiled at the obvious contrast with the cricket he had just witnessed on the maidan. Here, all the boys were in whites, and helmets were compulsory. Those who weren't batting or bowling practised their fielding. Coaches roamed around, encouraging here, gently chiding there. Parents had taken advantage of the holiday to check up on their bright hopes. Someone offered Ajay a seat, perhaps thinking him to be a potential donor.

He watched as one of the coaches tried to teach a young boy how to bowl a googly. The coach had set a tea towel at the far end of the net at which the boy had to aim. The boy kept trying but had little control over the ball, which flew into the roof and side of the netting. The coach kept his patience and continued to encourage the boy. 'Just try dipping your shoulder a little more,' he said, 'and point the back of your wrist to the sky.'

Ajay looked out onto the happy scene and remembered the terrible dread he used to feel on coming here. Often, he would be unable to sleep the night before, fearing the moment at 4.30 a.m. when his father would tap him on the shoulder and whisper, 'It is time, Ajay.' He would already be awake, listening to the dull whirring of the fan and the howling of wolves outside, a sick feeling penetrating the deepest parts of his body – a feeling he now understood as nerves but was too young to understand then. After his father came, he would duck down under the cover for one last feeling of warmth and safety before he carefully clambered over his sleeping sister and stepped out onto the hard, cold stone floor.

He would dress slowly, trying to delay time, but he was usually out of the house by five, just as the soft first light of the morning fell upon Kusumba. Sometimes he took a rickshaw to Garia Station, but mostly he walked. He would pass the yapping dogs scavenging in the rubbish tip, on past the silent bamboo grove and past the enormous red house in the centre of the village with its ornate gates, where two customs officers lived. 'They've got rich in the last ten years,' his mother always noted whenever they passed it, leaving unsaid what was common knowledge in the village.

Ajay hated the practice sessions at the Academy, especially when his father turned up for an hour or so before work. No other parents bothered to turn up, except during the holidays. Not only did his father embarrass him with his presence, but whenever Ajay was batting his father would position himself conspicuously, straight in his eyeline behind the bowler's arm. Ajay would immediately feel the tightening of his muscles and the draining away of all fluidity in his limbs. He could sense that his father was playing every ball himself, wincing and groaning each time Ajay was bowled out, or made a mistake, which was often for he was watching his father and not the ball. After every false shot he could see his father, with his sleeves rolled to the elbow and a cigarette dangling from his lips, ghosting the shot that ought to have been played. Whenever things went well, his father would clap and nod vigorously just to make sure that everyone knew that, yes, that is my son.

Even then, Ajay knew that he lacked the talent and the passion of some of the other boys. He had decent equipment and was well coached for his age, but he knew that the game didn't come naturally to him. Certainly, not as naturally as it came to Shivsagar Singh. Shivsagar was much shorter than Ajay and yet he was able to hit the ball twice as hard and twice as far with little apparent effort. Shivsagar came from a village four hours away and during the week he often slept in the tin hut, or inside the hollow rollers that were used for flattening the pitches. 'Why can't you make it look as easy as Shivsagar,' his father often complained. Ajay had no answer, except that he knew he would never make it look as easy as Shivsagar.

He also knew that Shivsagar, and some of the other village boys, deliberately falsified their ages in order to play in age-group matches that they were undoubtedly too old to play in. Ajay had no desire to hide his age. The Saturday matches, played on the small ground the Academy rented from the Army, were painful enough. His fear of fast bowling remained and the matches brought an added fear of failure. Inevitably, his father never missed a match, pacing the outfield and storing up enough criticisms and questions to last the entire journey home, and often the conversation during dinner.

Ajay was sure that he would have given the Academy up had it not been for his father's insistence and the presence of a coach called Naru. Naru was a former Indian cricketer – one of the few that Bengal had ever produced – with a ragged beard and a twinkle in his eye, who went everywhere with a parrot perched on his shoulder. The boys like to quip that the parrot talked more sense, but Ajay liked the fact that Naru didn't take himself or the game too seriously. Naru, in fact, saw much of his own childhood in Ajay and he knew that a passion for the game could never be forced. Like love, it happened of its own accord or not at all. Naru remembered how his own father had nearly knocked all the enjoyment of the game out of him at an early age. So, whenever Ajay went to him with a technical concern, his face screwed tight with tension and worry, Naru would shrug his shoulders, waggle his head and say, simply, 'technique is the servant not the master'.

Often, at the end of the practice sessions, Ajay's father would call Naru over to discuss his son's progress. Ajay would hear the sniggering of the other boys and he would feel the heat rising in his neck as his father, for the umpteenth time, asked the coach to check his son's grip. He would stand head bowed, looking at the ground, avoiding the gaze of the other boys. When he looked up at the coach, he did so apologetically. Naru would wink conspiratorially; pretend to move Ajay's top hand around the handle a little. 'There,' he would say, 'that's how Don Bradman used to hold it!'

There was just one more place to go now before Ajay felt that he could return home. He walked back to Shisha Pal, patted him on the shoulder and pointed to the giant floodlights of Eden Gardens. They walked to the car together.

'What was your mother's name, Shisha?'

'She was Lajabati, sir.'

'And your father?'

'He was B.D. Sharma.'

'What did he do?'

'He moved from the Punjab, sir, and he briefly tried the merchant navy. He didn't much like sea life though.

Back in the Punjab he struggled for work and that was when we moved to Calcutta.'

'Was he proud of you?'

'At first, he wanted me to learn shorthand and learn to type and become a clerk. I knew he was upset when I left school early and that lasted a long time. But the day I bought my first car I promised myself that I would teach my father to drive. Sat behind the wheel of my car he was the happiest man in Calcutta.'

Ajay contemplated the strange twists and turns of fate that had shaped his own life. If he had gone to England on the cricket scholarship it was likely that he would have never met Tanuja nor sipped tea with her in the cool courtyards of Tagore House, shaded by the deb-daru trees, discussing literature, discussing art and Indian politics.

The great stadium was empty and Ajay knew exactly where he wanted to go. D Stand was situated in between the old scoreboard and the new electronic scoreboard and it was where he and his father had sat many times. They were the cheap seats, just wooden plants unprotected from the sun. It was quite a climb and Ajay was wheezing by the time he arrived. He smiled at the fact that he was now grateful for the chance to sit on the seats that used to numb his back-side after six hours of sitting. The old scoreboard still showed the scores and players' names from the One Day International that had been played the week before and that was the only evidence that cricket was played in the stadium. He was the only person in the ground.

Ajay recalled the thrill he felt on coming here for the first time when he was nine years old. His father had carefully laid the tickets out the night before and his mother had prepared a huge picnic of luchis, fried bhekti and mutton cutlets. When they arrived a dense smog sat over the ground before the start of play. Ajay could hear the noise of the massive crowd, a dull murmur of anticipation, but could see nothing. Miraculously, before the start of play the fog lifted and the sight of the vast numbers of people, the colour, the noise of the firecrackers and their acrid smell would stay with him for the rest of his life.

His father would always watch the cricket intensely, turning to Ajay only to point out a tactical blunder or a missed opportunity. Only ever the mistakes. Much later, Ajay understood the reasons for his father's sourness. Every day his father left the house with his crisp, white handkerchief protruding from the top pocket of his jacket. Every day, he returned with it crumpled and smeared with sweat. The confident stride of the early morning was replaced with the shuffling steps of the early evening. The dominant man who barked orders at breakfast was replaced by the man who sat with his head inclined to the floor, so utterly defeated, at dinner-time. His father had often told Ajay and his friends that he worked 'in a bank', but Ajay knew him to be a lowly clerk, and knew also the frustration and bitterness this brought into his father's life.

He always brought a small transistor radio with him to Eden Gardens to listen to the commentary of Ajay Basu (the man after whom Ajay was named) who was the vocal link between Bengalis and the game they loved. Ajay could picture his father, now, hunched forward, one hand shielding his eyes from the sun, the other pressing the radio to his ear. Ajay had often told his sister that this was when his father was at his happiest. It made her envious because she looked upon the trips to Eden Gardens as a secret pact between father and son, one from which she was forever excluded.

Ajay descended the steps from D Stand and walked out onto the arena, looking around the vast, empty stands. He had made the long walk to the middle once before for Bengal U17s against Uttar Pradesh and he retraced those steps now. The dry, brittle grass crackled under his sandals until he reached the centre square, which was firm underfoot. The last time he made that walk he was sick with nerves. He had felt so small and insignificant. He remembered the sweat that had prickled his forehead and run into his eyes, stinging them and blurring his vision for an instant. His mouth was parched, his tongue sticking to the roof of his mouth. The jerky movements of his limbs betrayed his fear.

His father had inevitably taken the day off and for the only time in his life he was allowed to sit in the members' pavilion. Ajay wished he wasn't there; instead he tried to recall Naru's encouragement. Initially, his feet wouldn't move into the positions he wanted them to and the ball would miss the centre of his bat, sending shockwaves through his hands. With his first well-timed stroke the nerves began to disappear and his body felt his own again.

It was an innings he would always be proud of. Later, Naru would tell him that true courage was dealing with and overcoming your fears. After the match, one of the umpires presented him with the match ball.

For once he had looked forward to the journey home. Normally after a match his father could not contain himself and there were always enough questions about the game and Ajay's performance to last the hour's journey from Sealdah Station to Garia. This time his father was strangely silent, his right foot constantly tapping up and down. Ajay sensed his father's mood.

'What's the matter, father?'

'You could have done more, Ajay.'

'But I thought I had a good match.'

His father turned to him, his face bloated and puckered with emotion.

'For God's sake, Ajay. I work my fingers to the bone for you. I scrimped and saved so that I could send you to the Academy, so that I can buy you new equipment, so that we can attend the Test match every year, and this is how you repay me. You had a hundred there for the taking today and you just gave it away. You should never be satisfied. I've never been more disappointed in you.'

Ajay looked at this strange man and wondered, for a moment, exactly who he was. He knew then that he could never satisfy him, and there was silence for the rest of the journey home.

On the way home in the car now there was also silence between Ajay and Shisha Pal, as Ajay recovered from the disturbing memories the morning had brought. In his study he looked at the dozen or so books that he had had published and the periodicals that he had contributed to. His father had never read a line he had written.

Tanuja walked in to his study. A little broader than the slim girl he had met at Tagore House, but still lovely. She kissed the top of his forehead, lifted the glasses from his face and suggested that it was time for him to rest.

He sighed and looked at the white envelope – the envelope that had sparked off the morning's memories. It was still on his breakfast tray, unopened. He peeled off the stamp and tried to stick it to the wall, but it fluttered to the floor. His arthritic fingers lifted the envelope now, just as his father's had done one morning many years before.

When the letter had finally arrived, his father had called the family around. Even his grandmother had been woken from her slumbers and forced to stand and watch as Ajay's father fingered the edge of the envelope. Despite the fact that it was addressed to Ajay, his father made no move to release it from his grasp. Ajay's mother and sister sat as nervously as he, wondering whether he would be the first boy from the village to go to England. His father peeled back the seal, opened the letter and read it slowly. He read it again before he looked up to Ajay and his face broke into a huge smile. 'We've done it! You're going to England, to Lord's! You will get some proper coaching now!' He lifted both arms ready to embrace his son, so that the letter caught in the fan. Ajay ignored the old man's plea for an embrace, leaving him with both arms raised aloft, the letter still flapping in the fan. He rose slowly. For the first time in his life he prepared to challenge his father.

An Indian Marriage

JENNY COLGAN

SHE is arrayed for her wedding in a gossamer fine, red garment, which is embroidered with gold, and jewelled butterflies and other ornaments adorn her lustrous black hair. She is wearing precious gems in her ears, and her arms and wrists are covered with bracelets, while a golden band encircles her slender waist and anklets of gold shine on her feet.

The Ramayana

Cities reflect expectations. So Paris is full of red-rose sellers and menus for romantic dinners for two. New Yorkers feel quite justified in pushing you out the way if they don't think you're walking quickly enough. And Kolkata – well, you can find yourself doing some of the most peculiar sightseeing: there is a tourist trail of poverty, like a subcontinental version of the Victoria and Albert Museum, if the Victoria and Albert Museum were 37 degrees Centigrade, smelled foul and was trying its damnedest to give you a respiratory disorder.

Our guide for the day, adores the place. 'I think the people here – they're just much nicer and kinder than people in Europe.'

Lots of hearty nodding from us.

'And just on your left there you'll see the place they sacrifice goats. And here is where once upon a time women would hurl themselves onto the funeral pyre of their husbands and burn to death.'

'People always write about the bad Kolkata,' he continues. 'I really don't want you to do that. Now, I'm driving you through the red light district and here's the child prostitution section. They come here under false pretenses from Nepal. They live in cupboards. Many have HIV.'

Actually, Kolkata is in fact now so famous as a hideous destination that you can't even meet a child prozzie any more without tripping over four charity people trying to help her out and lots of other people standing around shaking their heads and taking artistic photographs for broadsheet magazines. A mynah bird hops about half-heartedly in the dust.

I decide I want to see how people live in other ways, escape from the guidebook and maybe, if I'm lucky, get someone to paint some of that beautiful swirly stuff on my hands. Is no-one having any fun around here?

Fortunately I am introduced to Polly, and her friend Subiha, in the large apartment Polly runs her beauty salon from. Polly is second-generation Chinese, with a gentle voice and the most peculiar English accent I've heard this side of Sheena Easton: Subiha is her good friend, a beautiful Muslim woman from Bangalore. Set in a tower, the rooms are spacious and airy.

'Have you been to our new shops?' says Polly. 'Very chic.'

'No, we've been to the railway station.'

She rolls her eyes. 'They always take people there.'

'Next they'll be taking you to the Mother Teresa home,' snorts Subiha.

'All this time we are trying to make people think better of Kolkata and you come and write these pieces.'

'I'm trying not to!' I protest vigorously. 'In fact, what are you doing now?'

'Well, we're very busy. There's a big fashion show in town.'

'That's what I mean!'

Polly tells me they will do a mendhi hand for me and, even better, they're going to let me watch her do a full bridal makeover on Subiha, in true *Girl's World* style. Subiha's already married, but Polly's doing some practice, which suits me fine.

Better than fine actually: weddings are a topic close to my heart at the moment, because all the signs are pointing to me having to organise one. (Boyfriend constantly dropping what he believes to be casual hints: 'Do you think you could put up with my incessant tool-buying for the rest of your life?'; 'Just out of interest, what do you like – gold or platinum?'; 'I'm just off to phone your dad. For, uhmm, no reason.')

Marriage translates literally in Hindi as 'taking the girl away for a special purpose'. Big in every culture, Indian weddings pretty much beat the band. The average number of guests is about seven hundred. Ceremonies last up to 4 days and can cost more than 700,000 rupees (the average monthly wage in West Bengal is 2500 rupees). There is dancing, there are gifts, there is ritual running around a fire and there is a lot of food. Imagine feeding and watering seven hundred of your nearest and dearest for days on end.

This scale of affairs isn't just confined to the rich. In fact, the further down the ladder you go, the more likely you are to splash out, as it becomes all-important to have one time in your life when you feel important. Many people get in terrible hock to money lenders for the rest of their lives. And the women's families pay for the entire thing.

There aren't so many real weddings taking place at this time of year, which is why Subiha is dressing up for me. I watch Polly delicately sweep thick kohl black eyeliner straight across her eyelid. April is considered an inauspicious month for brides. There is religious significance in this, but you suspect that the gods were being pragmatic that day, because the spring weather is so dusty and hot and awful it's simply not practical.

'Is that a good theory?' I ask Subiha. She gives me a half smile and Polly tells her to stop moving.

'I hear that February is not a very auspicious month to get married in Great Britain.'

Polly's salon is a light room covered in L'Oreal posters with a huge air-conditioning unit propped in the corner. It is in a solidly middle-class area of emergent educated middle-class Indians; doctors, chemists, bcomms (bachelors of commerce) and engineers. The rich go to smart name brand salons on Park Street; the poor do their own and each others' hair at home.

And, like everywhere, the middle class is emerging stronger than ever. Sixty per cent of West Bengali women can now read, which may not sound like much but craps on, for example, Egypt.

Although it's nothing on the scale of what's happened in Delhi and Bombay, with it's Gucci-clad 'international set', Kolkata is trying desperately hard to catch up. Large multinationals are disinclined to invest in the city with its history of labour problems – they prefer to head to Bangalore or places not quite so dusty. Yet shiny billboard advertisements for new technology and consumer products are everywhere. I hang around Polly's salon, trying not to get too much in the way. I interrupt as many conversations as I can and the chat obeys all the international rules about what you talk to your hairdresser about – your husband, your misbehaving kids and what you're thinking about wearing later.

It isn't easy to be a chic person in a dustbowl city piled on top of a disease-ridden swamp, but somehow people manage it here. Okay, the women manage it. The men stick to Tony Soprano-style golf tops and tan slacks – practical if not quite what you'd call sexy – but the woman are fabulous butterflies in pinks and orange saris. On the subway, the men and women have different compartments. The women squash in their seats all together, like plump posies.

The arranged marriage is still very much a feature, but these days it is becoming more common for the couple to be engaged, and then get to know each other first before the wedding. I suggest to Poll that this 'getting to know each other' thing might just be the death knell for arranged marriages.

She agrees, but Subiha is in favour. 'It means, no more "charging the bedclothes",' she says. Of course, I'm from the decadent West, where a woman will sleep with a man after meeting him only once. But in a funny way, things aren't so different here. Except in the East, you don't get to creep away extremely early in the morning holding your shoes in your hands and promising never to drink daquiris again. In India, you're stuck with him.

Add to this the amount of highly educated and successful Indian women all around the world who are coming home and infecting their families with their Western ways – trying to get an Indian woman educated in the West to agree to an arranged marriage is, they agree, well nigh impossible. ('Plus', adds Subiha in a quiet aside as Polly is mixing the colours for her forehead, 'often families try to fob off a mentally deficient or unpleasant male on the woman who is not here in the same country to know him'.)

Somewhat unsurprisingly, I am to hear many Indian men working in the West still like to stick with a traditional bride rather than the feisty, uppity, hello-darling-hey-why-don't-we-share-the-housework types they meet in the business world.

Arranged marriages won't last forever though, for a few reasons: gradual awareness of simultaneous Western laxness and affluence in areas of the globe without censored newspapers, but sadder and more likely, the facts of the matter are that better prenatal scanning facilities are ensuring that there is, on the way, a demographic that leaves no-one for a generation of young men to marry, about 934 girls for every 1000 boys. The women will probably find they have more of a say in the matter then.

'I don't think my daughters will have an arranged marriage,' says Subiha. 'They will get an education first.' Subiha now has her heavily kohled eyes done, which makes them look enormous. Her lips are coloured a deep coral. She stands up and unveils her pure silk printed gold sari. She looks unbelievably beautiful, and finally I can photograph her.

You're not allowed to get your photograph taken before you really get married because that might put the evil eye on you. In addition, while you're doing your make up you mark a black spot behind your right ear with a kohl pencil to ward off evil spirits. I must be lucky, then, because the dust of Kolkata is making me completely black throughout the neck area. Subiha has the painted white lines on her forehead embellished with tiny jewels; all the delicate gold filigree is handmade. The fashion among the more bling of the local girls had been putting the tiny ornaments all over their faces, but Polly doesn't like it: she thinks the diseased effect is rather unfortunate. And for the bride, wearing the most beautiful silks is no longer enough: they now have to be embossed with gold thread and are now considered not very *de trop* unless they are also covered in Swarowski crystals. That's before we get to the jewellery.

Subiha is at pains to point out that she is only wearing normal afternoon jewellery (gold necklace, jewelled bracelet, earrings, rings). Which means brides displaying as much dowry wealth as they possibly can – they must not wear anything borrowed – often sit underneath extremely heavy gold and diamond chains weighing their heads down for days on end in punishing heat. They look like a poster I passed at Homah Station – a woman laden with gold at her ears and throat.

They get married so young they scarcely remember it. It is a lot of pressure on them even to make sure the folds are straight on their saris.

'Seven hundred people will be watching,' says Subiha.

'Three hundred and fifty,' corrects Polly. 'Only the other women.'

The Indian age for getting married is eighteen, but religious law takes precedence over government law (I'm not convinced that's a good idea – the religion of Jenny says you're allowed to take Flakes from shops without paying for them which can't be right), so if you are Muslim, marriages at fifteen aren't uncommon in the countryside. Subiha, who is Muslim, was married at sixteen.

There is some consternation at the speed at which the world has changed. Mondira has popped in for a quick trim. She wears a neat brown and orange sari, and her short tidy hair has similar subtle streaks of colour in it. She tells me how disappointed she was when she arrived home one day to announce to her parents that she was going to be the first one in her family to be having a love match.

'That's fine darling,' they said. 'Is he from a nice family?'

'Now the girls, they pretend to listen to their mothers, then they get an education then they do what they like,' she says, smiling.

Chubby, talkative Sonia married across caste – she is from Kolkata – to a boy from Uttar Pradesh. For six years, from the ages of fifteen, they met in secret.

'My parents thought I was the perfect daughter!' she giggles. She has a perm and wears Indo-Western.

'I would always always be home at nine o'clock. I never asked to stay later or go to any bad parties.'

Finally, when he turned twenty-one she donned a sari for very the first time and went to visit his parents. They were delighted.

Maritha found the same. 'I am the first person ever in my family to marry for love,' she says. 'I met him when I was a student. I felt so brave. I marched up to my parents and I said I had met someone. But they weren't cross. I was a bit disappointed.'

Maritha is one of four daughters.

'My mother says I did it because women who don't have brothers don't know their place. But she didn't care. People would feel sorry for her and she would say "my daughters are my sons". And because of her I wasn't afraid of anything.'

You must go to the right school, you must get your qualifications, you must succeed while countries see

Indian labour as cheap and intelligent. With the diaspora and the progressive education of women; the media that goes with the new technology, the old ways are being swept away. And of course, bringing in some of our less savoury habits.

'If it's a love match,' says Mrs Vreetha (a stern-looking matriarchal character; steel haired and with enormous spectacles, she is older than Polly's predominant clientele of young mums), 'it just needs more checking as to the financial status, that's all.'

She looks at me. 'You know, here, it is very hard not to get married.'

'Am I too old to get married?' I ask Mrs V.

She looks at the other women.

'I once heard of someone thirty-four got married,' says Polly.

'Really?'

'To a foreign man of course.'

Everyone in the salon nods solemnly.

'It's all about *money*,' thunders Mrs Vreetha suddenly. 'Finance. Love match, arranged match – pff, what matters? You get tired after two months anyway. It's all a façade. Can he look after you? Can your family give him enough money to look after you? That's what's important.'

It occurs to me that in the films and books of India, they don't have the same strictures we do. In the West, the most popular story type is Cinderella – poor girl meets rich boy, hurrah! In Kolkata that makes no sense – the Romeo and Juliet prototype is more popular. Poor should marry poor, that's the best way, otherwise everyone gets dragged down.

'But these girls . . . the education.'

'It's not their fault,' says Mondira. 'It used to be you

wouldn't go out at night because of modesty. Now the girls can't go out at night because they get harassed.'

Everyone nods. Between the enchanting loose ladies of the television, and the still pervasive modesty of the people, it must be pretty tough being an adolescent boy here. Just yesterday, the newspaper reports, a boy of eighteen was arrested for 'Eve teasing' – the crime of verbally harassing a young woman on the street. This could even be a wolf whistle or following a woman down a road. Just as well it isn't the law in Britain; nothing would ever get built. Kolkata isn't really a late-night city anyway: the streets are literally lined with sleeping bodies.

I have noticed the lack of male gaze here, and wondered about it. I hoped it wasn't some kind of colonial hangover where you don't look at the white woman, saba. Or that I was just a huge, galumphing, plainly dressed, white, beef-eating, Anglo–Saxon milch cow, unattractive in the same way that Japanese men find European women unattractive. But speaking to these women I think it's just that the separation of men and women is so ingrained, it's instinctive not to look at women that way (and of course the nine-year-olds aren't wearing t-shirts which say 'shag me sideways').

What about divorce? I was somewhat shy of mentioning it, but everyone knows someone who's got divorced. It's still a thing of shame, but that doesn't mean it isn't massively on the increase. A lot of Bollywood movies romanticise the love match now, and *Titanic*, with its arranged marriage and flight to true love, made an absolute fortune here.

The girls encourage me to see a movie while I'm in town. They are advertising one at the moment I particularly like the look of. It is called *The Hero*, and in the TV ad has a gorgeous, lantern-jawed chap saving beautiful maidens, fighting enemies by flying over them and some excellent singing and dancing – all to a backdrop of alpine ice, snow, chalets and cable cars. The maidens look alarmingly underdressed. They're also advertising a remake of *The Getaway*. 'And the original film', it says on the English tickertape in the advertising feature, 'has no songs!!!'

I am on my way to get my mendhi hands done, the intricate lacy henna tracery most commonly drawn on brides and those close to them. Passing, I catch a glimpse of a sandy courtyard being prepared for a wedding. It is a sea of pink and white flowers and balloons, the orange dust below their feet being swept and swept again in a Sisyphean attempt to stop the grime of the city bespoiling the shocking freshness – in a city full of colours, the pure white is the most unusual of all, a good tactic of Mother Teresa's.

'How do people keep looking so clean and fresh here?' I ask Subiha while she's painting my hands.

'We change four times a day,' she says, as if I've just asked an incredibly stupid question, which I clearly have.

The mendhi looks amazing, like a lace tattoo. It gives one the uncomfortable sensation that you could take off your skin like a glove.

I make only one faux pas when having it traced on my hand: 'I bet you've never worked on skin that white before,' I said. What I mean is, I'm so used to my peely-wally see-through Celtic paleness, I've forgotten what it means.

'Actually my daughters are both extremely pale, says Suhiba. Doh. Mind you, I get my revenge later on.

'Do you live by yourself or with your parents?' she asks me.

'Actually, I live with my boyfriend.'

'Oah my gott! Of course.'

Mina is twenty-four and the only person I meet who is not married. She shrugs.

'I want to be a fashion designer.'

'You want to marry somebody smart, from Delhi, huh?' teases Polly.

'Well, I don't want to marry anybody from Kolkata,' she says sulkily. 'I would rather marry a foreigner.'

The other women laugh.

'I will marry a foreigner and go to Rome.' She tosses her new blonde highlights.

Mina is preparing for her brother's arranged marriage in a week's time. Again and again I am seeing families in which the brothers put up with arranged marriages and the sisters will not. Men really will do anything for a quiet life from their mothers.

She shows me the exquisite, elaborate invitation. It is a long genealogy of grandparents and parents on both sides, listing their full names: it's a complete record offered up for verification of the joining of the families so you can check their lineage and status.

It's impolite and extremely difficult to bring up the subject of caste without sounding accusatory. It's about as hard to discern as our own minuscule class variations. I realise quickly that when people say 'from here' they mean their own caste and 'from' Uttar Pradesh, or Bangalore, it is code for another caste.

The women say it's becoming a little easier to marry a little up or down provided a family has enough money. Consorting well out of caste is as unlikely as asking people if they marry goats; it's mentally difficult to conceive of, one reason why Arundhati Roy's book *The God of Small Things* made such an impact.

In fact, looking around me, it is little wonder that the great nineteenth-century novels these days are being written about India. Vikram Seth writes like Jane Austen because for both societies and their razor-thin gradations, a mutually beneficial marriage is not just desirable, but everything, when the chaos is only just beneath the surface of the beautiful Calcutta ladies, gliding swan-like through the heat.

A month after I got back, someone I'm very close to did indeed finally go down on one knee, in the pouring rain, and say, 'I want to be with you forever and not one second less will do. Will you marry me?'

And of course I said yes. And then I said, 'But a small wedding, right?'

Laughter Is a River Too

TONY HAWKS

I HADN'T been expecting to come to Kolkata and have a bloody good laugh but as it turned out, that's what happened. I laughed out loud, I laughed heartily, and, if I'd had the foresight to have brought it with me, I would have laughed enough to have fallen out of my chair.

My flight landed at 4.30 a.m. and I had expected the taxi ride to the hotel to be through deserted streets, but I soon learnt that there was already a bustling vibrancy about the place – cars and auto rickshaws were buzzing around with scant regard for the old British idea of driving on the left, ragged men pulled carts bearing eccentric loads, and the odd cow aimlessly milled about the place, no doubt rather chuffed that its sacred status meant it could wander freely, unhealthily munching at the bountiful rubbish which lined every street. When we passed a large park, I was surprised to see it teeming with people. It was as if there was some kind of event going on.

'What's happening?' I asked my driver.

'Nothing. It is like this every morning.'

'But it's 5.45. What are all these people doing? Where are they going?'

'They are exercising. Many people will walk for two hours around this park before they begin their working day.'

I stopped the taxi and got out to survey the scene for myself. Hundreds of citizens were involved in diverse activities including stretching, jogging, walking, meditating, and practising yoga. How different this is, I thought, to the sight that will greet you at the break of dawn in most British parks – a solitary jogger if you're lucky, a lonely lady with a dog, and a man in a raincoat who looks set to expose himself. A smallish boy walked past in a school uniform. He had no compunction about staring and I felt I had to say something.

'Good uniform!' I said.

'St Xavier's,' he said, 'the best school in Kolkata.'

I heard voices which seemed to be chanting 'Ho!' and 'Ha!' at regular intervals. This noise seemed to be emanating from a spot beyond some trees. I signalled to my driver to wait while I set off to investigate, and turning a corner I was greeted by the sight of about a hundred people standing in the shade of a huge banyan tree. The gathering, which seemed to be predominantly elderly, were all following the bellowed instructions of a man who stood before them, waving his arms. The men were separated from the women, and all were lined up, much like prisoners in an exercise yard. The 'Ho's and the 'Ha's continued, until suddenly everybody burst into hysterical laughter, throwing their heads back and waving their arms in the air. All very odd.

Weary from my flight, I began to wonder if this was some kind of weird hallucination brought on by fatigue. Like me, the park's passing joggers and walkers stared in amazement, except for one or two, who must have known something that we didn't. I watched as the throng beneath the tree indulged themselves in a very big laugh, which was followed by a flurry of hand shaking and goodbyes.

'Are you interested in joining us?' asked an elderly gentleman who had wandered over from the gathering.

'Joining what?'

'The Laughing Club,' said the man. 'We meet here

every morning at six o'clock. Why don't you come? You will enjoy the benefits which laughter can bring to your health.'

The man, who was almost evangelical in his enthusiasm, went on to assert that laughing artificially at some ungodly hour of the morning could help with asthma, arthritis, back pain, digestive problems, depression, fatigue, insomnia, obesity, rheumatism and a weak memory. Proud boasts indeed. I was dubious, but I responded as I always do when I'm being rather bullied into something, in a cowardly manner.

'Sounds good,' I said, 'I'll definitely try and get here in the morning, if I can.'

Naturally, I had absolutely no intention of going. Much as I like a laugh, I prefer not to force it, especially at a time when I should be neatly tucked up in bed, easing slowly towards consciousness.

I'd forgotten about my body clock, of course – the one that's buried somewhere inside you which is totally inaccessible when you need to shift it forward or back by five and a half hours. I'd overdone the resting on my first day in Kolkata, choosing to doze and sit by the pool in my hotel instead of embarking on a fatigued initial exploration of the city, and there was a frustrating consequence of this. I was wide awake at 4.45 a.m., and with not many options on how best to pass the time. There was only one thing for it.

As I made my way though the park, once again I was amazed by the scenes which greeted me. It was the crack of dawn but this public place of recreation was packed full of people who were using it for exactly that – public recreation.

'Good morning,' I said proudly as I walked into the compound of the Laughing Club at six o'clock on the dot.

'Aha! I see you have made it!' said the same fellow who had collared me the previous morning.

'Oh yes, I wouldn't have missed it for the world,' I said, stretching the truth just a tad. 'I am delighted to be here,' I added to the now beaming gentleman. I looked down at the name badge which adorned his chest. It read 'Commander Singh'. Commander? Was this Laughing Club some kind of military operation, I wondered? If it was, then its army wouldn't have made a formidable fighting force. I looked down the line of old ladies in colourful saris, limbering up ready for their workout, and then over to the venerable old gentlemen in predominantly Western clothing, most of which had gone out of fashion in the early Eighties. This was a body of people who wouldn't strike fear into the heart of an opposing army. No matter though – they were being trained to laugh at the enemy, a desperately underused military strategy and one which, in the right circumstances, might prove surprisingly successful.

A tall man in shorts with extremely knobbly knees smiled at me.

'Are you from America?' he asked.

'Stop talking! And get into a line!' barked another stern-looking man, before I had time to answer. Dutifully, everyone stopped talking and fell into line. I looked a little lost, not knowing what was expected of me, but Commander Singh leapt into position, pointing to a spot where he felt I should stand. I obeyed, fearful of a court martial. Shortly, I was to wish that I'd chosen a slightly different spot.

The man leading operations was a fit-looking 'sixty

something' who was slightly scary, on account of having one eye which was all white, with no pupil. He would have made a good James Bond villain, I thought. He lead us through an unreasonably thorough sequence of stretching exercises, which I found quite exhausting. Eyeballs were revolved, ears were tugged outwards and then poked into with our fingers, and every joint and muscle was elongated, tightened, constricted, relaxed, distended, all to the rhythm of the bellowed orders from our cockeyed leader. Only one of my organs was left unstretched, no doubt because to have had me stretching that in a public place would have led to an arrest. As ever, it would be down to me to stretch that in my own time.

I began to wonder why all this exertion was necessary for a group of people who just wanted a vigorous titter of a morning. This was hard work, especially for me, because it was patently obvious that all those years of not doing this kind of thing at six in the morning had left my body incredibly unsupple. All around me my venerable colleagues reached the positions with ease while I winced in agony, trying hard to haul my body into place. Kolkata was a very humid place, even this early, and I was beginning to sweat profusely. This was painful. Very painful, and not at all what I'd been expecting. When would we ever start the fun bit? When could we start laughing?

As it happened I caused some extracurricular laughter as a few of those around me began to notice what a state I was in. The man who still thought I might be American was smirking constantly, but soon he was to laugh out loud. This happened when I emerged, dripping in sweat, from a feeble attempt to touch my toes, only to reach upwards to the sky and feel a moist

deposit on my head. I looked up to see a bird fly off,*
looking, in my view, slightly smug and pleased with
itself.

Commander Singh, having seen my misfortune,
smiled and whispered to me.

'This, my friend, means you are lucky.'

Hmmm. How can a bird crapping on my head be
anything other than *un*lucky? What about Commander
Singh and the man with the knobbly knees, whom the
droppings had just missed? Had they both experienced
extreme bad luck by not having their hairdos soiled by
the mischievous bird? I think not.

Another twenty minutes of stretching exercises followed, in which time the sweat in my hair was mixing
with the recent bird droppings to create a radical and
unmarketable hair gel, guaranteed to deter any lover
from affectionately running their fingers through your
locks. To my relief though, we were finally ready to
start the laughing, and I was delighted that the 'fun bit'
could at last begin. The feeling didn't last long.

The boss-eyed leader instructed us all to throw our
heads back and to laugh hysterically, forcing the loud
noises from our diaphragms. This seemed to come easily to those around me, but I struggled to find the
sound, and when I did, it felt absurd. After all, I was
being asked to force a laugh, and I'd been brought up
in a culture where we only laugh when we find something funny, or when someone has said something
distinctly *un*funny and we want to mock them and
make them cry.

---

* The bird was later described to me as being correctly titled the
common mynah bird. In my view, you don't get much more common than taking a dump on someone's head.

The sound of everyone's laughs echoed through the surrounding banyan trees. I looked up to see passers-by stopping and looking at us all in amazement. I was embarrassed, particularly since as the only white boy present, I was the focus of attention. Everyone was looking to see what I was like at laughing hysterically, and frankly my efforts were laughable.

I decided to cheat, and I began to think of funny things. Like the cricket commentator Brian Johnston's comment after watching Ian Botham's dismissal when he stumbled into his own stumps after a sweep shot – 'Oh dear – he just couldn't get his leg over!' I successfully recreated in my head the sounds of the post-prandial wine-induced sniggering and giggling which followed the remark, and soon I was ready to let out a huge guffaw of my own. Deep breath, Tony – go for it!

'Ha! Ha! Ha! Ha! Ha! Ho!'

A round of applause from the onlookers. Hey, I could get good at this. Further efforts began to free up some part of me that usually remained dormant till after lunch. Yes, it felt strange to be forcing the laughs, but I'd got the hang of it now, and I was discovering that the process was making me feel wide awake, happy, and refreshingly alive. I was beginning to feel that this activity wasn't as daft as it had initially seemed.

'Please come back tomorrow,' Commander Singh requested, as I left the Laughing Club's small enclosure, myself now part of a bunch of people who all seemed to be glowing ever so slightly.

'All right, I will,' I replied.

And this time I meant it.

It's a funny thing, laughter. I'd spent a good proportion of my life trying to instigate it in others, and now I found myself in a city on the other side of the world, beginning my day by forcing myself to indulge in it – for health reasons. Could laughter really be that good for you? Could it, as the Laughing Club claimed, help prevent asthma, arthritis, back pain, digestive problems, depression, fatigue, insomnia, obesity, rheumatism and a weak memory?

Why do people enjoy laughing? Why do we constantly overhear exchanges like this? – 'How was last night?' 'Oh, it was a brilliant night – we had a great laugh!' Could it be that as humans we crave laughter because we have an inherent and instinctive sense that it contributes to our all round well-being?

I spent the day rejecting the touristy 'walking tour' suggested by my guidebook and instead I found myself wandering into alleys dominated by market stalls, and into a world of relentless commerce. Here, I simply stood and watched people. I guess my morning's experience had left me faintly obsessed and I now wanted to see what prompted laughter in the local population. Were the population of this bustling city getting enough of laughter's healing qualities in everyday life?

Certainly the foreign traveller in Kolkata doesn't have to worry in this department. For them there is plenty to amuse, not least the reckless driving (what you need to drive in India is good brakes, a good horn, and good luck), or copious hand-painted 'official notices' which seem to adorn every office lobby or shop-front. Not all of these notices get it quite right. A branch of the State Bank of India was equipped with a 'Compliant Box' on the wall, and one hotel I passed had a sign up saying 'Entry from back-side only' – enough to make you think twice about checking in.

Suddenly I was no longer the tourist, but the keen

sociologist, observing people as they go about their everyday business. These people seemed good-natured and content, but few were actually laughing. Oh dear, I thought to myself, I hoped they weren't losing out.

Still vaguely lost in these odd musings, I passed a huge advertising hoarding for an Indian movie. I looked up at it in all its garish and ostentatious magnificence and was immediately reminded of what a friend had said to me before I'd left.

'One thing you've got to do in India is to go and see a Bollywood movie in an Indian picture house. The atmosphere is incredible and it's an experience you won't forget.'

Well, it certainly seemed like a good way of spending the afternoon, especially since the city's humidity was beginning to get the better of me, and I'd noted that the cinema on the advertising hoarding had boasted air conditioning.

'Excuse me, but could you tell me where the Globe cinema is, please?' I asked a small but perfectly turned-out fellow on a street corner.

'Yes I can,' he answered precisely. 'You must take this street to your left and walk straight without hesitation. Then you must turn right after the big church.'

'Thanks,' I said, somewhat reeling from being told, in no uncertain terms, to walk without hesitation.

I set off, rather nervous that the man might be watching me just to see if I followed his instructions to the letter. So I marched steadfastly, without hesitation, not once breaking stride or dilly-dallying. And, as a result, I got hopelessly lost.

It would have been a scary experience had it not been for the fact that the people of Kolkata seem as peaceful and as unthreatening as a major city's population could be. Never mind that I was wandering aimlessly up dingy, narrow alleys and past doorways where down-trodden figures lurked, watching me with what I took to be fascination but which could just as easily have been disdain; I felt safe. I stopped for a while to watch a snake charmer, peering through the large crowd of locals who were gathered round the cross-legged show-man and his performing reptile. They turned and then cheered when they saw that a Westerner had stopped to view proceedings and the snake charmer's eyes lit up. Forthwith, he doubled his efforts to get his trusty cobra to do his bit. I felt embarrassed that a better show was now being given because a wealthy Westerner had arrived on the scene – someone who had the capacity to toss in more money than the rest of the crowd put together – so I quickly threw in a handful of rupees and moved on . . .

. . . On still further into parts of Kolkata which featured nowhere on my tourist map. I was perspiring heavily and was beginning to feel tired. I stopped on a street corner to rethink my strategy. As I often do when deep in thought, I ran my fingers through my hair, for-getting that it was caked in the digested aftermath of a common mynah bird's breakfast.

'Shit!' I said, being unexpectedly literal, and making a mental note not to shake anybody's hand until I'd had a chance to wash.

Then I felt a tap on the shoulder. I jumped round in shock, to be greeted by the gnarled face of an old man.

'You want me take you?' he asked, grinning a tooth-less grin.

'What?' I replied, still momentarily shaken.

'Me. I take you. Now.'

This didn't sound good. It didn't sound good at all.

'I take you,' he repeated, this time pointing to a sad, dilapidated rickshaw which was upended by the road-side a few yards away. It looked like it had been dumped. Apparently not though. It was more than ready for commercial use, and the wizened figure before me was its owner.

'Me. I take you. Come,' he said, gently tugging at my sleeve.

I would have laughed. I would have laughed a big healthy laugh but I didn't. I didn't because, although the sight of a man twice my age and half my strength want-ing to pedal me around the city in his rickshaw was funny, it was also sad. Very sad. I would have refused his offer, if it hadn't been for the fact that the fare was probably going to provide him with his next meal, and by the look of him, one that was long overdue.

'Could you take me to the Globe cinema?' I asked, already knowing the answer.

The old man beamed, nodded and ushered me into the rickshaw's seat while he mounted the bicycle part of the contraption and began forcing his bodyweight down onto the pedals to get it moving. The sun beat down and I tried not to feel guilty as I sat back and watched my sticklike rickshaw wallah struggle through the overcrowded streets.

It took us about fifteen minutes to reach the picture house, by which time the old man was bathed in sweat and I was consumed with guilt. It wouldn't have been so bad if, after I'd handed over the fare and a handsome tip, he hadn't insisted on shaking my hand.

The picture house had clearly been built back in the days when there was more money in Kolkata than in the City of London, and pleasingly it still looked the part, if a little jaded. I wandered into the art deco foyer and found myself surrounded by an eager crowd, none of whom seemed particularly surprised to see a Westerner turning up to see a Hindi film. I bought my ticket, and then was almost swept up the grand staircase and into the vast auditorium by the sheer weight of enthusiastic and vocal customers, all anxious to take their seat for the forthcoming spectacle.

The levels of excitement were high because today's movie was so 'hot'. *The Hero*, as it was called, was doing great business in India right now, and was gaining much publicity because it was the biggest-budget Bollywood movie ever made.

I found myself a seat near the front of the balcony beside an extended family who took up the rest of the row. They were constantly up and down in their seats exchanging colourful sweets and unidentifiable miscellany. The father, who was next to me, looked at my hair and scowled, no doubt unimpressed by my choice of hair gel. The opening credits rolled, the audience gasped in anticipation, and I braced myself for three hours of full-on entertainment.

Not being altogether fluent in Hindi, some of the gentler nuances of the plot were lost on me, but I can reveal that the story centred around *The Hero* who was a kind of Indian James Bond with greasy, combed across hair (actually, not that dissimilar to mine at the time). He began the film dressing up in lots of ludicrous disguises for spying purposes and occasionally waving a gun about, before heading off to Kashmir where he upped the ante and single-handedly killed scores of pesky Pakistani soldiers, while jumping in the air and shouting a lot. Then he fell in love with a local shepherd girl who never went anywhere without a baby goat, which she stroked obsessively. Quality stuff.

It had been billed as an adventure/comedy/romance but unfortunately it only delivered in two of these categories. When we came to the scenes in the film which I reckoned were supposed to be the funny bits, I looked down my row to see the response of the extended family alongside me. Straight faces. Long faces, almost. Clearly, the comedy just wasn't working. All the more disappointing for me, the man who had now become the student of laughter.

I'm afraid I can't tell you how the film ends, not because I don't want to spoil it for you – the director had handled that side of things most adroitly – but because I left during the intermission. Lazy, I know, but I had three sound reasons. My bottom was getting sore on the hard seat; the film felt like a cross between *Last of the Summer Wine*, *The Terminator* and *Carry On Camping*; and the expressions on the faces of those around me suggested that there was a general consensus that I should go home and wash my hair.

'You are most welcome once again,' said Commander Singh, with a little bow of his head.

'Morning,' I said, conscious of just how 'morning' it was.

I'd struggled to make this session. The body clock was reverting to normal and I was slipping back into the world where early mornings were vaguely obscene.

I was greeted warmly by a number of the other members, who all looked delighted to see me again. Perhaps it was because I was the youngest person here. Commander Singh was busying himself, generally ordering people about and being commander-like. I could do that, I thought to myself as he passed before me and nodded congenially.

'Can I be a commander?' I asked him mischievously, attempting to exploit the wave of good will around me.

'What?'

'Can I be a commander, like you? I've been here three mornings in a row now – surely that means I can be a commander now?'

Before the bemused man could respond to my perfectly unreasonable request, we were all barked at by a more senior Kommandant, and ordered to fall into line for another rigorous routine of stretching and cackling. It wasn't long before my head was thrown back in laughter once again, and I found myself looking up into the thick green foliage of the banyan tree, with my mouth wide open. I couldn't help thinking that it was an open invitation to the common mynah bird to go one better than yesterday and to relieve himself directly into my mouth.

Following another intensive workout of nearly every part of the body totally unconnected with it, we reached the point of laughter once again. A small crowd of onlookers had gathered, particularly interested in me just as they had been the previous morning. I began to feel it was important that these people saw that I was not the weak link in the club. I wanted to show them that I was no beginner at this laughing business – I was, after all, a veteran of three days now. I decided that I should go for a very big laugh indeed; a laugh that would see off any critics; a laugh to end laughs.

'Ha ha ha ho ho hi hi ha ha ho ha!' I went.

But somehow it didn't feel big enough.

'Ho ho ho, ha ha ha, hi hi hee hee, ha hah hoooooo!'

Better, but I was still being outperformed both in

volume and length of laugh by two others in the group. This time I elected to really put my back into it. I leant back, threw my arms in the air, and I *really* went for it.

'HA HA HA HA HO HO HO HO HEE HEE HEE HEE HAH HAH HA HI HI HO HO HAAAAAAAH!!!!!'

I finished my laugh with my head flung forward. I hung there for a few moments, well aware that I had expended a huge amount of energy and that I might not be able to summon enough to haul myself back into an upright position. When I did eventually straighten up I realised two things: that the laugh had impressed a good deal, and that everyone in the club was looking over and smiling approvingly; and that an acute shooting pain halfway up my body meant that I'd pulled a muscle in my back.

Bugger.

I'm not blessed with a high pain threshold, and I'm sure the back pain would have been tolerable to another, but for me it just wasn't acceptable. The discomfort was ruining my sightseeing day. By the time I reached the Hooghly river and the Howrah Bridge, I was beginning to whinge to myself about the pain.

'This is a right royal pain in the arse!' I lamented, with anatomical inaccuracy.

Before me was an extraordinary sight. The amazing Howrah Bridge is surely the busiest in the world, crossed by 100,000 vehicles a day, and probably ten times as many pedestrians. It may have been stunning to observe thousands of people crossing one bridge carrying anything from fruit to engine parts, but my back hurt, and that was enough to spoil the experience. I needed a fix, and I needed one quick.

'Do you know where I can get a massage?' I asked sheepishly, in the hotel reception.

God I felt seedy.

'I've strained my back slightly, you see,' I explained to the nice young man, who I felt convinced was thinking that I really wanted a prostitute. 'It doesn't have to be a woman,' I added hastily. 'A man would be fine.'

'You want a man?' he replied, eyebrows raised.

Oh dear. I was making things worse.

'No, it doesn't have to be a man, it's just that . . .'

Fortunately, he'd turned away to make a phone call before I could dig the hole any deeper.

An hour later there was a knock on the door of my hotel room. I answered it to a stocky fellow, thick set, with a low centre of gravity – he resembled a kind of Indian Maradona.

'Massage?' he said.

'Yes,' I replied, rather taken aback.

The man introduced himself as Sunil and came into my room and set up his massage table. If the hotel receptionist had seen his brief as being one of providing me with a masseur/se that I didn't fancy, then he had excelled himself. I looked at the brutish man across the room from me, and I just hoped that he would not be expecting to supplement his income by supplying 'extras'.

After an awkward exchange in which we tried to establish the nature of the required massage without the use of a common language, the man set about his task. I'd agreed to a 'full body massage', mainly because these were the only English words he managed to mumble, but I'd failed to alert him to the problem in my back, despite numerous efforts. Whether I wanted it or not, a full body massage was what I was going to get. I uttered a little prayer that he shared the same loose definition of the word 'full', and I stripped to my pants and lay down.

A painful and nervous half hour followed, but I'm pleased to say that the burly man made no forays into the hallowed area of my underpants. Instead, Sunil pulled, pushed and slapped my body into submission and I felt a tension leave my body. When he reached my back he did something, I know not what, but I felt the pain which had plagued me all day lift from my body. I wondered if Sunil had extra healing powers.

'Thank you Sunil,' I said as he packed away his massage table. 'You could make a fortune in England.'

Sunil wobbled his head from side to side in nervous deference, clearly not understanding a word I'd said. Maybe the fortune would be difficult to attain until he extended his English vocabulary beyond the three words 'full body massage'.

The healing of my back left me able to sleep well that night. So soundly, in fact, that I slept through the last Laughing Club of my stay. When I'd gone to bed I'd told myself I wanted to get up early the following morning and go to the club, but I guess the truth was that I didn't want to *really*. I could try to pretend that it hadn't been a conscious decision to remain unconscious at the crucial time, but even though this argument might have stood up in a court of law, it didn't carry much weight in my heart's conscience. The truth was that the Laughing Club was too much like hard work and it happened too early. I needed less of a rigorous workout and I needed it at 11.30 a.m.

I felt guilty at breakfast, not least because I hadn't said goodbye to the Commander, the Kommandant, or any of the other morning colleagues with whom I'd had such a good laugh. I hadn't said thank you either – and the tuition I'd received at the Laughing Club had all been free. I decided that I needed to make amends in some way. Give something back, if not to the Laughing Club itself, then somewhere else. How I would do this, I was still unsure as I left the hotel for my final day in the city, but I hoped that something might come to me.

It was late morning when the idea arrived. I'd spent the morning wandering and observing, seeing at first hand how people really lived out their lives on the street. Mothers showered their children on street corners, men slept in doorways, kids played in front of their father's market stalls dodging in and out of lorries, carts and rickshaws, and it all seemed perfectly normal. This was Kolkata life, and it was an entertaining show. But I'd bunked in without buying a ticket. By the time I'd reached Howrah Bridge, I knew what to do about it.

It was long after morning rush hour, but you wouldn't have known it. Hordes of people swarmed around, among whom were many eager rickshaw wallahs, who eyed me longingly. I was potential business – and, for one of them I was about to be very good business indeed.

It was a few minutes before I saw the right fellow. He was slumped in his rickshaw, looking exhausted and altogether not that enamoured with life. He had white hair and a matching neatly trimmed grey moustache which turned downwards acutely at each end of his top lip, making it resemble an upside-down smile. His clothes were grubby, tattered and torn, and it looked like he needed the fare but was too jaded to compete for it. He was perfect.

'Rickshaw please,' I said as I drew alongside him.

The man, although confused that I had chosen him

ahead of all his much more eager colleagues, immediately jumped out of his tiny chariot and ushered me into the cushioned seat. He'd got a job without even trying. It was his lucky day. It was about to get luckier still.

'What is your name?' I asked.

'Ramesh.'

'Okay, Ramesh, first we agree a price,' I said to him firmly. 'How much to the Mahatma Gandhi Road?'

'Twenty rupees,' he replied without hesitation.

This was probably an inflated price given that I was a Westerner, but it was still less than the cost of a Mars bar back home in the UK, and since this was to be an unusual journey, why not begin it in an unconventional manner? Without the almost compulsory haggling.

'Okay, let's go!' I said, moving to the front of the rickshaw and taking hold of the shafts.

Ramesh stepped forward and stood over me possessively, saying something brusquely in Bengali. I guessed it was something like 'What, in God's name, are you doing?'

'It's Okay,' I said, as soothingly as I could, '*I* want to pull the rickshaw. I want to see what it's like for you guys. You get in. This ride's on me.'

The rickshaw wallah was unhappy. Perhaps he believed that I was under the impression that I'd just bought the rickshaw off him, and was about to make off with it.

'It's Okay,' I repeated. '*You* sit on the seat. I'll pull *you*.'

Again Ramesh shook his head. I nodded. He shook his head again, and I nodded again. This went on for some time, until a small crowd had gathered to watch, and until I eventually said the magic words.

'Okay, if you don't sit in the seat,' I enunciated firmly, 'you don't get the twenty rupees.'

This had the desired effect and Ramesh, albeit some-what reluctantly, climbed into the seat of his own rickshaw.

Once the perplexed Ramesh was ensconced in the seat, the crowd let out a big cheer, and the first wave of laughter began. I set off, finding the rickshaw easier to pull than I'd expected. Simple designs are often the most brilliant, and the Kolkata rickshaw offers a smooth ride, is easily manoeuvrable, and provides excellent cornering. (Eat your heart out, Jeremy Clarkson.)

Now I was actually moving one about myself I could see how the transport policy of Kolkata's authorities was absurd. They want to ban these rickshaws, concen-trating on building flyovers to accommodate the forthcoming plague of motor cars.

The effort required to pull the rickshaw may have been less than I expected but what made it really tough was the 35 degree heat and the stifling humidity. After only a few paces the sweat was beginning to drip from my brow, something which only served to make the spectacle more hilarious for the amazed onlookers. I ploughed on through the beaming smiles and joyous chuckles. Children pointed and women cackled, and there were countless genuine double takes as people struggled to take in the reality of the scene before them – the daft white man pulling the old rickshaw wallah. I was joined by a posse of young men who acted as chaperones, helping clear the way when I came upon a congested section of street. A car pulled alongside me and the driver wound down his window.

'Only in India!' he said, before accelerating away.

People on buses waved and smiled, street traders and their customers froze in mid-transaction as they caught a glimpse of the unusual spectacle, but most of the roadside throng simply threw their heads back and laughed. Big raucous laughs, worthy of the Laughing Club itself.

As I arrived at the Mahatma Gandhi Road, wet through and to a huge cheer, I realised that my work here was done. In the last quarter of an hour alone I had created enough laughs to ease a good proportion of the city's arthritic and digestive problems. Well, I liked to think so anyway.

As I stood there dripping with sweat among the small crowd, their hands reaching out from all directions to shake mine, I began to lament not being able to stay longer in this city. In the few days I'd spent milling about Kolkata's busy streets and loitering in its parks, I'd grown fond of the Bengali people and their warmth and good humour. I'd learnt from the practitioners of the laughter therapy too, and my, it feels terrific to know that every future laugh I raise can be of benefit to someone's health.

And by the way, have you heard the one about the group of authors who headed off to Kolkata? . . .